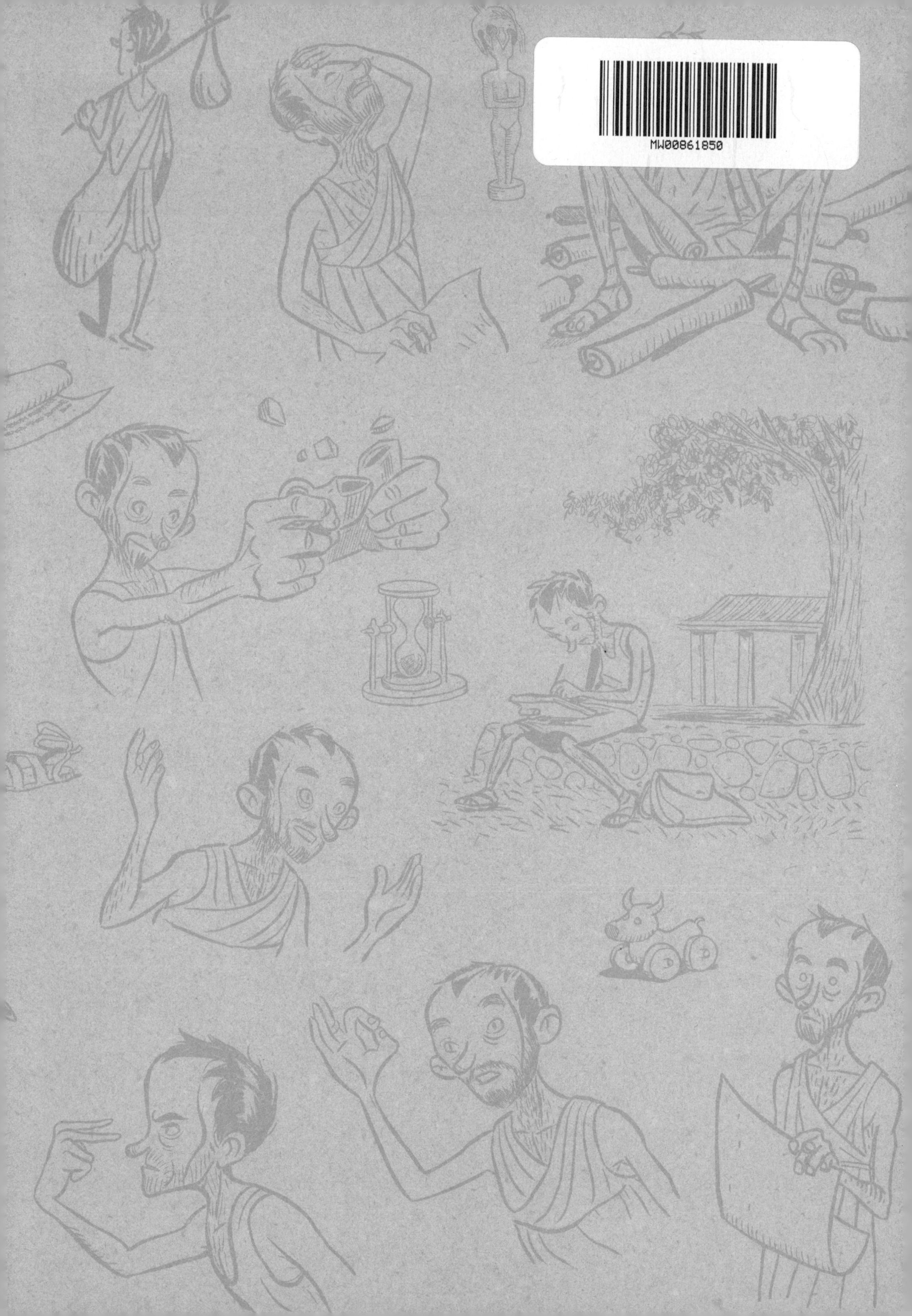

ARISTOTLE

A GRAPHIC BIOGRAPHY

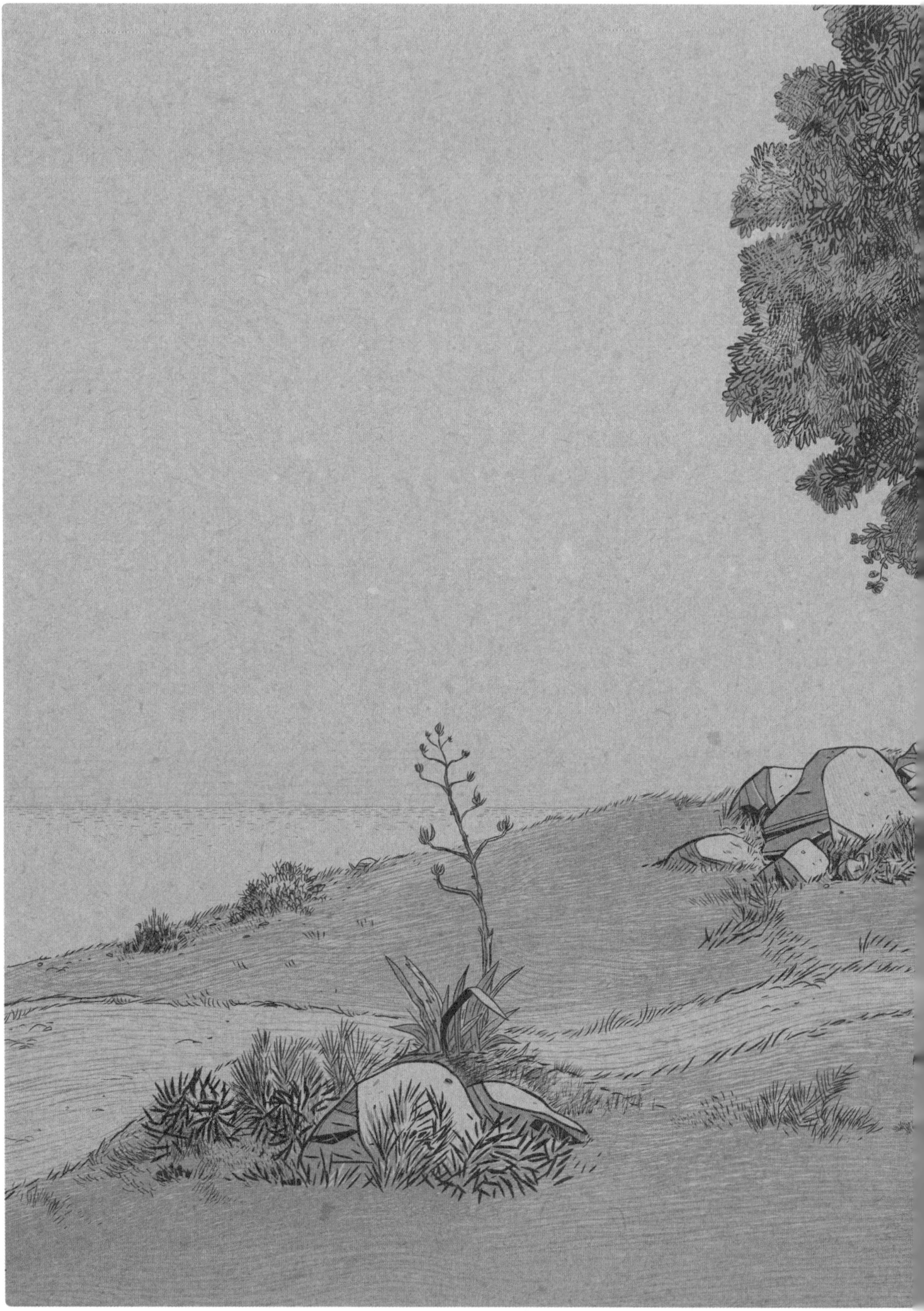

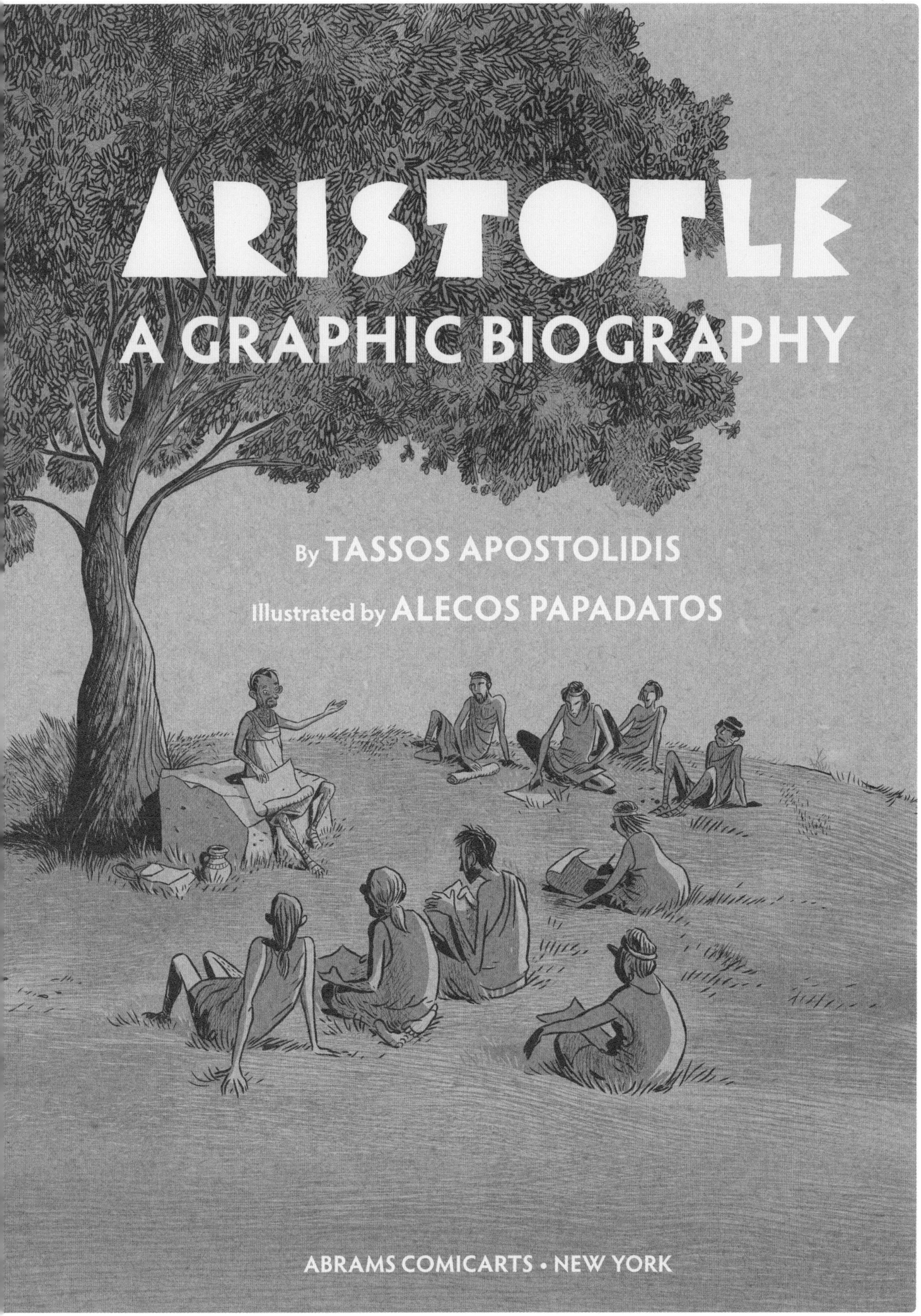

ARISTOTLE

A GRAPHIC BIOGRAPHY

By TASSOS APOSTOLIDIS

Illustrated by ALECOS PAPADATOS

ABRAMS COMICARTS • NEW YORK

ARISTOTLE

The hero of our story! The great Greek scholar and philosopher had an exceptional life. And you'll discover that, for the most part, his theories are still relevant today.

THEOPHRASTUS

A student of Aristotle, he became first an associate, then a close friend and eventually his successor at the Lyceum. He narrates our tale.

PLATO

Philosopher, student of Socrates, and teacher of Aristotle, he founded the Academy. He and Aristotle respected each other greatly, but often disagreed.

HERMIAS

He was Aristotle's greatest supporter. To show his appreciation, Aristotle composed "Hymn to Virtue" in his honor, which ended up causing him a lot of problems.

PYTHIAS

Hermias's niece and a brilliant biologist—even if the term didn't exist at the time. She was first Aristotle's associate, then his wife. She followed him wherever he went.

PYTHIAS II

Pythias and Aristotle's daughter, named after her mother out of love, but also perhaps because he had sensed something...

PHILIP II OF MACEDONIA

The great monarch is primarily known for being Alexander's father.

ALEXANDER THE GREAT

Before he became the great strategist and conqueror, he was Aristotle's student. He would later say that his rich, full life was owed to his master. That's saying something!

HERPYLLIS

Aristotle's companion at the end of his life. She gave him a son, Nicomachus, for whom he wrote "Nicomachean Ethics," a book that even today is still one of the most read in the world.

NICANOR

Son of Proxenus, Aristotle's guardian. When the child lost his parents, Aristotle adopted him and gave him the same affection he himself had been given.

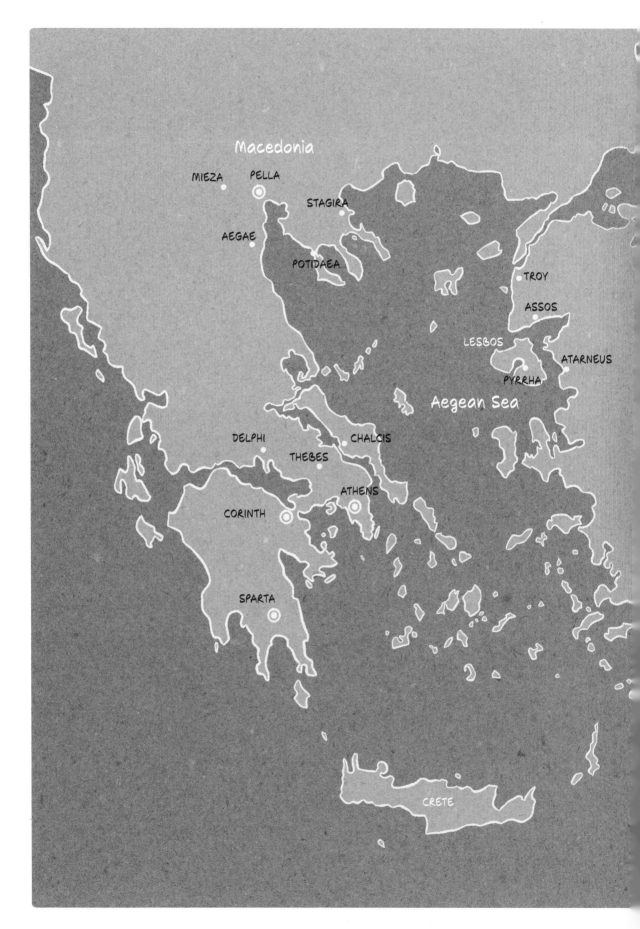

Macedonia

MIEZA
PELLA
STAGIRA
AEGAE
POTIDAEA
TROY
ASSOS
LESBOS
ATARNEUS
PYRRHA

Aegean Sea

DELPHI
CHALCIS
THEBES
ATHENS
CORINTH

SPARTA

CRETE

CHRONOLOGY
(All dates are BCE)

5th Century: called "The Age of Pericles," this was the Golden Age of Athenian democracy. Art and literature reach their pinnacle, and the city is at the peak of its economic, social, political, and cultural development.

469: Birth of Socrates.

431-404: The Peloponnesian War between Athens and Sparta, which ends with the defeat of Athens.

428: Birth of Plato.

399: Trial and death of Socrates.

389-387: Plato's first stay in Syracuse. Upon his return, he founds the Academy.

398: Birth of Hermias, philosopher and friend of Aristotle, who becomes ruler of Atarneus in Asia Minor.

384: Birth of Aristotle in Stagira, in Macedonia.

382: Birth of Philip II of Macedonia, Alexander the Great's father.

370: Birth of Theophrastus. Philosopher, friend, and associate of Aristotle, and his successor as the head of the Lyceum.

367: Aristotle goes to Athens to study at the Academy.

359: Philip accedes to the Macedonian throne.

356: Birth of Alexander the Great, son of Philip and Olympias.

347: Death of Plato. Aristotle leaves Athens for Assos, in Asia Minor, under Hermias's protection.

345: Hermias is made prisoner by the Persians, who accuse him of collaborating with the Macedonians. Aristotle agrees to move to the island of Lesbos, as proposed by Theophrastus.

343: Philip calls upon Aristotle to take charge of Alexander's education.

340: Death of Hermias. Aristotle writes "Hymn to Virtue" in his honor.

338: End of Alexander's education; he becomes viceroy.

336: Assassination of Philip. Alexander takes the Macedonian throne and prepares the Panhellenic campaign against the Persians.

335: Aristotle returns to Athens and founds the Lyceum, where he teaches, assisted by Theophrastus and other eminent philosophers.

334: Birth of Pythias II, Aristotle's daughter, who has the same name as her mother.

326: Death of Pythias, Aristotle's wife. He decides to live with Herpyllis, the slave who manages his household. She gives him a son, whom Aristotle names Nicomachus after his father.

326-323: Period of intense activity for Aristotle at the Lyceum: teaching, writing, research.

323: Death of Alexander. Aristotle, threatened by the anti-Macedonians in Athens, takes refuge in Chalcis, on a property he inherited from his mother.

322: Aristotle dies from a stomach illness.

318: Theophrastus makes the Lyceum a philosophy school characterized as a "peripatetic school."

310: Euclid writes the "Elements."

306: Epicurus founds a philosophy school in Athens, which he calls the Garden.

301: Zeno of Citium founds his philosophy school, the Stoic school, in Athens.

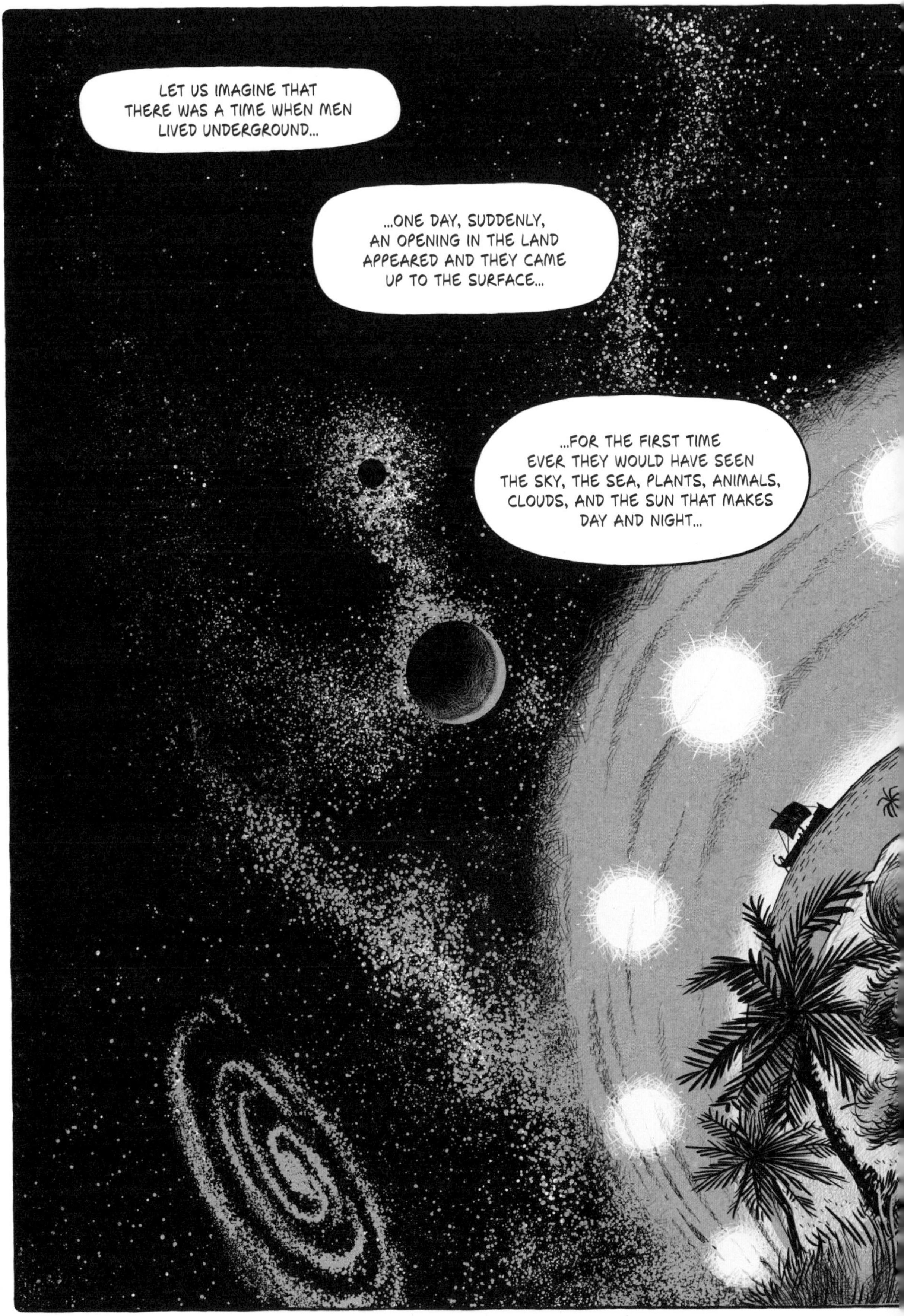
LET US IMAGINE THAT THERE WAS A TIME WHEN MEN LIVED UNDERGROUND...
...ONE DAY, SUDDENLY, AN OPENING IN THE LAND APPEARED AND THEY CAME UP TO THE SURFACE...
...FOR THE FIRST TIME EVER THEY WOULD HAVE SEEN THE SKY, THE SEA, PLANTS, ANIMALS, CLOUDS, AND THE SUN THAT MAKES DAY AND NIGHT...

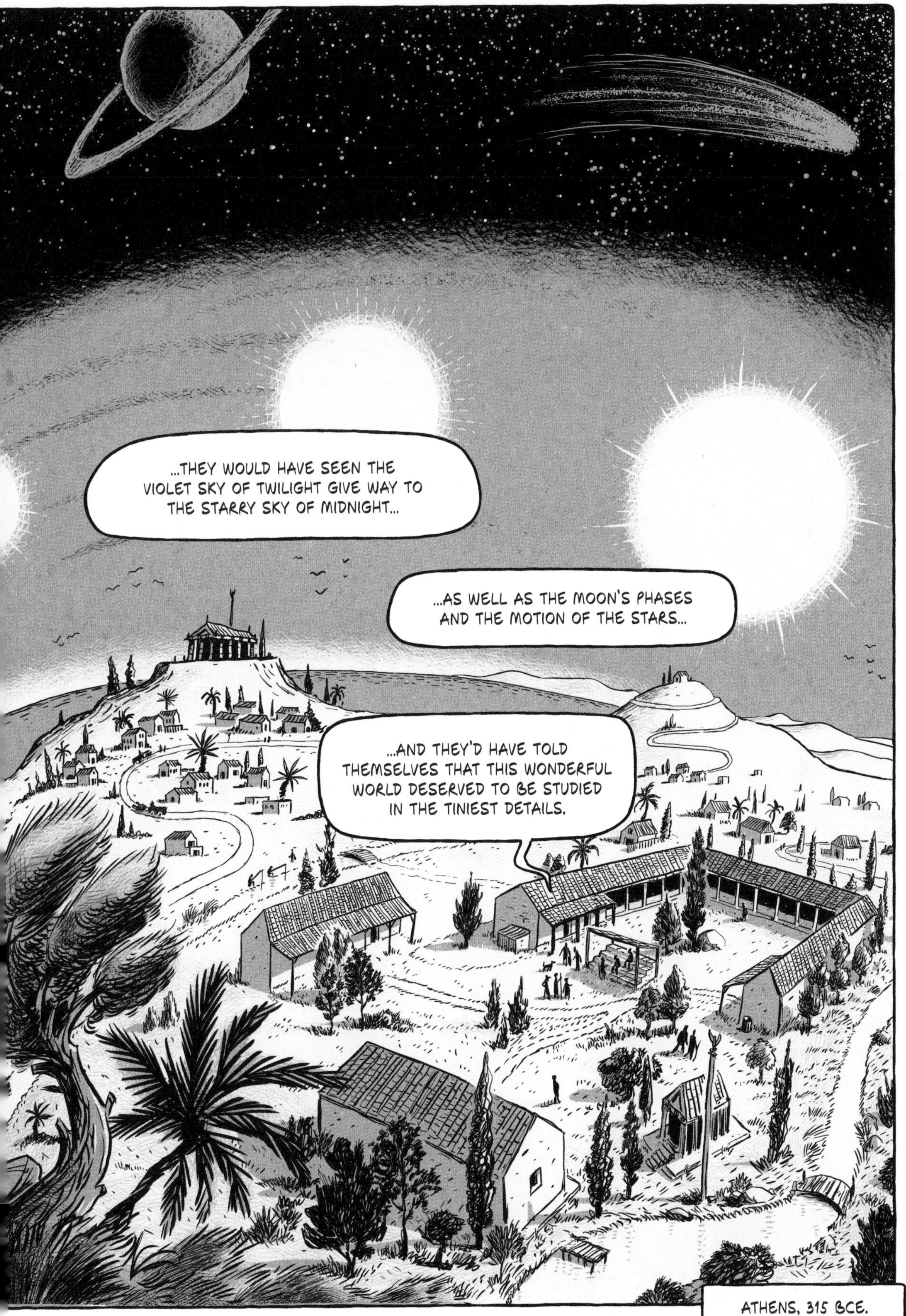
...THEY WOULD HAVE SEEN THE VIOLET SKY OF TWILIGHT GIVE WAY TO THE STARRY SKY OF MIDNIGHT...
...AS WELL AS THE MOON'S PHASES AND THE MOTION OF THE STARS...
...AND THEY'D HAVE TOLD THEMSELVES THAT THIS WONDERFUL WORLD DESERVED TO BE STUDIED IN THE TINIEST DETAILS.
ATHENS, 315 BCE.

DON'T FORGET WHAT ARISTOTLE SAID. THE THIRST FOR KNOWLEDGE AND THE DESIRE TO DISCOVER NATURE ARE INNATE IN EVERY MAN.

YOU WERE SO LUCKY, THEOPHRASTUS, TO SPEND ALL THOSE YEARS BY THE MASTER'S SIDE!

IT'S TRUE, ARISTOTLE CHANGED MY LIFE! HE MADE ME HIS ASSOCIATE, HIS FRIEND, AND, JUST BEFORE HE DIED, THE DIRECTOR OF THE LYCEUM.

IT'S AN ENORMOUS RESPONSIBILITY, THIS LEGACY!

HAS OUR SCHOOL, THE LYCEUM, ALWAYS BEEN CALLED THE "PERIPATETIC SCHOOL," THE "SCHOOL OF THE WALKERS" IN A WAY?

NO! THAT NICKNAME'S FAIRLY RECENT!

BACK IN THE DAY, ALL THAT WAS HERE WAS THE GYMNASIUM, THE WOODS, AND APOLLO'S TEMPLE. THAT HASN'T DISAPPEARED, OF COURSE.

ARISTOTLE LOVED TEACHING HIS STUDENTS IN THE GYMNASIUM HALLS, WHICH WERE ALSO CALLED "WALKWAYS."

THANKS TO FUNDING GRANTED TO US BY ALEXANDER THE GREAT, WE RENTED BUILDINGS WHERE WE SET UP CLASSROOMS.

WE ALSO HAD LABORATORIES, A LIBRARY, AND HOUSING FOR PHILOSOPHERS AND STUDENTS WHO CAME FROM OTHER CITIES. THIS PRACTICE STILL GOES ON TODAY.

AND SOME CLASSES ARE EVEN STILL HELD IN THE WALKWAYS!

THUS THE NAMES...

..."PERIPATETIC SCHOOL"...

...AND "PERIPATETIC PHILOSOPHERS"!

EXACTLY!

IN CLASS I'LL TELL YOU ABOUT ARISTOTLE AND MY LIFE WORKING WITH HIM, AS WELL AS WHAT HE SHARED WITH ME ABOUT HIS LIFE DURING OUR LONG CONVERSATIONS.

11

I'LL TELL YOU ABOUT THAT GREAT GREEK PHILOSOPHER FROM MACEDONIA, THE HONORS BESTOWED UPON HIM AND THE OFFENSES HE ENDURED.

I'LL TALK ABOUT HIS LOVE OF NATURE, HIS RESPECT FOR HIS PARENTS AND ANCESTORS, HIS GREAT IDEAS, HIS THEORIES...

...ABOUT THE UNCEASING WAR WAGED AGAINST HIM BY THE ORATORS AND SOPHISTS, ABOUT THE WORRIES AND FEARS HE FACED AS A METIC*...

...AND ABOUT HIS OWN WEAKNESSES.

BUT I'LL BEGIN BY GIVING YOU THE HISTORICAL CONTEXT, WHCCH YOU ABSOLUTELY HAVE TO BE FAMILIAR WITH.

*Foreigner living in Athens without the rights of a citizen.

12

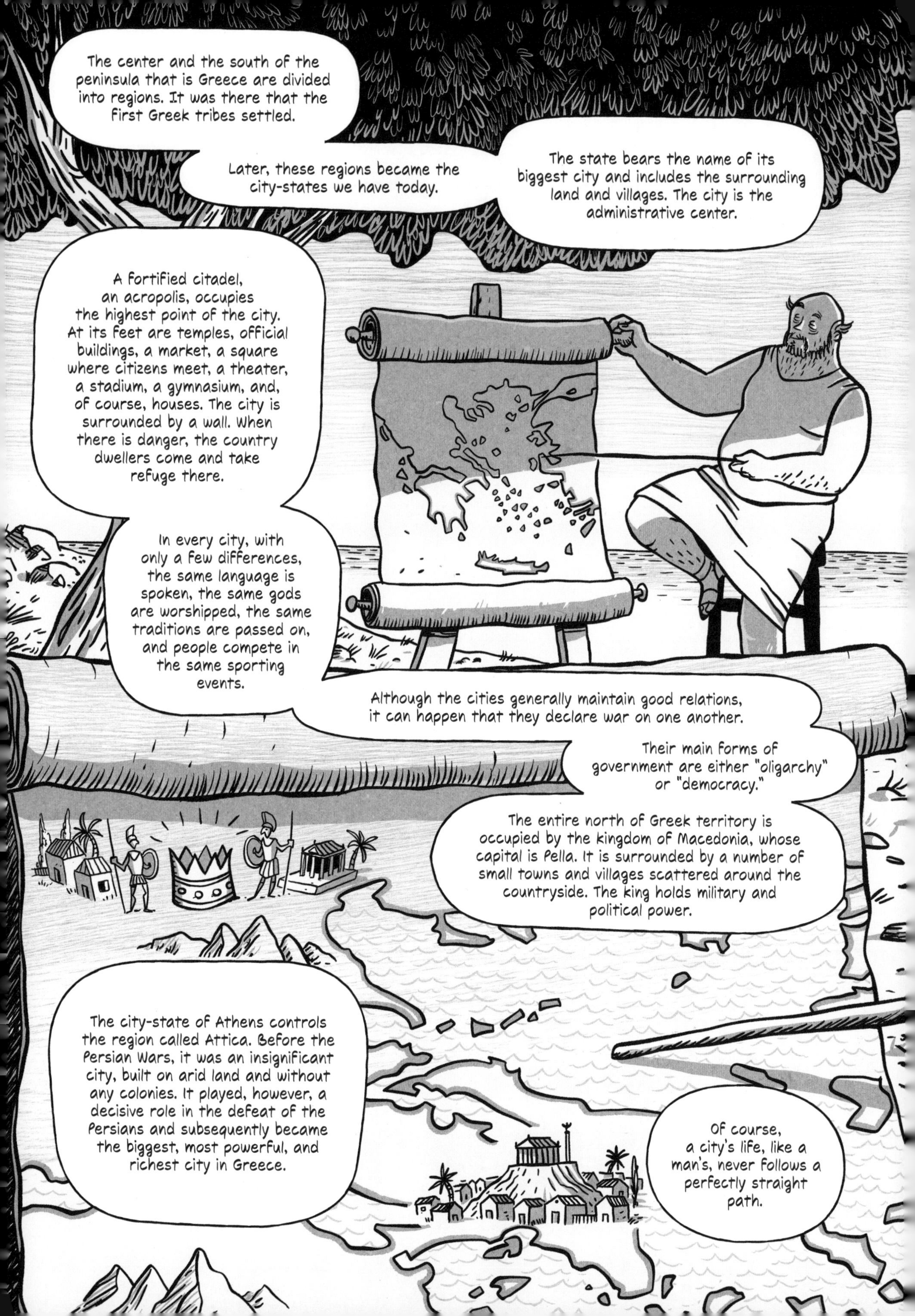
The center and the south of the peninsula that is Greece are divided into regions. It was there that the first Greek tribes settled.
Later, these regions became the city-states we have today.
The state bears the name of its biggest city and includes the surrounding land and villages. The city is the administrative center.
A fortified citadel, an acropolis, occupies the highest point of the city. At its feet are temples, official buildings, a market, a square where citizens meet, a theater, a stadium, a gymnasium, and, of course, houses. The city is surrounded by a wall. When there is danger, the country dwellers come and take refuge there.
In every city, with only a few differences, the same language is spoken, the same gods are worshipped, the same traditions are passed on, and people compete in the same sporting events.
Although the cities generally maintain good relations, it can happen that they declare war on one another.
Their main forms of government are either "oligarchy" or "democracy."
The entire north of Greek territory is occupied by the kingdom of Macedonia, whose capital is Pella. It is surrounded by a number of small towns and villages scattered around the countryside. The king holds military and political power.
The city-state of Athens controls the region called Attica. Before the Persian Wars, it was an insignificant city, built on arid land and without any colonies. It played, however, a decisive role in the defeat of the Persians and subsequently became the biggest, most powerful, and richest city in Greece.
Of course, a city's life, like a man's, never follows a perfectly straight path.

- LIFE NEVER FOLLOWS A PERFECTLY STRAIGHT PATH!

WE OFTEN FIND OURSELVES AT A CROSSROADS.

WE MUST THEREFORE CHOOSE THE DIRECTION TO FOLLOW, GUIDED ONLY BY A "MUST" OR A "MUST NOT"!

- IF I UNDERSTAND CORRECTLY, ARISTOTLE, LIFE IS A JOURNEY OF MORAL CHOICES.

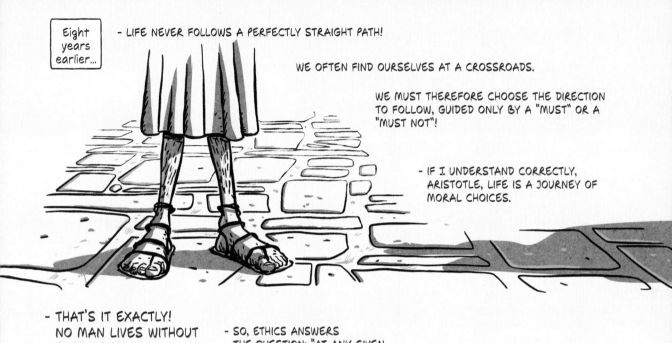

- THAT'S IT EXACTLY! NO MAN LIVES WITHOUT PRECISE MORAL CONCEPTS.

- SO, ETHICS ANSWERS THE QUESTION: "AT ANY GIVEN MOMENT, WHAT MUST I DO?"

- VERY WELL PUT!

- AND IN THE END, HOW WILL I KNOW "WHAT TO DO"?

- IT'S SIMPLE: DO WHAT A VIRTUOUS MAN WOULD DO!

- YES!... BUT, UM, HOW WILL I RECOGNIZE A VIRTUOUS MAN?

- HE'S THE MAN WHOSE VIRTUES SET HIM APART!

- AND WHAT IS MEANT BY "VIRTUES"?

- VIRTUES ARE FEATURES THAT LEAD TO SELF-FULFILLMENT.

- SO HOW WILL I BE ABLE TO BECOME VIRTUOUS?

- BY AVOIDING TWO EXTREMES: LACK AND EXCESS.

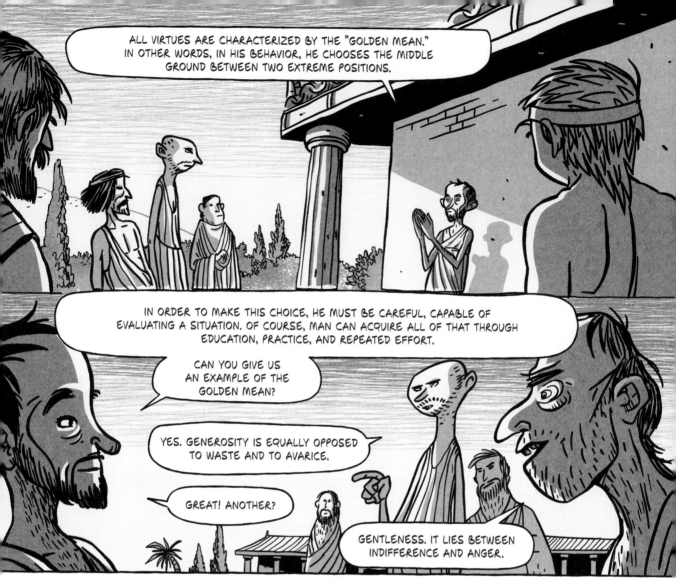

ALL VIRTUES ARE CHARACTERIZED BY THE "GOLDEN MEAN." IN OTHER WORDS, IN HIS BEHAVIOR, HE CHOOSES THE MIDDLE GROUND BETWEEN TWO EXTREME POSITIONS.

IN ORDER TO MAKE THIS CHOICE, HE MUST BE CAREFUL, CAPABLE OF EVALUATING A SITUATION. OF COURSE, MAN CAN ACQUIRE ALL OF THAT THROUGH EDUCATION, PRACTICE, AND REPEATED EFFORT.

CAN YOU GIVE US AN EXAMPLE OF THE GOLDEN MEAN?

YES. GENEROSITY IS EQUALLY OPPOSED TO WASTE AND TO AVARICE.

GREAT! ANOTHER?

GENTLENESS. IT LIES BETWEEN INDIFFERENCE AND ANGER.

ARISTOTLE! THIS MESSAGE HAS JUST ARRIVED FROM BABYLON!

BABYLON?

ALEXANDER IS DEAD !

Alexander, the great king of Macedonia, had died.
He who had continued his father Philip's work and succeeded at uniting the city-states of Greece into a single state, only to then conquer Asia, was no more.

AND SO IN ATHENS, ALL THOSE WHO REFUSED THIS HEGEMONY SEIZED THE OPPORTUNITY TO DO WHAT THEY COULD TO FREE THEMSELVES FROM ANY MACEDONIAN PRESENCE.

DEMOPHILUS...

...PRIEST OF THE GODDESS DEMETER, INITIATED IN THE ELEUSIAN MYSTERIES...

...AND EURYMEDON...

...FROM ISOCRATES'S SCHOOL OF RHETORIC, A RIVAL OF THE LYCEUM...

...BOTH OF WHOM HAD REASONS TO WANT TO GET RID OF ARISTOTLE.

HAVE YOU HEARD, EURYMEDON?

ALEXANDER IS DEAD!

THAT'S WHAT I HEARD, DEMOPHILUS. BUT ARE WE CERTAIN OF IT?

OR IS IT JUST A RUMOR, LIKE THAT TIME THE THEBANS GOT TAKEN IN? DO YOU REMEMBER?

OF COURSE I REMEMBER! THEY BELIEVED ALEXANDER WAS DEAD AND THEY REVOLTED! AS A RESULT, HE CHOPPED THEM TO BITS!

BUT THIS TIME IT'S TRUE!

THEY EVEN SENT A MESSAGE TO ARISTOTLE!

ARISTOTLE?

HMM!

SO, HOW ABOUT WE START WITH HIM?

GO ON...

YOU'RE FAMILIAR WITH THE RECIPE FOR GETTING RID OF UNDESIRABLE PEOPLE.

YES, BUT...

WE'LL HAVE TO FIND AN ACCUSER, A PRETEXT, SOMETHING.

WELL...

...YOU'LL BE THE ACCUSER!

ME?

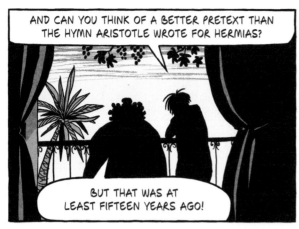

AND CAN YOU THINK OF A BETTER PRETEXT THAN THE HYMN ARISTOTLE WROTE FOR HERMIAS?

BUT THAT WAS AT LEAST FIFTEEN YEARS AGO!

SO WHAT?

DON'T YOU THINK IT'S A CRIME, THAT IT'S UNGODLY, TO WRITE A POEM FOR A DEAD MAN IN THE FORM OF AN APOLLONIAN HYMN?

SURE, BUT...

HERE IT IS!

LISTEN!

"O VIRTUE, O BEAUTY, O STRENUOUS LABOR, THE WORK OF A LIFETIME! FOR YOU, EVEN DEATH IS A SWEET FATE! O VIRTUE, TO CONQUER YOU, THERE'S NO ONE IN GREECE WHO DOES NOT HONOR HIS EFFORT, HIS TOIL!" ETC., ETC.

WELL? I'M LISTENING!

UM, YEAH...

BESIDES, HERMIAS WAS A FRIEND OF THE MACEDONIANS!

SURE, OF COURSE, BUT STILL...

YOUR REACTION BAFFLES ME!

NO, YES. YOU'RE RIGHT.

IT WAS A CRIME! AWFUL AND UNGODLY!

ARISTOTLE MUST BE CHARGED, TRIED...

...AND SENTENCED TO DIE!

18

Not long after, before the conspirators could act, I went to Aristotle's home...

SO, IT'S DECIDED? YOU'RE LEAVING?

YES, THEOPHRASTUS, I AM!

NOW THAT ALEXANDER IS DEAD, I'M NO LONGER ABLE TO STAY IN ATHENS.

IT'S TRUE, THE ANGER TOWARD MACEDONIANS KEEPS GETTING WORSE!

IT DOES. AND I AM A MACEDONIAN!

BESIDES, I DON'T WANT TO LET THE ATHENIANS COMMIT A SECOND CRIME AGAINST PHILOSOPHY.

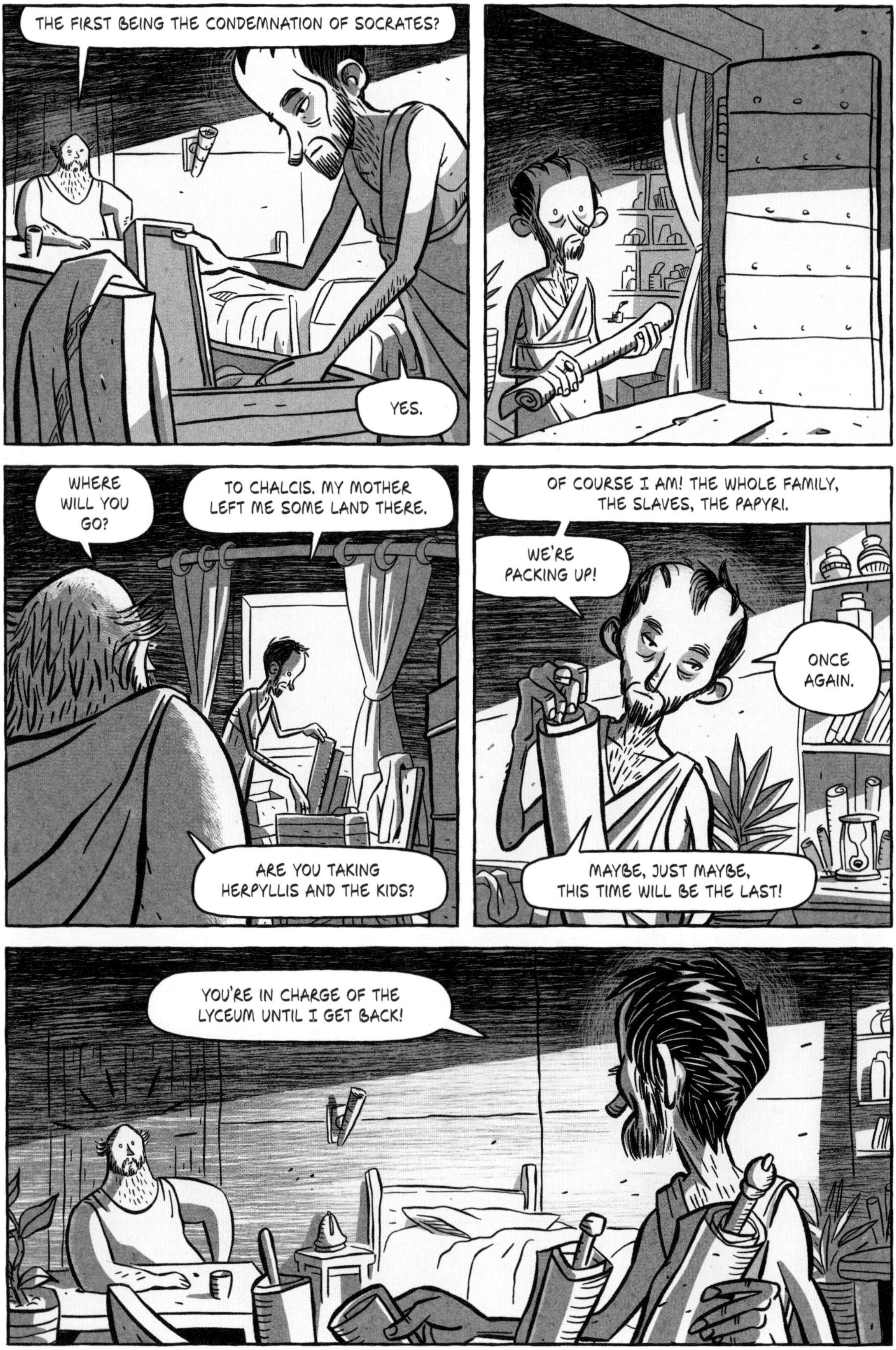
THE FIRST BEING THE CONDEMNATION OF SOCRATES?
YES.
WHERE WILL YOU GO?
TO CHALCIS. MY MOTHER LEFT ME SOME LAND THERE.
ARE YOU TAKING HERPYLLIS AND THE KIDS?
OF COURSE I AM! THE WHOLE FAMILY, THE SLAVES, THE PAPYRI.
WE'RE PACKING UP!
ONCE AGAIN.
MAYBE, JUST MAYBE, THIS TIME WILL BE THE LAST!
YOU'RE IN CHARGE OF THE LYCEUM UNTIL I GET BACK!

A few days later...

ALONG WITH PYTHIAS, ARISTOTLE'S 11-YEAR-OLD DAUGHTER, HERPYLLIS, ABOUT 30 AT THE TIME, RIDES IN THE FIRST WAGON. SHE HOLDS NICOMACHUS, HER 2-YEAR-OLD SON, IN HER ARMS.

TELL ME, ARISTOTLE, WHAT DOES ATHENS MEAN TO YOU?

ATHENS? IT'S A MAGNIFICENT CITY WHERE I LIVED FOR MORE THAN THIRTY YEARS! BUT SOMETHING TERRIBLY UGLY HIDES BEHIND ITS BEAUTY: SYCOPHANTS, THOSE SLANDEROUS PROFESSIONAL LIARS!

HEEYA!

- WHAT ARE YOU THINKING, ARISTOTLE?
  - THANKS FOR BEING BY MY SIDE, HERPYLLIS!
  - BUT OF COURSE!

- YOU ASKED WHAT I WAS THINKING?
  I WAS THINKING ABOUT MY FIRST TIME IN ATHENS.
  I WAS 17 YEARS OLD, I WAS FROM THE COUNTRY.
  I'D HEARD ABOUT THE CITY AND THE PEOPLE WHO LIVED THERE,
  BUT WHEN I SAW IT, I WAS LITERALLY STUNNED.
  EVERYTHING SEEMED SO BIG,
  SO SHINY!

Everything seemed big and shiny to him!

FIGS!!!

LEECHES!!!

MY FISH IS FRRRESH!

ΜΗΔΕΙΣ
ΑΓΕΩΜΕΤΡΗΤΟΣ
ΕΙΣΙΤΩ ΜΟΙ
ΤΗ ΘΥΡΑ

"ONLY GEOMETRISTS ALLOWED INSIDE!"

OH! THAT'S THE ENTRANCE TO PLATO'S "ACADEMY"!

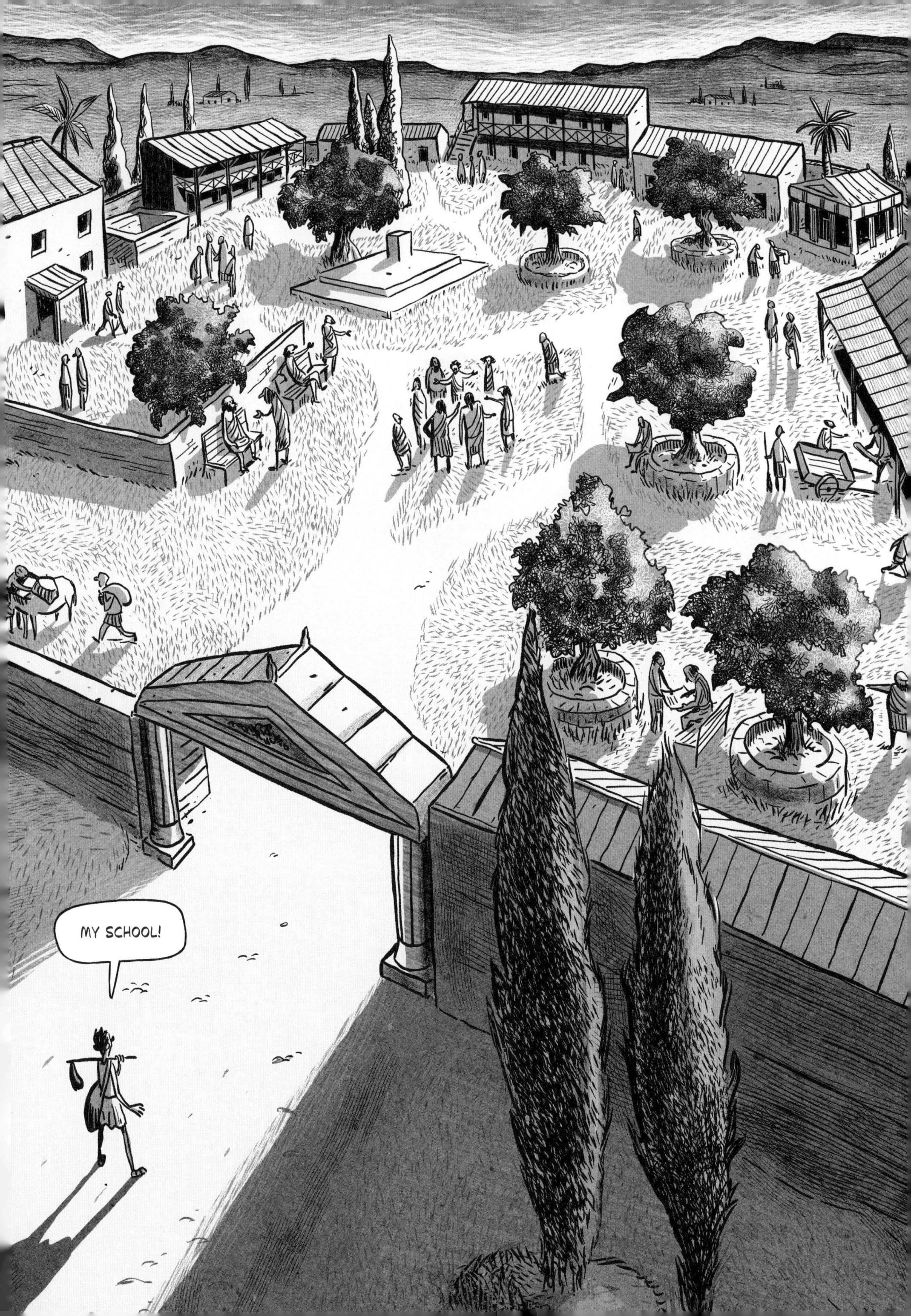
MY SCHOOL!

Aristotle was born in Stagira, in Macedonia. His father, Nicomachus, was a doctor in the court of King Amyntas III, Alexander's grandfather. His family is said to be descended from Asclepius, the god of medicine. Aristotle lost his mother and father when he was very young.

A relative, Proxenus of Atarneus in the Troad, became his guardian, and he lived with him through his adolescence. He encouraged Aristotle to choose the Academy for his advanced studies. Proxenus had Plato's first dialogues in his papyrus library.

As you know, the dialogues are philosophical writings in a particular style. They're like plays, and it's their dialogue that transmits the teachings of the great philosopher Socrates. Of course, Aristotle, a studious pupil, read them over and over again, and thus familiarized himself with the settings where the dialogues took place: generally in the Agora, the Athenian market, or a gymnasium, or a rich man's house.

He also knew about the Peloponnesian War, the civil war that the dialogues often allude to. He discovered in them the work of the sophists Protagoras, Gorgias, Hippias, as well as the politicians of the time: Alcibiades, Nicias, Charmides... He also discovered in the dialogues those burning questions that men ask themselves, such as: "What is it that defines ethical behavior?" "What is the best way to educate citizens?" "Why are laws important?" "What is the best form of government?"

I'M ARIST—

ARISTOTLE!

OH!

HERMIAS! AM I EVER SO GLAD TO SEE YOU!

- DID YOUR CLASSMATES SCARE YOU? THEY DO THAT TO ALL THE NEW STUDENTS, BUT THEY'RE NOT BAD GUYS.

  - I HOPE NOT!

   - PROXENUS WROTE, SAID YOU'D BE HERE.

    - DO YOU REMEMBER OUR ENDLESS CONVERSATIONS IN THE HOUSE IN ATARNEUS?

- OF COURSE I REMEMBER! I ALSO REMEMBER HOW HE WANTED US TO BE FRIENDS!

  - I THINK HE HAD SOMETHING ELSE IN MIND!

   - HE MIGHT HAVE! HA HA HA! HE'S THE ONE WHO SENT ME TO THE ACADEMY, TOO!

    - YES, I KNOW!

  - I'VE BEEN HERE ALMOST A YEAR! COME ON! I'LL INTRODUCE YOU TO THE DIRECTOR!

PLATO?

NO, EUDOXUS. HE'S A MATHEMATICIAN AND ASTRONOMER.

PLATO RETURNED TO SICILY AFTER HE TURNED 61.

HE'S TRYING TO CONVINCE DIONYSIUS, THE RULER OF SYRACUSE, TO APPLY HIS POLITICAL IDEAS!

- I KNOW THOSE IDEAS. THEY'RE IN "THE REPUBLIC." I'VE READ THAT WORK. DO YOU THINK THAT PLATO HAS ANY CHANCE OF GETTING HIS IDEAS IMPLEMENTED?

NONE! HE ALREADY TRIED 20 YEARS AGO. TOTAL FAILURE!

IS THAT WHEN HE WAS ARRESTED AND SOLD AS A SLAVE?

EXACTLY! LUCKILY, A CYRENIAN RECOGNIZED HIM AND BOUGHT HIM IN ORDER TO SET HIM FREE. SO HE CAME BACK TO ATHENS AND FOUNDED HIS SCHOOL, THE ACADEMY.

BONG!

OH, LOOK! EUDOXUS! EUDOXUS!

EUDOXUS, MEET ARISTOTLE. I TOLD YOU ABO—

I THINK THAT TWENTY-SEVEN SPHERES WILL SUFFICE FOR STUDYING THE MOTIONS OF THE PLANETS AND STARS.

AND WHAT DO YOU THINK, MY BOY?

FOR NOW, I DON'T HAVE AN OPINION BECAUSE I DON'T HAVE THE KNOWLEDGE. WHEN I DO, I'LL GIVE YOU AN ANSWER.

HA HA HA!

EXCELLENT. YOU PASSED THE TEST!

COME ON, I'LL SHOW YOU TO YOUR ROOM.

MOST OF THE TEACHERS AND NEARLY ALL THE STUDENTS LIVE HERE, CLOSE TO THE CLASSROOMS. THAT WAY THEY DON'T WASTE TIME GETTING AROUND, AND THEY CAN SPEND THEIR DAYS TOGETHER.

SO IN A WAY, YOU COULD SAY IT'S A SORT OF CLOSED SOCIETY?

YES, A LITTLE, LIKE THE PYTHAGOREANS HAVE IN KROTON.

YOU LIKE IT?

IT'S JUST WHAT I NEED!

THEN GET SETTLED IN! I'LL COME GET YOU WHEN IT'S TIME FOR DINNER.

THANKS, HERMIAS!

GOOD EVENING. ARISTOTLE'S GOING TO BE IN YOUR GROUP.

WELCOME! MY NAME IS XENOCRATES.

I'M CORISCUS!

AND I'M ERASTUS!

CLINIAS.

AND I'M PHILOLAUS. WE'RE TWINS!

HAVE A SEAT! I'LL GO GET YOU SOME FOOD. STARTING TOMORROW, YOU CAN SERVE YOURSELF IN THE KITCHEN.

- WHERE ARE YOU FROM?
- STAGIRA.

- WHERE'S THAT?
- IN THE CHALCIDICE. IT'S A COLONY FOUNDED BY PEOPLE FROM CHALCIS AND ANDROS.

- A MACEDONIAN, THEN!
- YES, A MACEDONIAN!
- I HEARD YOUR DAD WAS A DOCTOR.
- YES, HE WAS KING AMYNTAS OF MACEDONIA'S DOCTOR. BUT MY PARENTS DIED WHEN I WAS LITTLE, AND ONE OF MY RELATIVES IN ATARNEUS TOOK ME IN. HE HANDLED MY INHERITANCE AND GOT ME AN EDUCATION! THAT'S WHY I'M HERE TODAY!

- SO, WAS IT IN ATARNEUS THAT YOU MET HERMIAS?
- YES, HE WAS A CLOSE FRIEND OF MY GUARDIAN.
- I HEARD HE'S A EUNUCH!
- A LOT OF SLAVES ARE.
- DID YOU SAY SLAVE?
- YES, HERMIAS WAS THE SLAVE OF EUBULUS, THE ATARNEAN RULER. YOU DIDN'T KNOW THAT? THANKS TO HIS INTELLIGENCE AND MANY GREAT QUALITIES, HE GAINED HIS FREEDOM.

- HERMIAS IS AN EXCEPTIONAL MAN. SOMETHING TELLS ME HE'S GOT A BRIGHT FUTURE!
- SHH! HE'S COMING.

I SUGGEST THAT TOMORROW, BEFORE CLASSES START, XENOCRATES AND YOU GO TO THE MARKET. YOU CAN GET ANYTHING YOU NEED THERE.

SOUNDS GOOD!

YES, OF COURSE! THANK YOU!

ARE YOU ATHENIAN, XENOCRATES?

NO, I'M A METIC AS WELL. I COME FROM CHALCEDON, A TOWN NEAR BYZANTIUM.

HERE, OUTSIDE THE CITY WALLS, IS THE PUBLIC CEMETERY. JUST ON THE OTHER SIDE OF THE WALLS ARE WORKSHOPS. POTTERY WORKSHOPS, FOR THE MOST PART.

THAT HILL THERE IS THE PNYX. THAT'S WHERE THE CITY'S ECCLESIA MEETS. IT'S THE ASSEMBLY OF ATHENS'S FIFTY THOUSAND CITIZENS.

IT'S ALSO WHERE THE MOST IMPORTANT DECISIONS GET MADE.

THAT BIG BUILDING IS THE BOULEUTERION, WHERE THE BOULE, OR THE COUNCIL OF THE FIVE HUNDRED, MEETS.

ITS ROLE IS TO WRITE THE PROPOSALS THAT WILL BE SUBMITTED TO THE ECCLESIA. IT ALSO OVERSEES THE SIX HUNDRED MAGISTRATES, THE ARCHONS, WHO MAKE UP THE EXECUTIVE POWER.

HA HA HA! TELL ME, IS THIS A CLASS?

NO, JUST A CONVERSATION BETWEEN FRIENDS!

- SURE! SO, TO CONTINUE OUR CONVERSATION, WHAT ABOUT THE MILITARY LEADERSHIP? AND THE JUDICIARY?

- THAT'S WHAT I WAS ABOUT TO TELL YOU! THE ONLY MAGISTRATES WHO AREN'T CHOSEN BY DRAWING LOTS ARE THE TEN GENERALS. THEY LEAD THE ARMY AND DETERMINE ATHENS'S FOREIGN POLICY.

- AND THE JUDICIARY?

- TWO BODIES EXERCISE JUDICIAL POWER: THE HELIAIA, WHICH IS MADE UP OF SIX THOUSAND HELIASTS, CIVILIAN JUDGES CHOSEN BY LOT, AND THE AREOPAGUS, WHICH TRIES PREMEDITATED AND RELIGIOUS CRIMES.

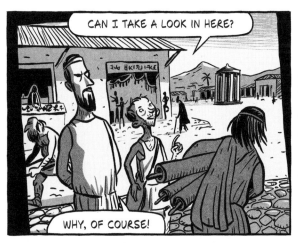

CAN I TAKE A LOOK IN HERE?

WHY, OF COURSE!

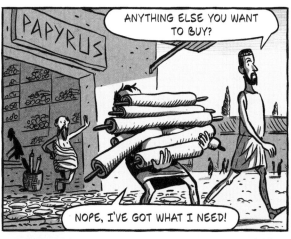

ANYTHING ELSE YOU WANT TO BUY?

NOPE, I'VE GOT WHAT I NEED!

THE STREETS OF ATHENS ARE SO NARROW THAT PEOPLE KNOCK AS THEY LEAVE THE HOUSE, SO THEIR DOORS DON'T WHACK A PASSERBY WHEN THEY OPEN THEM.

FASCINATING!

BANG!

HE SHOULD'VE KNOCKED.

At the Academy, pupils mainly learned... higher mathematics.

PLATO SAYS THAT FOR EVERYDAY CALCULATIONS, A BASIC FAMILIARITY WITH GEOMETRY AND ARITHMETIC IS ENOUGH. SUCH OPERATIONS CAN BE DONE BY SLAVES.

BUT TO ELEVATE HUMAN INTELLIGENCE, WE NEED HIGHER MATHEMATICS! FOR IT IS BY TRYING TO UNDERSTAND THESE CONCEPTS THAT MAN TOUCHES UPON...

...PHILOSOPHY AND THE IDEA OF ETHICS. MATHEMATICS AND ETHICS SHARE SOME COMMON POINTS, SUCH AS "DETERMINANTS," "ORDER," AND "SYMMETRY."

LEADERS, TO GIVE YOU AN EXAMPLE, MUST KNOW HIGHER MATHEMATICS, BECAUSE HIGHER MATHEMATICS LEADS TO PHILOSOPHICAL REFLECTION, AND THAT GUARANTEES AN ETHICAL MANNER OF GOVERNING!

HIGHER MATHEMATICS MIGHT VERY WELL HELP US WITH PHILOSOPHICAL REFLECTION AND WITH GOVERNING WELL, BUT AS YOU CAN SEE, LEODAMAS, THEY PUT US IN A TRICKY SPOT. EVERYONE ELSE HAS LEFT.

THE UNIVERSE, AS YOU SEE IT IN THIS MODEL OF CONCENTRIC SPHERES, HAS AT THE CENTER OUR SPHERICAL, IMMOBILE EARTH. THE STARS MOVE ALONG THE OUTER SPHERE. EACH ONE COMPLETES A FULL CIRCLE IN ONE DAY AND ONE NIGHT.

BUT TO REPRESENT THE MOTION OF THE FIVE PLANETS—MERCURY, VENUS, MARS, JUPITER, AND SATURN—I NEEDED FOUR SPHERES FOR EACH ONE OF THEM. THEY DO ACTUALLY MOVE ALONG A CIRCLE, BUT THEY DO IT IN AN IRREGULAR WAY!

AND FINALLY, TO REPRESENT THE MOTION OF THE MOON, I NEEDED THREE SPHERES, JUST AS I DID FOR THE SUN. IN TOTAL, THERE ARE 27 SPHERES!

27 SPHERES...

EUDOXUS...

...THAT'S A DESCRIPTION, NOT PROOF!

MY JOB IS TO NOTICE PHENOMENA, NOT TO PROVE THEM!

YOU WERE SO INSOLENT. YOU SHOULDN'T HAVE BEEN!

ON THE CONTRARY, HERMIAS! I HOLD EUDOXUS IN HIGH ESTEEM AND ALL I DID WAS GIVE HIM MY POINT OF VIEW.

FOR THE TIME BEING, IT SEEMS A LITTLE PREMATURE TO BE JUDGING YOUR TEACHERS. START BY LISTENING TO THEM AND WORKING.

I'M DOING JUST THAT!

LIBRARY

And of course, philosophy was taught...

THE WORD "PHILOSOPHY" IS MADE UP OF THE VERB "PHILO," TO LOVE, AND THE NOUN "SOPHIA," WISDOM. WISDOM IS KNOWLEDGE OF THE CAUSES OF THINGS THAT ALLOWS US, BEYOND JUST EXPLAINING PHENOMENA, TO DISCERN WHAT IS GOOD AND JUST.

THAT'S SPEUSIPPUS, PLATO'S NEPHEW. A PHILOSOPHER AND MATHEMATICIAN.

OH! I SEE!

A PHILOSOPHER IS SOMEONE WHO LOVES WISDOM AND, WITH OTHERS, SEEKS IT OUT.

AS PLATO SAYS, EVERY OBJECT IN OUR ENVIRONMENT THAT WE PERCEIVE THROUGH OUR MIND IS THE REFLECTION OF AN ETERNAL, UNCHANGEABLE "IDEA" LOCATED IN THE WORLD OF IDEAS!

SO WHAT IS REAL IS NOT THE WORLD IN WHICH WE LIVE, BUT A CERTAIN WORLD OF IDEAS SOMEWHERE!

SHH!

TRY AS I MIGHT, THIS IS ONE OF PLATO'S THEORIES I SIMPLY CANNOT SWALLOW!

YOU CAN TELL HIM THAT WHEN HE GETS BACK TO ATHENS! HA HA HA!

OBVIOUSLY!

I'LL ALSO TELL HIM THAT THE ONLY REALITY IS THE ONE WE PERCEIVE WITH OUR SENSES.

HE'LL BE THRILLED!

MAN'S SOUL AND HIS BODY ARE TWO DIFFERENT THINGS!

WHY ARE YOU ALL SO OBSESSED WITH THIS THEORY, SPEUSIPPUS?

SHH!

BEFORE BIRTH, A MAN'S SOUL IS IN THE HEAVENS, IN THE WORLD OF "IDEAS." THUS, IT HAS CONTEMPLATED EVERY ONE OF THEM.

BUT AT BIRTH, WHEN THE SOUL IS INCARNATED IN THE BODY, IT FORGETS THEM.

IT MUST THEREFORE REMEMBER THEM!

THUS, THE TRUTH TOWARD WHICH KNOWLEDGE STRIVES IS BUT THE REMINISCENCE OF IDEAS.

HMM...

I PERSONALLY THINK THAT TO REACH THE TRUTH AND KNOWLEDGE, WE MUST BEGIN WITH OUR EXPERIENCES IN THE WORLD...

...THE WORLD AROUND US, WHICH OUR SENSES REVEAL TO US.

THESE EXPERIENCES ARE DEVELOPED BY THE INTELLECT IN ORDER TO FORM...

...CONCEPTS, THE SCIENCES, AND THE ARTS!

REALLY?

WELL...

...TEACH THAT TO YOUR STUDENTS, IF YOU EVER HAVE ANY!

WHICH I HIGHLY DOUBT!

Teachers and students at the Academy weren't obliged to embrace Plato's theories.

In fact, everyone freely expressed their own points of view, all while working in collaboration with the others to advance research in a number of different fields.

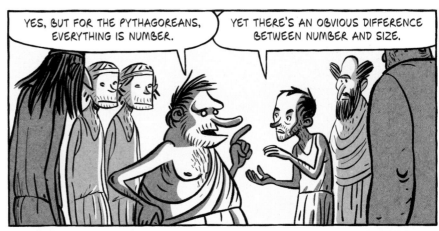

YES, BUT FOR THE PYTHAGOREANS, EVERYTHING IS NUMBER.

YET THERE'S AN OBVIOUS DIFFERENCE BETWEEN NUMBER AND SIZE.

Of course, sometimes there was friction!

GET OUT! IMMEDIATELY!

Aristotle was in Athens and at the Academy at the best possible moment. He found there learned men and conditions that allowed him to make the most of his abilities, to satisfy his desire to learn, to develop his thought, and to support his theories.

I'M TELLING YOU, SIZE IS DIVISIBLE. TAKE A RIBBON. WE CAN CUT IN TWO, THEN CUT THE HALVES IN TWO, AND SO ON AND SO ON.

YOU MEAN THAT THE RIBBON AND THUS ALL SIZES ARE MADE UP OF ELEMENTS THAT ARE INFINITELY DIVISIBLE?

He studied long and systematically the opinions and theories of philosophers of his time as well as those before him. He closely examined every thesis before either adopting or rejecting it.

He benefited from all the books he found at the school or that he bought. He attended class, took notes, and wrote summaries and outlines. Most of all he studied, studied, studied!

EXACTLY! EACH NUMBER, ON THE OTHER HAND, IS MADE UP OF INDIVISIBLE UNITS. AND THE ONLY POINT THAT NUMBER AND SIZE HAVE IN COMMON IS THAT ONE IS USED TO MEASURE THE OTHER. DO YOU GET IT?

AND WHAT DO YOU GET NOW THAT LEODAMAS HAS KICKED YOU OUT?

One day...

AND WE CAN DO IT?

THAT'S WHAT I'M SAYING! YOU IN?

I'M IN!

PYTHIONIKE WAS PERFECT!

AND MELISSA SO SWEET!

AND ARISTOTLE SO SLOW, DON'T YOU THINK?

WELL...

YES!

LET'S GO SEE! I'M WORRIED!

THUS, MOTION IS ENTELECHY, OR THE ACT OF MOVING IN AND OF ITSELF!

REALLY?

THAT'S A NICE RING YOU HAVE!

GLYKERA, LISTEN CLOSELY! IT'S BECAUSE OF ENTELECHY THAT MATTER TAKES FORM!

OH... MATTER IS LOVELY!

FOR WITHOUT FORM, MATTER IS INDETERMINATE.

IT IS? INDETERMINATE?

LET ME EXPLAIN. MATTER IS THE POTENTIAL OF THAT WHICH FORM WILL MAKE OF IT ONCE ACTUALIZED.

I SEE... POUR ME A LITTLE MORE OF THAT PURE WINE!

They usually cut it with water.

PSST!

WHAT?

MMMM!

WHAT ARE YOU TWO DOING?

WHAT ARE YOU TELLING HER?

WELL, WE'D FINISHED, SO I WAS EXPLAINING MY THEORY TO HER!

OH! I'VE DRUNK TOO MUCH! I'M SEEING DOUBLE!

YOU HAVE DRUNK TOO MUCH, BUT THOSE TWO ARE TWINS!

About two years later at the Academy...

ARISTOTLE, HAVE YOU HEARD THE NEWS?

I HEARD SOME TALK.

THE SATRAPS UNDER ARTAXERXES HAVE REVOLTED WITH THE HELP OF SPARTA AND ATHENS.

NO, NO! NOT THAT!

BEFORE THAT, THERE WAS THE THEBAN ALLIANCE WITH SPARTA AGAINST ATHENS!

PLATO IS BACK!

OH!

SPEUSIPPUS HAS ASKED US TO GATHER OUT ON THE SQUARE!

RIGHT NOW!

I HEARD YOU.

YOU CAN'T SEE OR HEAR ANYTHING!

COME ON! LET'S GO OVER THERE!

I'VE JUST RETURNED FROM A LONG, UNPLEASANT TWO-YEAR STAY IN SICILY...

...WHICH DID NOT MEET MY EXPECTATIONS.

AGAIN!

WHICH IS WHY I DECIDED TO STAY AND DEVOTE MYSELF ENTIRELY TO THE ACADEMY, WHICH IS OPERATING QUITE WELL AND TAKING IN NEW STUDENTS.

YOU, YOUNG MAN! YES, YOU, THE SCRAWNY LITTLE ONE WITH SHORT HAIR AND SMALL EYES AND SKINNY LEGS AND LOTS OF RINGS. WHAT'S YOUR NAME?

MY NAME'S ARISTOTLE! HOW COULD YOU SEE ALL THAT FROM SO FAR AWAY?

I CAN SEE FAR AWAY, BUT NOT UP CLOSE!

SO YOU'RE ARISTOTLE OF STAGIRA, YES?

THAT I AM!

SON OF NICOMACHUS AND PHAESTIS, WARD OF PROXENUS OF ATARNEUS, IN THE TROAD?

EXACTLY! HOW DO YOU KNOW ALL THAT?

- HA HA HA! I KNOW A LOT MORE THAN THAT! EUDOXUS, SPEUSIPPUS, AND SOME OTHERS WROTE ME ABOUT YOU!

- OH NO! I GET THE MESSAGE! SORRY ABOUT MY "AGAIN" A FEW MINUTES AGO. IT JUST POPPED OUT!

- ALRIGHT, ALRIGHT! ANYWAY, YOU WEREN'T WRONG. I'D ALREADY GOTTEN STUCK IN SICILY TWENTY YEARS AGO. I SHOULDN'T HAVE MADE THE SAME MISTAKE. "WISE MEN DON'T REPEAT THEIR MISTAKES."

- IS THAT ONE OF YOURS, MASTER?

- ALRIGHT, ALRIGHT. I ALSO KNOW THAT YOUR EDUCATION IN ATARNEUS FOLLOWED GREEK IDEALS: INDIVIDUAL LIBERTY, PARTICIPATION IN PUBLIC AFFAIRS, AND EQUALITY!

- IT'S TRUE. MY GUARDIAN MADE SURE OF IT!

BEFORE COMING TO THE ACADEMY, I'D ALREADY READ A FEW OF YOUR DIALOGUES: "LACHES," "CHARMIDES," "THE APOLOGY"...

ALRIGHT, ALRIGHT!

TELL ME WHAT YOU LIKED BEST IN THE "CHARMIDES"!

I SUPPOSE THE CLARITY OF YOUR APPROACH TO THE QUESTION OF WISDOM!

I'VE HEARD THAT YOU READ A LOT.

ALL THE TIME! I CAN'T LEARN BY LISTENING, THE WAY SOME CAN!

WHATEVER WORKS!

IN THE ACADEMY'S LIBRARY I FOUND AND READ YOUR OTHER DIALOGUES, THE PYTHAGOREAN THEORIES, THE POEMS OF ANTIMACHUS...

ALRIGHT, ALRIGHT...

ANY THOUGHTS ON ANTIMACHUS?

I THINK HIS POEMS ARE AS GOOD AS THOSE OF THE ELEGIAC POET MIMNERMUS, BUT HE HAS A MORE FORMAL APPROACH TO POETRY.

IN HIS POEM "LYDE," NAMED FOR HIS MISTRESS...

ALRIGHT, ALRIGHT!

PLATO DISLIKES ERUDITION, OR WHEN KNOWLEDGE OR INTELLIGENCE IS PUT ON DISPLAY.

OH, SO NOW YOU TELL ME!

AND HE SPEAKS DISPARINGLY OF THOSE "WHO FEED OFF THE KNOWLEDGE OF OTHERS"!

SO WHO DID HE WRITE ALL THOSE DIALOGUES AND TREATISES FOR? HUNDREDS OF COPIES OF THEM ARE OUT THERE! THE COPYISTS COULD LIVE OFF HIS WORK ALONE!

At that time, the slave who read texts out loud to students at school was called "anagnost," "reader." So if someone said "I read a treatise," he actually meant he'd heard it read. Aristotle, however, read the texts himself and studied them. That's why Plato made fun of him by calling him "the reader." But the habit was slowly adopted by his fellow students, as well as by many others. People began to prefer learning by reading rather than by listening.

Plato had also given Aristotle another nickname: "noûs," "the mind," borne before him by the philosopher Anaxagoras, who said that the mind puts into order everything that had until that point been mixed up!

IS THIS WHERE YOU LIVE?

YES.

CAN I COME IN?

BUT OF COURSE!

THIS IS CLEARLY THE READER'S ROOM!

LAO TZU?

YES, THE FATHER OF TAOISM.

SIDDHARTA GAUTAMA? CONFUCIUS?

NOT WELL KNOWN IN GREECE.

WHERE DID YOU GET THESE TEXTS? AND IN TRANSLATION!

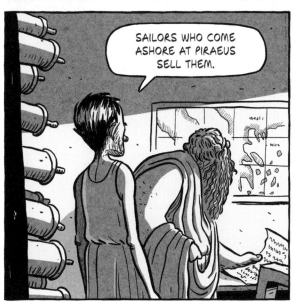

SAILORS WHO COME ASHORE AT PIRAEUS SELL THEM.

I ALSO HAVE WRITINGS BY THALES, HERACLITUS, PARMENIDES...

ALRIGHT, ALRIGHT!

- I ALSO LEARNED AT THE ACADEMY TO CLASSIFY BY SUBJECT ALL OF EXISTING KNOWLEDGE IN ORDER TO ACCESS IT EASILY IN THE FUTURE WHEN DOING RESEARCH.

- ALRIGHT! I WAS RIGHT WHEN I SAID THAT YOU'RE "THE MIND" OF THE ACADEMY, YOU GENIUS!!!

- YOU EXAGGERATE!

- NOT AT ALL! I WEIGH MY WORDS!

I THINK PLATO TRULY APPRECIATES YOU.

WE'LL SEE!

BECAUSE I HAVEN'T TOLD HIM YET THAT I DISAGREE WITH HIS "THEORY OF IDEAS."

DO YOU REALLY THINK THAT WAS THE MOMENT TO TELL HIM?

I FIND ARISTOTLE PERCEPTIVE, STUDIOUS, HARD-WORKING, AND HE READS A LOT.

YES, BUT...

BEFORE HIM, NO ONE HAD CLASSIFIED KNOWLEDGE BY SUBJECT.

YES, BUT...

IN A WAY THAT ALLOWS EACH CATEGORY TO BE STUDIED SEPARATELY, ACCORDING TO SCIENTIFIC METHODS!

YES, BUT... HE'S ALSO DEVELOPING HERETICAL THEORIES WHICH—

ALRIGHT, ALRIGHT!

44

REALLY? HERETICAL THEORIES?

AND THAT'S WHY, THEOPHRASTUS, THE ACADEMY WAS SUCH A THRIVING COMMUNITY OF LEARNED MEN.

IT CULTIVATED PERSONAL REFLECTION, ACCEPTED THE FREEDOM OF ONE'S OWN POINT OF VIEW, AND ENCOURAGED RESEARCH!

EXACTLY!

WHICH DOESN'T MEAN ALL POINTS OF VIEW WERE NECESSARILY ACCEPTED BY EVERYONE...

...OR THERE WASN'T JEALOUSY OR RIVALRY.

GIVE ME A HAND, CRITON!

I'M GOING TO START BY TALKING TO YOU ABOUT EDUCATION IN ATHENS AT THE TIME OF ARISTOTLE.

I'LL GIVE YOU A FEW HISTORICAL AND SOCIOLOGICAL ELEMENTS AS PROOF OF THE ASPIRATIONS OF CITIZENS THAT FURTHERED THE BLOSSOMING OF PHILOSOPHY.

As is still the case today, only boys went to school. A schoolmaster taught them to read and write, a cithara player taught them music, a gymnastics coach taught them physical exercises. They were mostly taught the Homeric epics. Afterward, those who wanted to could go to specialist teachers to learn a trade. They became doctors, sculptors, builders, or naval architects.

There was no systematic theoretical education until the sophists arrived. These teachers traveled around Greece and were paid to teach young people how to speak well and persuade their audience. According to them, the ability of students to succeed was no longer down to physical strength or courage, but was rather a question of intelligence and theoretic agility.

The philosophers agreed with them on this point, yet remained more theoretical in their methods. They sought the truth, the origins and causes of the existence of beings, and to know what a thing is and why it is the way it is.

After winning the Persian Wars, Athens created the Delian League, uniting a hundred and forty city-states, from the islands and the east coast of the Aegean Sea to Thrace and the Propontis. The cities paid Athens a tribute in order to obtain its "protection." In this way it became the greatest military, political, and economic power in all of Greece.

THRACE

Propontis

MACEDONIA

Aegean Sea

PERSIAN EMPIRE

ATHENS

CRETE

What's more, the system of direct democracy was a demanding one, since it required the participation not just of representatives, but all citizens.

The Athenians felt the need for a basic knowledge of politics, sociology, and ethics in order to fulfill with dignity the duties that their city assigned them. From then on, power would belong to those who were capable of convincing the greatest number of citizens...

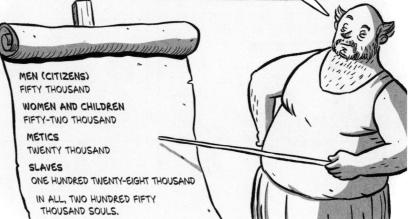

THE CITY-STATE OF ATHENS PRACTICED DIRECT DEMOCRACY. IT WASN'T VERY LARGE AND HAD A SMALL NUMBER OF CITIZENS. ITS POPULATION COULD BE BROKEN DOWN AS SUCH.

MEN (CITIZENS)
FIFTY THOUSAND

WOMEN AND CHILDREN
FIFTY-TWO THOUSAND

METICS
TWENTY THOUSAND

SLAVES
ONE HUNDRED TWENTY-EIGHT THOUSAND

IN ALL, TWO HUNDRED FIFTY THOUSAND SOULS.

...thus, the need to learn rhetoric, that is to say, the art of speech and argumentation.

Rhetors, sophists, and philosophers flocked to Athens to teach. Their classes touched on a number of subjects and were adapted as much to the needs as to the intellectual aspirations of their citizen-students.

Men now took an interest in familial and social interpersonal relationships, as well as in the application of law and in the pursuit of happiness.

At the same time, Athens had provoked the anger of allied cities by interfering in their domestic affairs.

As for Sparta, it did not look favorably upon the expansionist policies of Athens.

Add to that the end of the Persian threat, and you'll better understand first the allies' uprising, then the Peloponnesian War pitting Athens against Sparta.

Thirty years of civil war weakened all of the cities, but most of all sounded the death knell for Athenian grandeur.

And yet it was at that time that tragedy, comedy, historiography, the arts, and, of course, philosophy flourished in the city, attracting an ever-growing number of artists and writers from all around the Mediterranean.

47

The war ended in the defeat of Athens.

The tyrannical government imposed by the victors didn't last more than a year.

Democracy was re-established with trust and hope, despite the economic difficulties.

The Athenians attempted to restore their mastery of the sea, and they created the Second Athenian League, whereby the islands and coastal cities promised each other mutual protection.

The partisans of democracy were the small farmers, small-business owners, and landless peasants. Its main opponents were the aristocratic land owners, who had never been able to take back power.

The citizens were faced with new challenges, which had to be met with discernment.

For answers to their questions, to their worries, to their troubles, the Athenians turned once again to the practitioners of philosophy.

WHAT IS THE BEST FORM OF GOVERNMENT?

DEMOCRACY. AND IT COULD BE IMPROVED IF THOSE WHO GOVERN WERE ELECTED BY THE PEOPLE INSTEAD OF CHOSEN BY LOT.

WHAT MAKES A CITIZEN A GOOD CITIZEN?

WHEN ONE IS CAPABLE TO BOTH RULE AND BE RULED.

WHAT IS THE BEST EDUCATION FOR CITIZENS?

LEARNING AND PHYSICAL ACTIVITY.

EACH PERSON'S OWN TEMPERAMENT IS ALSO IMPORTANT.

PLATO, THE PEOPLE ARE HUNGRY TO LEARN. PERHAPS WE SHOULD INCREASE THE NUMBER OF OUR CLASSES AND HIRE ADDITIONAL TEACHERS?

I THOUGHT ABOUT THAT TOO, BUT CIRCUMSTANCES ARE NOT FAVORABLE FOR INVESTING. BESIDES, SOMETHING'S GOING ON WITH THE MACEDONIANS.

SPEAKING OF MACEDONIANS, I THINK ARISTOTLE IS NOW READY TO DO SOME TEACHING. HE'S BEEN HERE WITH US FOR NEARLY TEN YEARS!

I ENTIRELY AGREE! BUT HE DIDN'T WAIT FOR US TO ASK! HE'S ALREADY STARTED! COME AND SEE.

YES, TAKE NOTES DURING CLASS, BUT WHILE YOU'RE READING AS WELL. MAKE OUTLINES AND WRITE THEMATIC SUMMARIES.

PHILOSOPHY CONSISTS OF THINKING ABOUT SUBJECTS THAT WEIGH ON OUR DAILY LIVES, ABOUT WHAT IS HAPPENING AROUND US, OR ABOUT ANYTHING THAT HAS AN IMPACT ON OUR BEHAVIOR, OUR POLITICS...

WE WANT TO ATTAIN KNOWLEDGE THAT'S ACQUIRED THROUGH THE OBSERVATION OF THE WORLD WITH OUR SENSES.

KNOWLEDGE THAT THE INTELLECT WILL THEN DEVELOP IN ORDER TO LEAD US TO THE TRUTH.

THERE ARE TWO MAIN WAYS TO EXPLAIN AN EVENT OR A PHENOMENON: EITHER TO DETERMINE ITS "MATERIAL CAUSE," MEANING "BY WHAT MEANS" IT HAPPENED...

...OR TO DETERMINE ITS "FINALITY," MEANING "THE REASON FOR WHICH" IT HAPPENED.

LET'S TAKE A PHENOMENON AND EXPLAIN IT IN THE TWO WAYS. PHANIAS, WHEN IT RAINS, WHY DOES IT RAIN?

WELL, BECAUSE THERE ARE CLOUDS!

EXACTLY! CLOUDS ARE THE MATERIAL CAUSE OF RAIN!

NOW YOU, LYCANDER, ANSWER MY QUESTION IN THE OTHER WAY: WHY DOES IT RAIN?

TO WATER THE EARTH AND GIVE US WATER TO DRINK.

BRAVO! I SEE THAT YOU HAVE UNDERSTOOD THE DIFFERENCE!

WHICH RESPONSE SEEMS TO BE THE MOST RELEVANT?

MAYBE THE SECOND ONE?

WITHOUT WATER, NEITHER WE NOR NATURE WOULD EXIST!

GREAT! LET'S CONTINUE!

IF WE WISH TO UNDERSTAND THE WORLD, WE MUST UNDERSTAND EVERYTHING THAT'S IN IT. IMAGINE THAT THE WORLD IS A BOX, LIKE THIS ONE, FOR EXAMPLE, FULL OF MANY THINGS.

IF WE TRY TO UNDERSTAND WHAT THE BOX IS BUT DON'T KNOW ITS CONTENTS, WE'RE NOT GOING TO GET ANYWHERE.

BUT WHEN WE'VE EXPLAINED EVERYTHING THAT'S INSIDE THE BOX, THEN WE'LL UNDERSTAND EVERYTHING THAT IS RELATED TO THE WORLD.

???

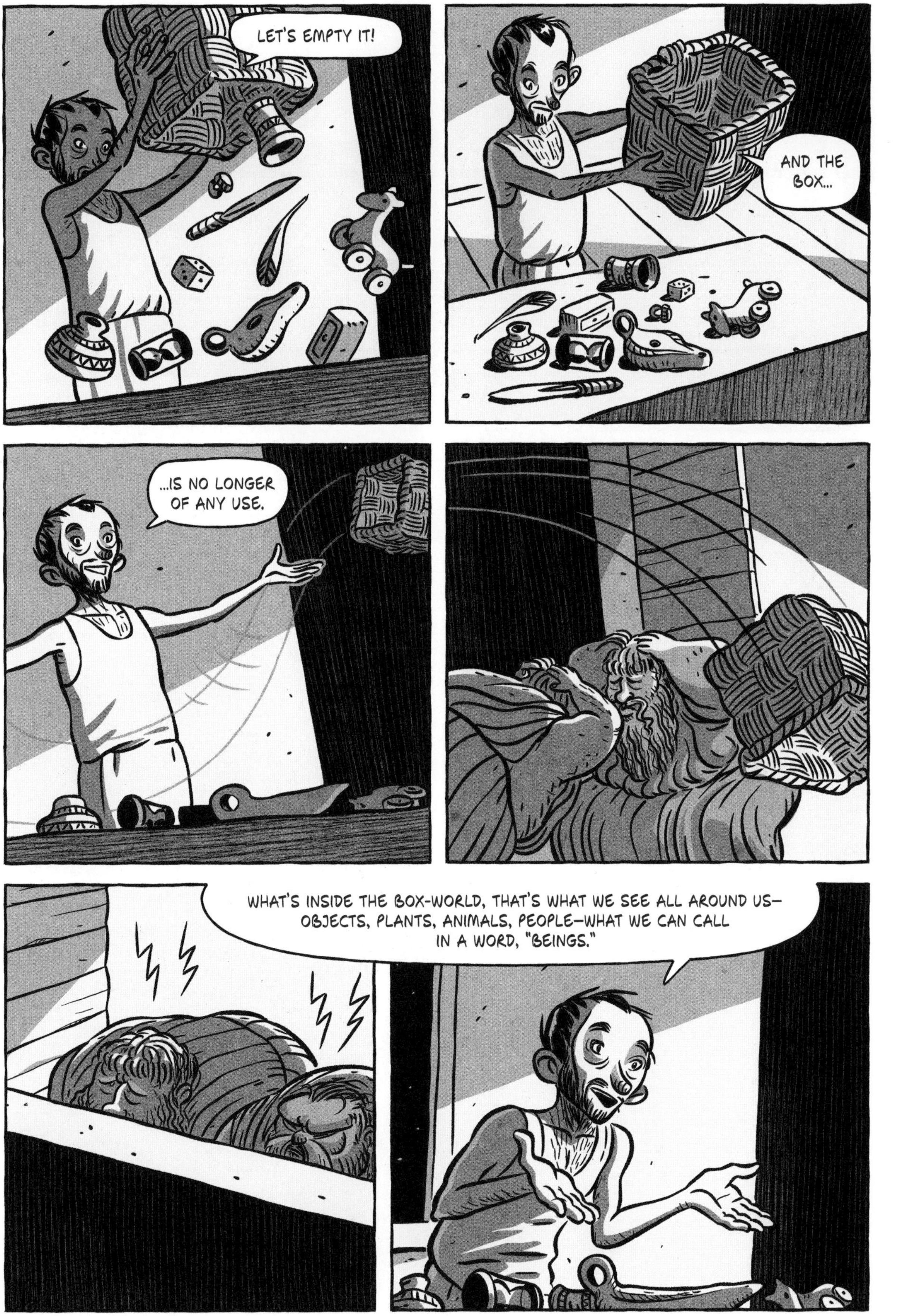
LET'S EMPTY IT!
AND THE BOX...
...IS NO LONGER OF ANY USE.
WHAT'S INSIDE THE BOX-WORLD, THAT'S WHAT WE SEE ALL AROUND US—OBJECTS, PLANTS, ANIMALS, PEOPLE—WHAT WE CAN CALL IN A WORD, "BEINGS."

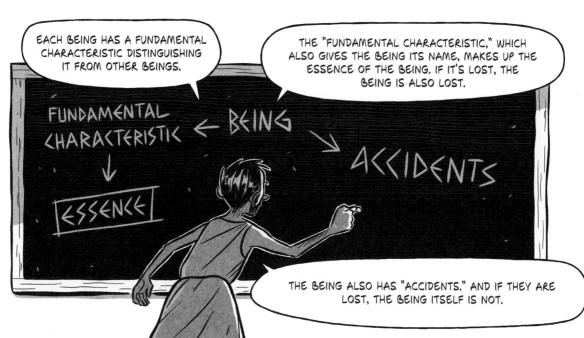

EACH BEING HAS A FUNDAMENTAL CHARACTERISTIC DISTINGUISHING IT FROM OTHER BEINGS.

THE "FUNDAMENTAL CHARACTERISTIC," WHICH ALSO GIVES THE BEING ITS NAME, MAKES UP THE ESSENCE OF THE BEING. IF IT'S LOST, THE BEING IS ALSO LOST.

THE BEING ALSO HAS "ACCIDENTS." AND IF THEY ARE LOST, THE BEING ITSELF IS NOT.

FOR EXAMPLE?

LOOK AT THIS YELLOW OIL LAMP!

IF WE WERE TO PAINT IT WHITE, IT WOULD STILL BE AN OIL LAMP.

THUS, ITS COLOR IS NOT NECESSARY FOR THE EXISTENCE OF THE LAMP!

EXACTLY! COLOR IS AN "ACCIDENT."

BUT IF I BREAK THE LAMP...

CRAC

ALL THAT REMAIN ARE PIECES OF TERRA-COTTA.

52

SO "LAMP" IS THE SUBSTANCE OF THE BEING, THAT IS TO SAY, ITS "FUNDAMENTAL CHARACTERISTIC"!

BEINGS, CONCRETE THINGS SUCH AS A TREE OR A TABLE, OR ABSTRACT NOTIONS SUCH AS JUSTICE OR MERCY, ARE GRAMMATICAL SUBJECTS. THE "ACCIDENTS" ARE PREDICATES.

IT'S A WAY FOR YOU TO REALIZE THAT "ACCIDENTS" DON'T EXIST IN AND OF THEMSELVES. ALL THEY DO IS QUALIFY BEINGS.

"WHITE" ON ITS OWN DOESN'T REFER TO ANY BEING, WHEREAS "THE WHITE OIL LAMP" DOES.

WOW, MASTER! WHAT YOU SPOKE ABOUT TODAY ALONE MAKES STUDYING PHILOSOPHY WORTHWHILE!

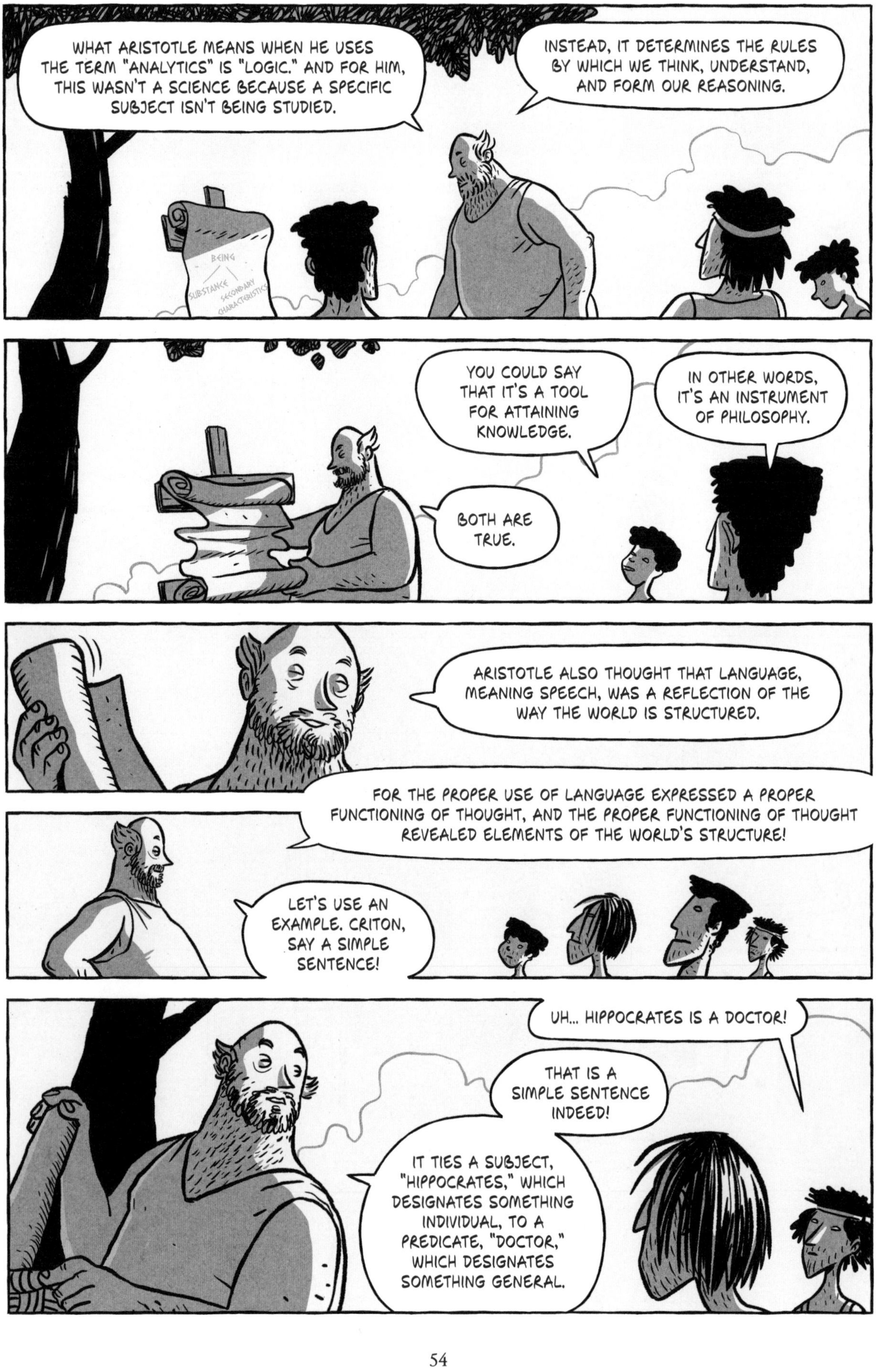
WHAT ARISTOTLE MEANS WHEN HE USES THE TERM "ANALYTICS" IS "LOGIC." AND FOR HIM, THIS WASN'T A SCIENCE BECAUSE A SPECIFIC SUBJECT ISN'T BEING STUDIED.
INSTEAD, IT DETERMINES THE RULES BY WHICH WE THINK, UNDERSTAND, AND FORM OUR REASONING.
BEING
SUBSTANCE
SECONDARY CHARACTERISTICS
YOU COULD SAY THAT IT'S A TOOL FOR ATTAINING KNOWLEDGE.
IN OTHER WORDS, IT'S AN INSTRUMENT OF PHILOSOPHY.
BOTH ARE TRUE.
ARISTOTLE ALSO THOUGHT THAT LANGUAGE, MEANING SPEECH, WAS A REFLECTION OF THE WAY THE WORLD IS STRUCTURED.
FOR THE PROPER USE OF LANGUAGE EXPRESSED A PROPER FUNCTIONING OF THOUGHT, AND THE PROPER FUNCTIONING OF THOUGHT REVEALED ELEMENTS OF THE WORLD'S STRUCTURE!
LET'S USE AN EXAMPLE. CRITON, SAY A SIMPLE SENTENCE!
UH... HIPPOCRATES IS A DOCTOR!
THAT IS A SIMPLE SENTENCE INDEED!
IT TIES A SUBJECT, "HIPPOCRATES," WHICH DESIGNATES SOMETHING INDIVIDUAL, TO A PREDICATE, "DOCTOR," WHICH DESIGNATES SOMETHING GENERAL.

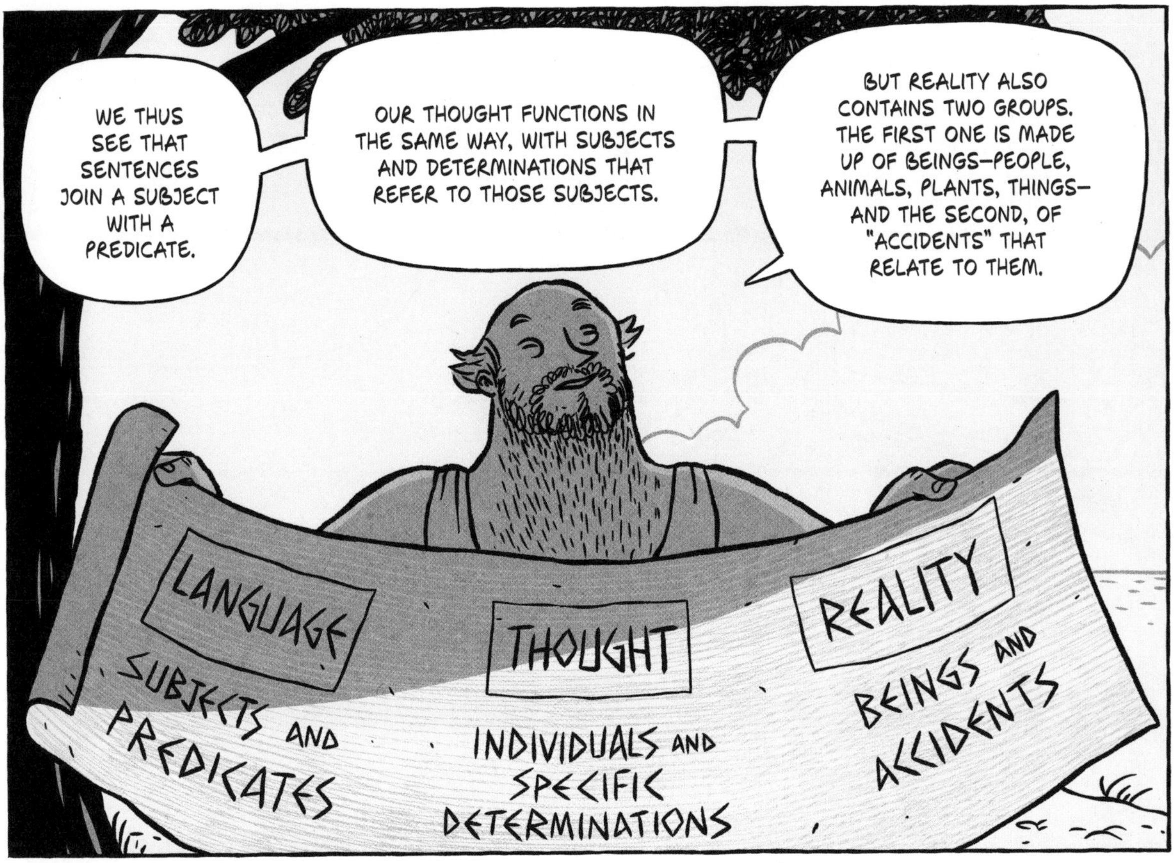
WE THUS SEE THAT SENTENCES JOIN A SUBJECT WITH A PREDICATE.
OUR THOUGHT FUNCTIONS IN THE SAME WAY, WITH SUBJECTS AND DETERMINATIONS THAT REFER TO THOSE SUBJECTS.
BUT REALITY ALSO CONTAINS TWO GROUPS. THE FIRST ONE IS MADE UP OF BEINGS—PEOPLE, ANIMALS, PLANTS, THINGS—AND THE SECOND, OF "ACCIDENTS" THAT RELATE TO THEM.
LANGUAGE
SUBJECTS AND PREDICATES
THOUGHT
INDIVIDUALS AND SPECIFIC DETERMINATIONS
REALITY
BEINGS AND ACCIDENTS

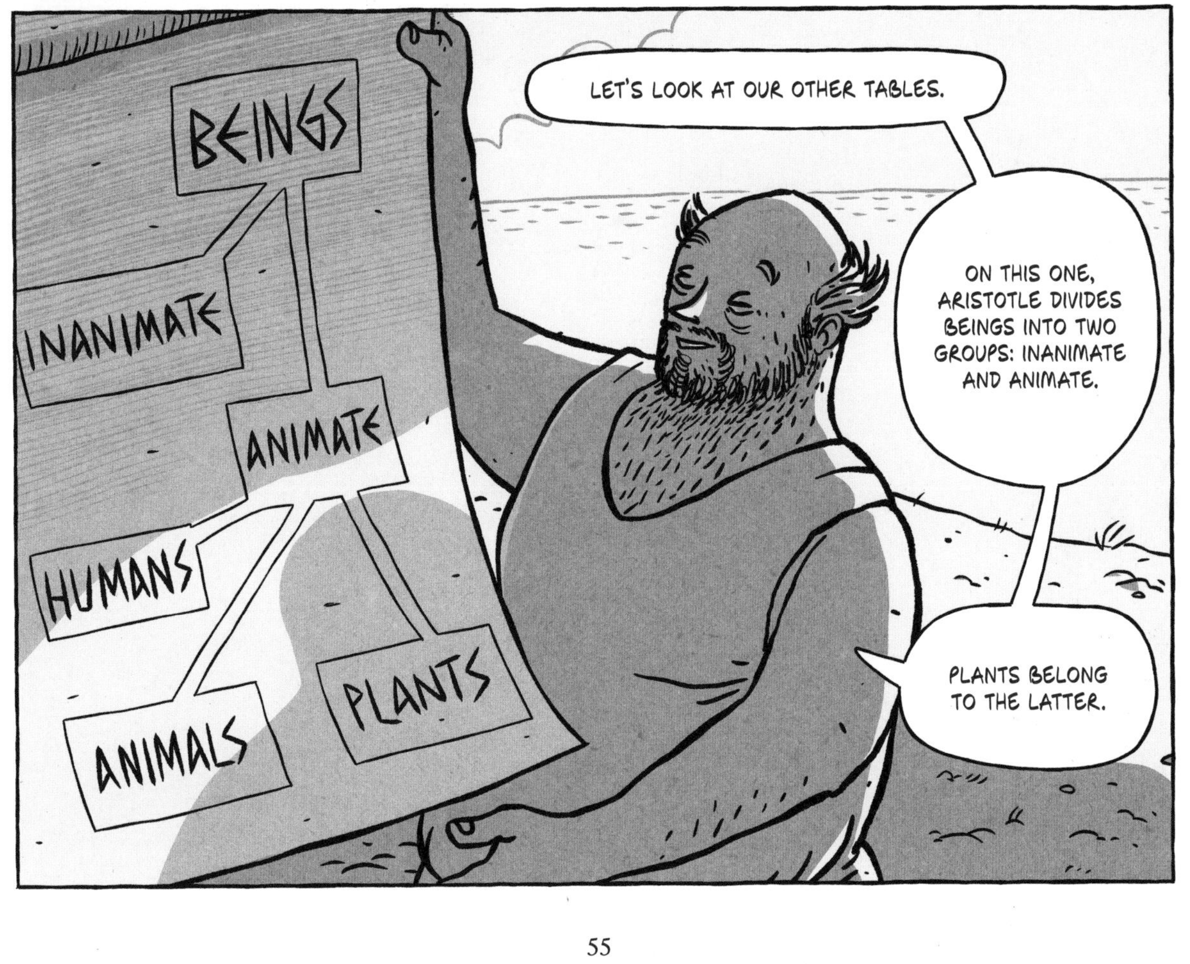
LET'S LOOK AT OUR OTHER TABLES.
BEINGS
INANIMATE
ANIMATE
HUMANS
ANIMALS
PLANTS
ON THIS ONE, ARISTOTLE DIVIDES BEINGS INTO TWO GROUPS: INANIMATE AND ANIMATE.
PLANTS BELONG TO THE LATTER.

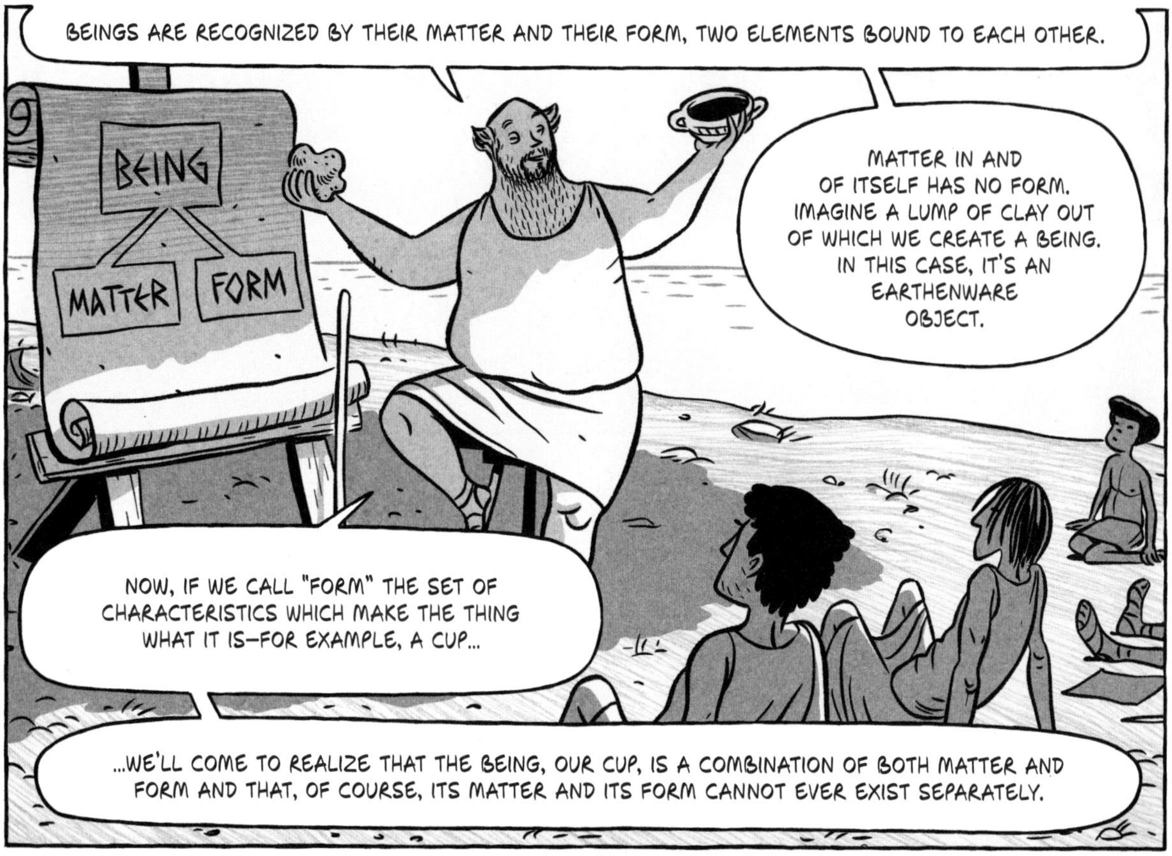
BEINGS ARE RECOGNIZED BY THEIR MATTER AND THEIR FORM, TWO ELEMENTS BOUND TO EACH OTHER.
BEING
MATTER
FORM
MATTER IN AND OF ITSELF HAS NO FORM. IMAGINE A LUMP OF CLAY OUT OF WHICH WE CREATE A BEING. IN THIS CASE, IT'S AN EARTHENWARE OBJECT.
NOW, IF WE CALL "FORM" THE SET OF CHARACTERISTICS WHICH MAKE THE THING WHAT IT IS—FOR EXAMPLE, A CUP...
...WE'LL COME TO REALIZE THAT THE BEING, OUR CUP, IS A COMBINATION OF BOTH MATTER AND FORM AND THAT, OF COURSE, ITS MATTER AND ITS FORM CANNOT EVER EXIST SEPARATELY.

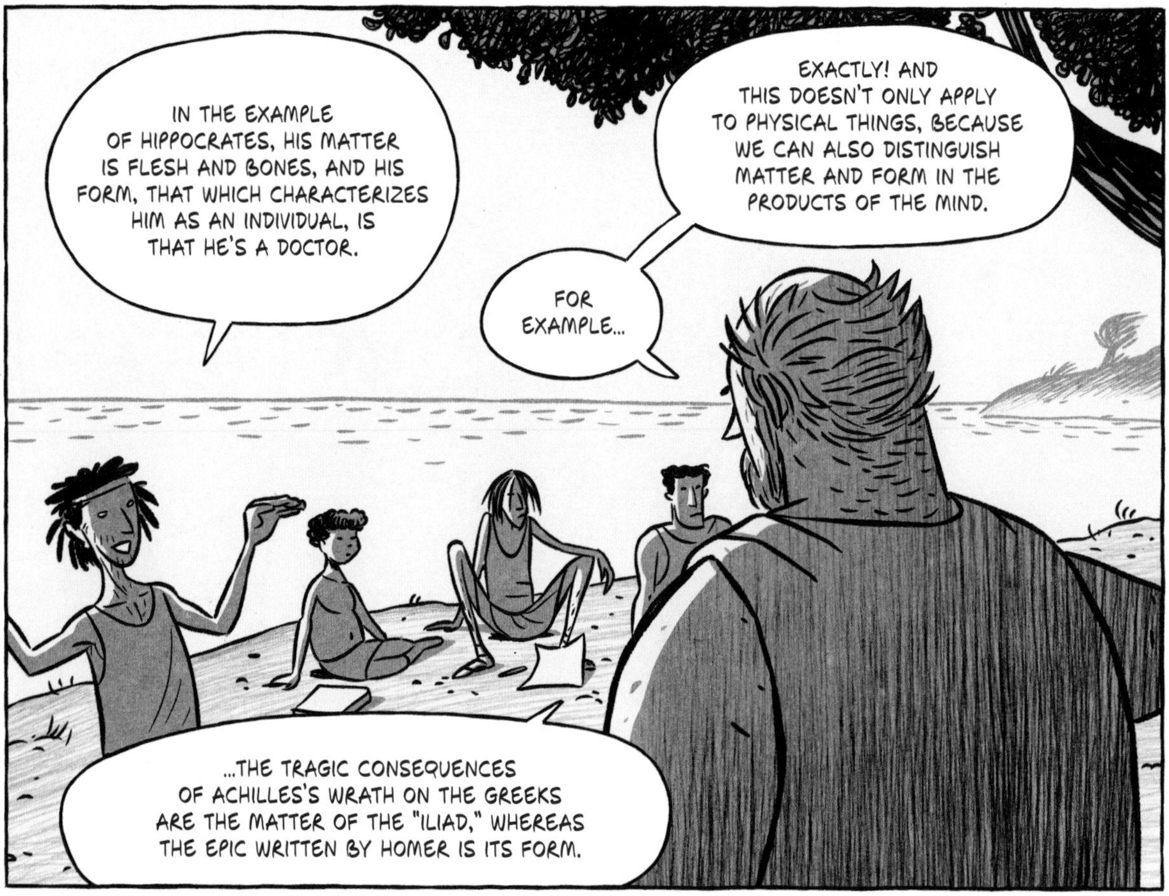
IN THE EXAMPLE OF HIPPOCRATES, HIS MATTER IS FLESH AND BONES, AND HIS FORM, THAT WHICH CHARACTERIZES HIM AS AN INDIVIDUAL, IS THAT HE'S A DOCTOR.
EXACTLY! AND THIS DOESN'T ONLY APPLY TO PHYSICAL THINGS, BECAUSE WE CAN ALSO DISTINGUISH MATTER AND FORM IN THE PRODUCTS OF THE MIND.
FOR EXAMPLE...
...THE TRAGIC CONSEQUENCES OF ACHILLES'S WRATH ON THE GREEKS ARE THE MATTER OF THE "ILIAD," WHEREAS THE EPIC WRITTEN BY HOMER IS ITS FORM.

TO CONCLUDE, WE'LL TALK ABOUT "CATEGORIES," WHICH ARE THE SET OF WAYS IN WHICH A PREDICATE CAN BE ATTRIBUTED TO A SUBJECT TO QUALIFY A BEING.

TO BEGIN WITH, WE CAN TALK ABOUT A THING AS A SUBSTANCE. SUBSTANCE REFERS HERE TO THE INDIVIDUAL. THE NINE "CATEGORIES" THAT THEN FOLLOW REFER TO ALL THE OTHER THINGS THAT WE CAN SAY ABOUT THE SUBSTANCE. LET'S APPLY THIS TO MY DOG. ETOLOS, GIVE IT A GO!

SUBSTANCE — THE DOG·

QUALITY — BROWN FUR

QUANTITY — ABOUT TWO CUBITS

RELATION — THEOPHRASTUS'S DOG

TIME — AFTERNOON

PLACE — ENTRYWAY

POSITION — SITTING

POSSESSION — HUNGER

ACTION — WAGGING ITS TAIL

AFFECTION — GLUTTONY

THESE CATEGORIES MIGHT ALSO BE QUESTIONS THAT WE ASK OURSELVES IN ORDER TO BETTER UNDERSTAND THE BEING BY LEARNING MORE ABOUT IT.

- ARISTOTLE HAS CALLED YOUR IDEA "FORM" AND LINKED IT TO MATTER TO MAKE THE BEING.
- THERE ARE OTHER POINTS ON WHICH WE'RE IN DISAGREEMENT, BUT THERE ARE ALSO MANY ON WHICH WE'RE NOT!

- BUT THAT'S NOT ALL.
- WHAT ELSE?
- HE BRINGS DEAD ANIMALS INTO HIS ROOM AND CUTS THEM OPEN!
- WHY?
- HE'S PERFORMING "DISSECTIONS," HE SAYS, TO SEE WHAT THEIR INSIDES ARE LIKE.
- NOW, THAT'S SERIOUS!
- HE ALSO COLLECTS INTELLIGENCE ON THE POLITICAL REGIMES OF DIFFERENT CITIES!
- TO WHAT END?
- HE GATHERS IT FOR ANALYSIS AND COMPARISON.
- HE'S WASTING HIS TIME! I'LL GO TALK TO HIM RIGHT NOW!

- AS YOU KNOW, PHILOLAUS, KNOWLEDGE IS A CONVICTION CONCERNING THE EXISTENCE, NATURE, OR CONDITION OF A BEING, BASED ON REASONING.

DO YOU REMEMBER THAT DAY SPEUSIPPUS GOT ANGRY WHEN I SAID THAT THE INTELLECT STARTED WITH EXPERIENCE, AND FROM THERE IT PROGRESSIVELY DREW OUT CONCEPTS AND DEVELOPED THE SCIENCES?

OF COURSE! IT CAUSED QUITE A HUBBUB!

WELL, TODAY NO ONE DISPUTES THAT MAN CAN ACQUIRE CERTAIN, VALID KNOWLEDGE THANKS TO SCIENCE, WHICH IS...

ENOUGH, ARISTOTLE. WE'RE HERE!

...A SYSTEM OF TRUE PROPOSITIONS THAT REFER TO A PRECISE SUBJECT, WHETHER IT BE MATHEMATICS, PHYSICS, HEALTH...

GOOD EATS
PUBLIC AND PRIVATE BANQUETS

HEY, CORISCUS!

HELLO!

ARE THE OTHERS HERE?

THEY'RE INSIDE!

REALLY, ARISTOTLE, YOU ARE ELEGANCE IN THE FLESH! ALL COVERED IN SILK AND JEWELRY!

YOU KNOW THAT I LIKE TO DRESS WELL!

IS THAT ALL?

AND TO EAT WELL, TOO.

IS THAT ALL?

I DO ALSO LIKE PRETTY GIRLS!

TONIGHT YOU CAN SEE CALLIDA. SHE'S DANCING HERE AT "GOOD EATS" FOR THE FIRST TIME!

IS SHE PRETTY?

ALL THE GIRLS WHO WORK AT "GOOD EATS" ARE BEAUTIFUL!

CALLIDA WORKS AT "GOOD EATS"...

...THUS, SHE IS BEAUTIFUL!

COME TAKE A SEAT!

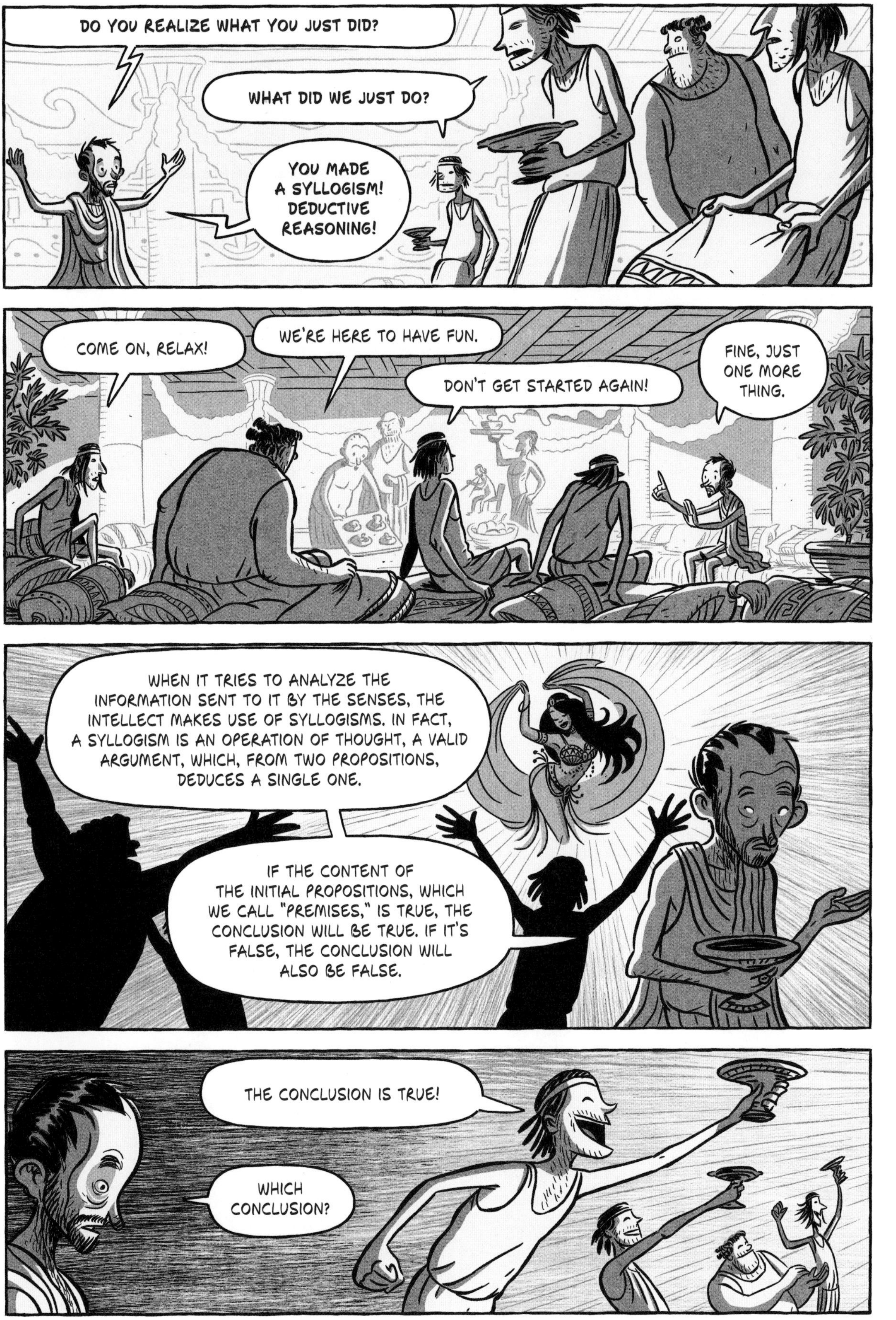
DO YOU REALIZE WHAT YOU JUST DID?
WHAT DID WE JUST DO?
YOU MADE A SYLLOGISM! DEDUCTIVE REASONING!
COME ON, RELAX!
WE'RE HERE TO HAVE FUN.
DON'T GET STARTED AGAIN!
FINE, JUST ONE MORE THING.
WHEN IT TRIES TO ANALYZE THE INFORMATION SENT TO IT BY THE SENSES, THE INTELLECT MAKES USE OF SYLLOGISMS. IN FACT, A SYLLOGISM IS AN OPERATION OF THOUGHT, A VALID ARGUMENT, WHICH, FROM TWO PROPOSITIONS, DEDUCES A SINGLE ONE.
IF THE CONTENT OF THE INITIAL PROPOSITIONS, WHICH WE CALL "PREMISES," IS TRUE, THE CONCLUSION WILL BE TRUE. IF IT'S FALSE, THE CONCLUSION WILL ALSO BE FALSE.
THE CONCLUSION IS TRUE!
WHICH CONCLUSION?

- ABOUT CALLIDA! SHE'S GORGEOUS!
- ON THAT SUBJECT, SYLLOGISMS, IN ACCORDANCE WITH THE FUNCTIONING OF THOUGHT...
- DO YOU WANT ME TO TELL YOU HOW MY THOUGHT FUNCTIONS WHEN I LOOK AT CALLIDA?
- ...SO, THIS REASONING CAN BE DIVIDED INTO TWO CATEGORIES: DEDUCTIVE SYLLOGISMS, WHICH, STARTING WITH GENERAL PREMISES, LEAD TO A PARTICULAR CONCLUSION, AS IN THE CASE OF CALLIDA...
  ...AND INDUCTIVE SYLLOGISMS, WHICH, STARTING WITH SPECIFIC PROPOSITIONS, LEAD TO A GENERAL CONCLUSION. HOW ABOUT ANOTHER EXAMPLE OF A DEDUCTIVE SYLLOGISM?
- HOW ABOUT YOU GIVE US A REST!

LISTEN! ALL MEN ARE MORTAL, CLINIAS AND PHILOLAUS ARE MEN. THUS, CLINIAS AND PHILOLAUS ARE MORTAL!

GO TO HELL, KILLJOY!

IS THAT THE ONLY EXAMPLE YOU COULD COME UP WITH?

NO! I'VE ALSO GOT AN EXAMPLE OF AN INDUCTIVE SYLLOGISM!

HAAAA HA HAAAAA

IF WE'VE ONLY EVER SEEN WHITE SWANS, WE DEDUCE THAT ALL SWANS ARE WHITE, UNTIL WE ACTUALLY SEE A BLACK SWAN. AT THAT POINT OUR CONCLUSION BECOMES FALSE.

IS THAT WHAT YOU SEE THERE, ARISTOTLE? A BLACK SWAN?

IT'S TRUE THAT INDUCTIVE REASONING IS WEAKER THAN DEDUCTIVE REASONING.

LOOK AT THAT! I'M SPEECHLESS!

WHAT'S HE GOT THAT WOMEN LIKE SO MUCH?

HE MUST SURELY HAVE A CERTAIN ACCIDENT THAT WE HAVE NO WAY OF KNOWING ABOUT!

DO YOU THINK HE'S GOING TO TALK HER EARS OFF WITH ALL THOSE SYLLOGISMS, CONCLUSIONS, AND ENTELECHIES?

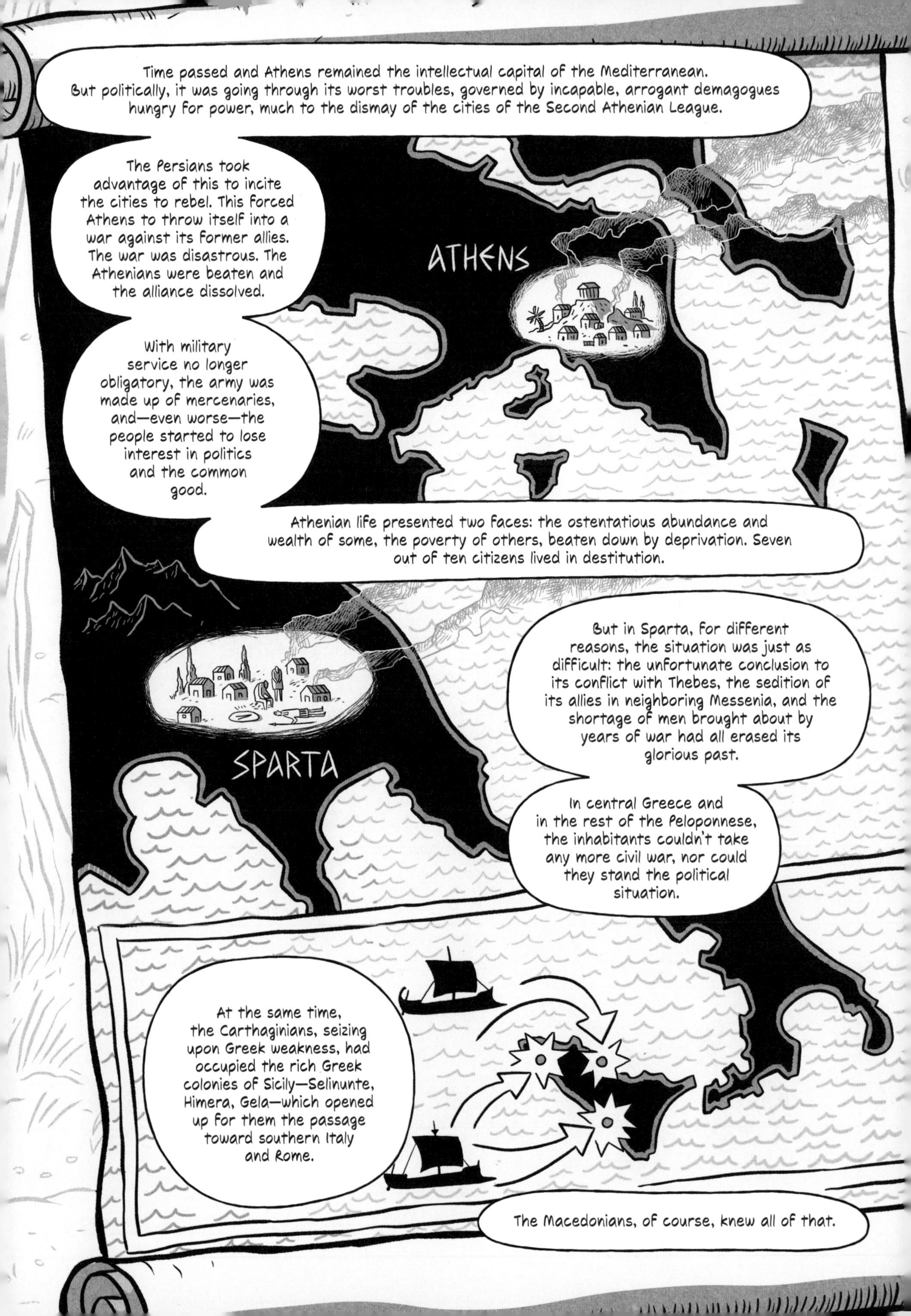
Time passed and Athens remained the intellectual capital of the Mediterranean. But politically, it was going through its worst troubles, governed by incapable, arrogant demagogues hungry for power, much to the dismay of the cities of the Second Athenian League.
The Persians took advantage of this to incite the cities to rebel. This forced Athens to throw itself into a war against its former allies. The war was disastrous. The Athenians were beaten and the alliance dissolved.
ATHENS
With military service no longer obligatory, the army was made up of mercenaries, and—even worse—the people started to lose interest in politics and the common good.
Athenian life presented two faces: the ostentatious abundance and wealth of some, the poverty of others, beaten down by deprivation. Seven out of ten citizens lived in destitution.
But in Sparta, for different reasons, the situation was just as difficult: the unfortunate conclusion to its conflict with Thebes, the sedition of its allies in neighboring Messenia, and the shortage of men brought about by years of war had all erased its glorious past.
SPARTA
In central Greece and in the rest of the Peloponnese, the inhabitants couldn't take any more civil war, nor could they stand the political situation.
At the same time, the Carthaginians, seizing upon Greek weakness, had occupied the rich Greek colonies of Sicily—Selinunte, Himera, Gela—which opened up for them the passage toward southern Italy and Rome.
The Macedonians, of course, knew all of that.

ARISTOTLE, THE MACEDONIAN PHILOSOPHER WHO TEACHES AT THE ACADEMY IN ATHENS...

YES, ANTIPATER, I KNOW WHO HE IS!

...CLAIMS THAT THE CARTHAGINIANS HAVE ONE OF THE BEST FORMS OF GOVERNMENT.

YES, I KNOW, I KNOW!

THE CARTHAGINIANS THREATEN ROME, BUT I DON'T THINK—

PARMENION, A GENERAL WITH YOUR EXPERIENCE OUGHT TO KNOW THAT...

...ANY POWERFUL ARMY, WHETHER NEAR OR FAR, IS AN ENEMY ARMY!

PHILIP, MY KING, YOU'VE CRUSHED THE PAEONIANS, THE ILLYRIANS, THE THRACIANS, THE CHALCIDIAN CITIES... WHY ARE YOU WORRIED ABOUT SUCH DISTANT ENEMIES?

BECAUSE MY MIND CAN SEE FAR!

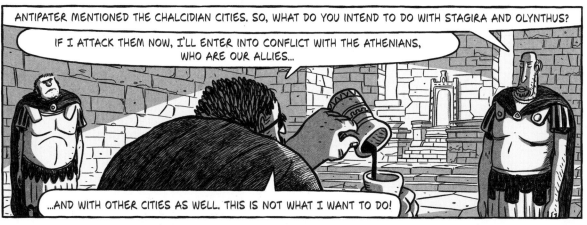

ANTIPATER MENTIONED THE CHALCIDIAN CITIES. SO, WHAT DO YOU INTEND TO DO WITH STAGIRA AND OLYNTHUS?

IF I ATTACK THEM NOW, I'LL ENTER INTO CONFLICT WITH THE ATHENIANS, WHO ARE OUR ALLIES...

...AND WITH OTHER CITIES AS WELL. THIS IS NOT WHAT I WANT TO DO!

ALL THE CITIES OF CENTRAL AND SOUTHERN GREECE ARE SO WEAKENED THAT WERE I TO ATTACK THEM, IT WOULD ONLY WORSEN THE SITUATION.

AND I WANT THEM UNITED AND READY TO FIGHT...

...SO I CAN MAKE USE OF THEIR FORCES FOR MY CAMPAIGN AGAINST THE PERSIANS.

Macedonia owes its name to its ancestor Macedon, the son of a Peloponnesian king.

The Macedonians are in fact descendants of the Argeads, an offshoot of the Dorian tribe of the Temenides. According to legend, their ancestor Temenus was the great-grandson of Heracles.

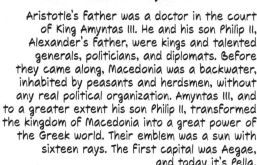

Aristotle's father was a doctor in the court of King Amyntas III. He and his son Philip II, Alexander's father, were kings and talented generals, politicians, and diplomats. Before they came along, Macedonia was a backwater, inhabited by peasants and herdsmen, without any real political organization. Amyntas III, and to a greater extent his son Philip II, transformed the kingdom of Macedonia into a great power of the Greek world. Their emblem was a sun with sixteen rays. The first capital was Aegae, and today it's Pella.

After the Peloponnesian War and the defeat of Athens, Amyntas decided to ally with Thebes, a rising power at the time. To cement this alliance, he sent there as a hostage his son Philip, fourteen years old at the time. This forced stay was decisive in Philip's education and the formation of his personality. He learned the art of war alongside the great generals Pelopidas and Epaminondas.

When Philip became king, he first neutralized all pretenders to the throne. Then, through some ingenious military, political, and diplomatic maneuvering, he distanced Macedonia from every threat. By strengthening the unity of all facets of the kingdom—military, administrative, demographic, and territorial—he made it into a robust state that stretched from the largely dominated Chalcidian peninsula to the Haemus Mountains. To solidify his friendship with Molossians of Epirus, he married Olympias, the daughter of King Neoptolemus. From their union were born Alexander and Cleopatra. After a siege of several months, he took Methone, an Athenian colony on the Thermaic Gulf. During battle, Philip received a serious headwound and lost his right eye.

He did not wish to conquer the central and southern Greek cities in warfare. Instead, he won "friends" over to his cause in each city with money, in order to secure their support for his policies.

His goal was to unite Greece under his leadership and then launch a Panhellenic campaign against the Persians.

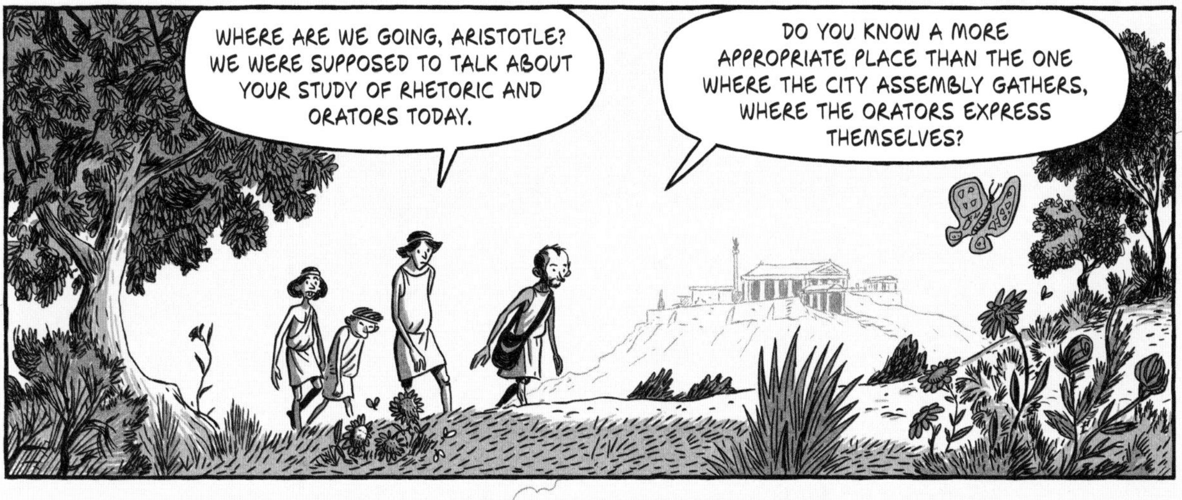
WHERE ARE WE GOING, ARISTOTLE? WE WERE SUPPOSED TO TALK ABOUT YOUR STUDY OF RHETORIC AND ORATORS TODAY.
DO YOU KNOW A MORE APPROPRIATE PLACE THAN THE ONE WHERE THE CITY ASSEMBLY GATHERS, WHERE THE ORATORS EXPRESS THEMSELVES?

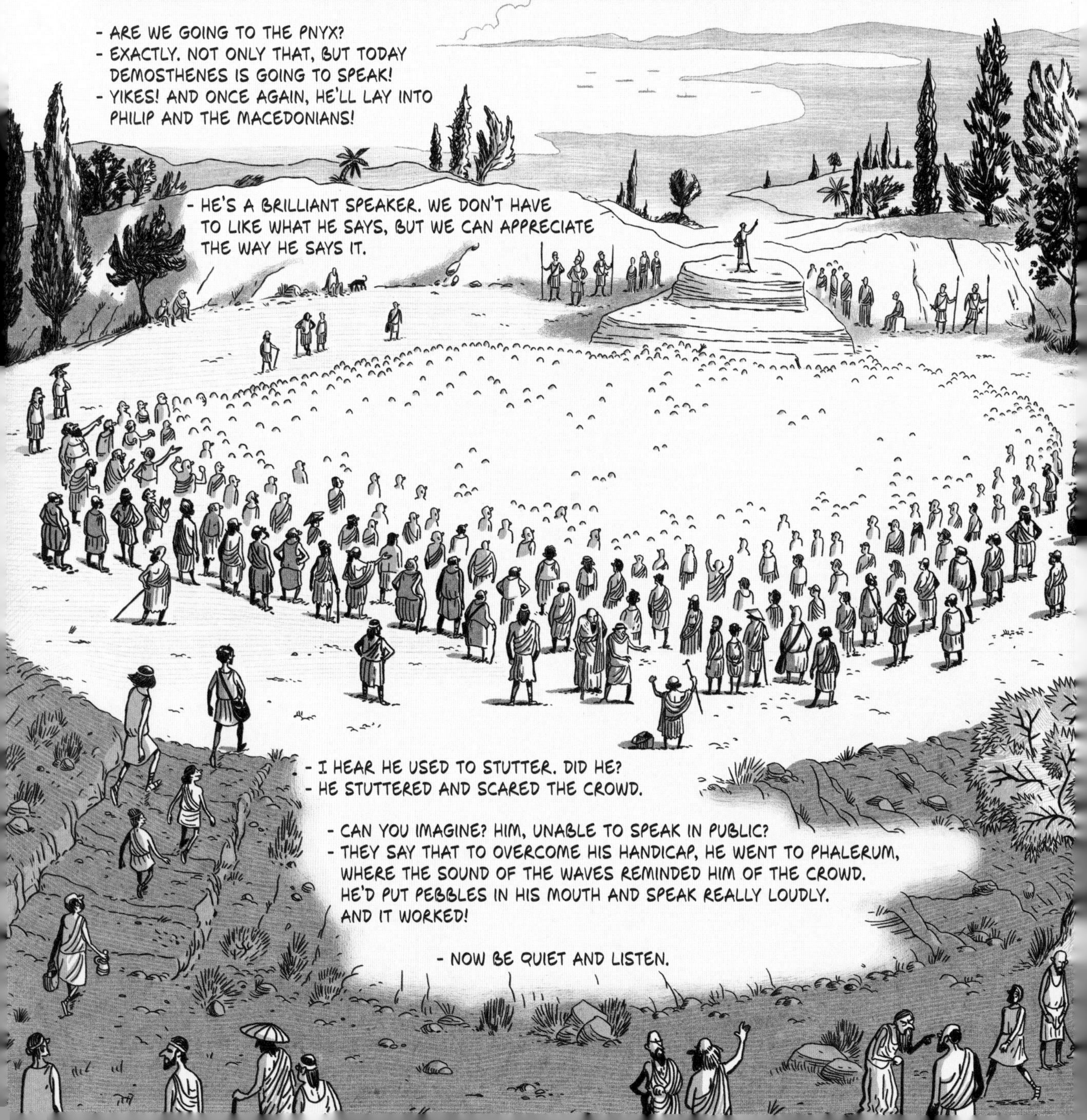
- ARE WE GOING TO THE PNYX?
- EXACTLY. NOT ONLY THAT, BUT TODAY DEMOSTHENES IS GOING TO SPEAK!
- YIKES! AND ONCE AGAIN, HE'LL LAY INTO PHILIP AND THE MACEDONIANS!
- HE'S A BRILLIANT SPEAKER. WE DON'T HAVE TO LIKE WHAT HE SAYS, BUT WE CAN APPRECIATE THE WAY HE SAYS IT.
- I HEAR HE USED TO STUTTER. DID HE?
- HE STUTTERED AND SCARED THE CROWD.
- CAN YOU IMAGINE? HIM, UNABLE TO SPEAK IN PUBLIC?
- THEY SAY THAT TO OVERCOME HIS HANDICAP, HE WENT TO PHALERUM, WHERE THE SOUND OF THE WAVES REMINDED HIM OF THE CROWD. HE'D PUT PEBBLES IN HIS MOUTH AND SPEAK REALLY LOUDLY. AND IT WORKED!
- NOW BE QUIET AND LISTEN.

CITIZENS OF ATHENS, I HOPE THAT MY WORDS WILL INCITE YOU TO MAKE DECISIONS IN THE BEST INTEREST OF THE CITY.

PHILIP IS A CRAFTY ONE, BUT HE'S NOT AS DREADFUL AS THEY SAY!

IN THE PAST, I ADVISED YOU TO SEND A POWERFUL ARMED BRIGADE INTO MACEDONIA, TO HARASS HIM AND KEEP HIM FROM TURNING TOWARD SOUTHERN GREECE.

YOU DIDN'T DO IT, AND LOOK AT THE RESULTS! HE'S CONQUERED NEARLY ALL OF OUR ALLIED CITIES, INCLUDING AMPHIPOLIS AND POTIDAEA, AND HAS MADE IT AS FAR AS THERMOPYLAE!

TODAY WE HAVE A GOLDEN OPPORTUNITY! PHILIP IS THREATENING OLYNTHUS, WHICH SEEKS OUR HELP.

WHAT ARE YOU DOING HERE, ARISTOTLE? WHEN DEMOSTHENES SPEAKS, YOU DISAPPEAR!

WATCH OUT, MACEDONIAN! WE'RE ALL A BIT ON EDGE!

WE MUST GIVE THEM THIS HELP AND SEND AN ARMY TO BEAT PHILIP ON HIS OWN TURF.

DON'T WORRY. THAT'S BEEN HAPPENING TO ME A LOT LATELY!

THIS WILL WEAKEN MACEDONIAN MORALE AND SPARE US THE CONSEQUENCES OF A WAR ON OUR OWN NATIVE SOIL.

"OUR OWN NATIVE SOIL." WHAT A PHRASE!

LET'S GO! WE'RE BOTHERING EVERYONE!

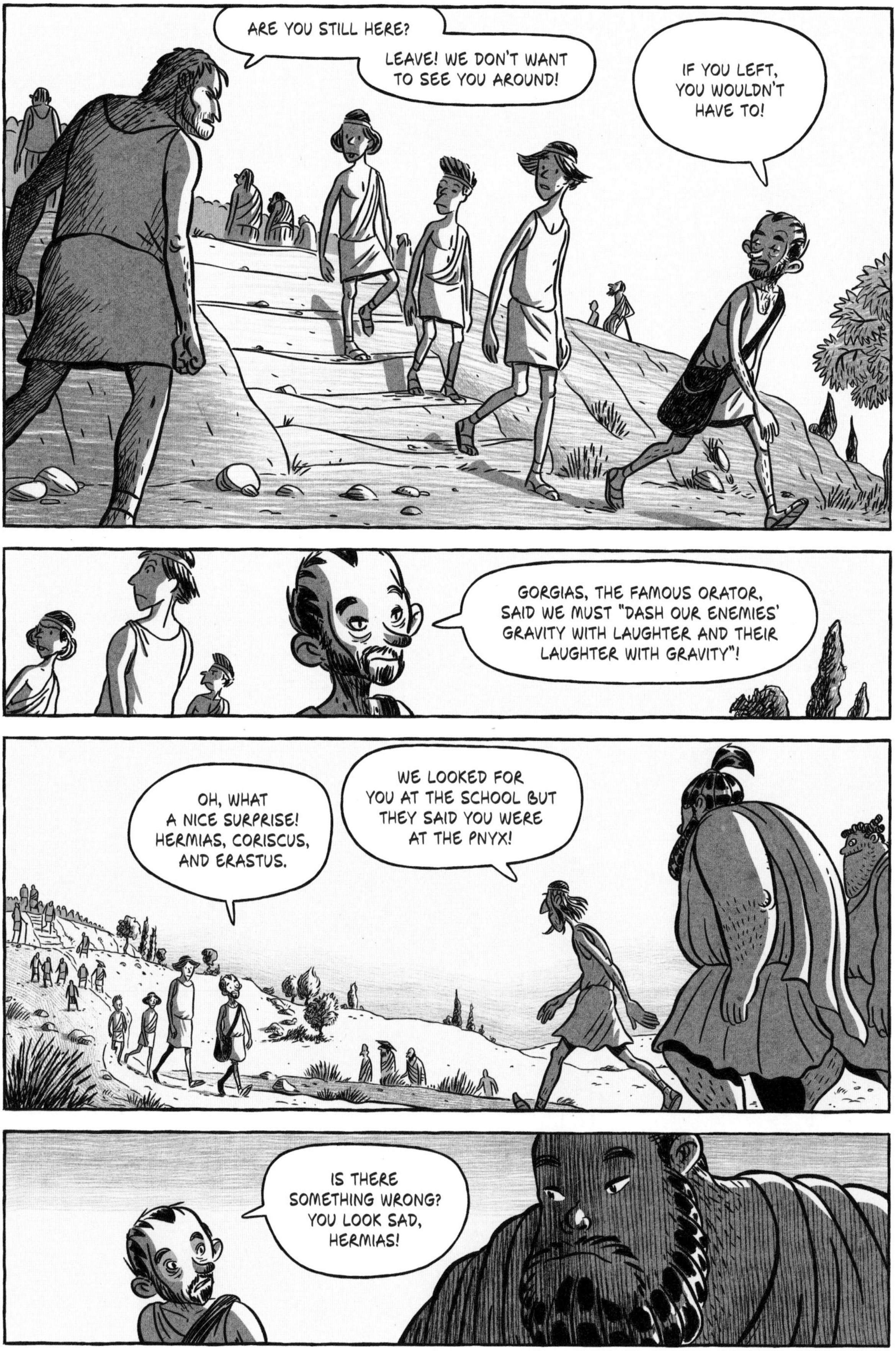
ARE YOU STILL HERE?
LEAVE! WE DON'T WANT TO SEE YOU AROUND!
IF YOU LEFT, YOU WOULDN'T HAVE TO!
GORGIAS, THE FAMOUS ORATOR, SAID WE MUST "DASH OUR ENEMIES' GRAVITY WITH LAUGHTER AND THEIR LAUGHTER WITH GRAVITY"!
OH, WHAT A NICE SURPRISE! HERMIAS, CORISCUS, AND ERASTUS.
WE LOOKED FOR YOU AT THE SCHOOL BUT THEY SAID YOU WERE AT THE PNYX!
IS THERE SOMETHING WRONG? YOU LOOK SAD, HERMIAS!

EUBULUS IS QUITE ILL! I DON'T KNOW IF I'LL GET THERE IN TIME, BUT I'M LEAVING IMMEDIATELY FOR ATARNEUS.

IT'S POSSIBLE I'LL TAKE HIS...

YOU'LL TAKE HIS PLACE, I'M SURE OF IT!

HERMIAS, RULER OF ATARNEUS!

WE'LL SEE!

I'M REALLY GOING TO MISS YOU!

YOU KNOW THAT IF YOU EVER NEED ANYTHING, ANYTHING AT ALL, ANYWHERE, I'LL ALWAYS BE THERE FOR YOU AND THE OTHERS.

THANKS!

AND THANKS FOR ALL YOU'VE DONE FOR ME, ESPECIALLY WHEN I FIRST ARRIVED.

I'M SO, SO PROUD OF YOU!

SAY HELLO TO PROXENUS AND HIS FAMILY FOR ME! WE HAVEN'T BEEN IN TOUCH IN A WHILE.

I WILL!

SAFE TRAVELS.

GOODBYE!

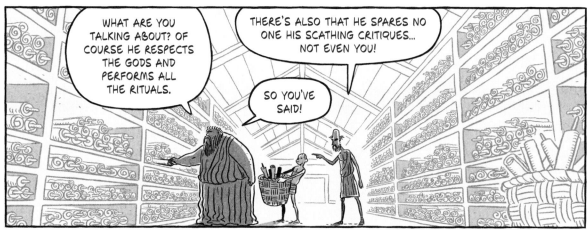

WHAT ARE YOU TALKING ABOUT? OF COURSE HE RESPECTS THE GODS AND PERFORMS ALL THE RITUALS.

THERE'S ALSO THAT HE SPARES NO ONE HIS SCATHING CRITIQUES... NOT EVEN YOU!

SO YOU'VE SAID!

HE FLAUNTS HIS KNOWLEDGE BECAUSE HE THINKS HE'S SUPERIOR!

BUT HE IS!

HE'S POMPOUS AND HE HAS NO SENSE OF HUMOR!

ALRIGHT! WE'LL COME TO YOU FOR A LAUGH.

NOBODY UNDERSTANDS HIS THEORIES! IT'S NOT ENOUGH FOR HIM TO TAKE ON DIFFICULT SUBJECTS: HIS WAY OF TEACHING THEM MAKES THEM EVEN MORE DIFFICULT!

I KNOW THAT ARISTOTLE INSPIRES MORE ADMIRATION THAN AFFECTION.

I ALSO KNOW WHY YOU KEEP SPEAKING ILL OF HIM TO ME.

REST ASSURED! IT WILL BE TO YOU THAT I'LL PASS THE TORCH!

NOT BECAUSE YOU'RE THE BEST, BUT BECAUSE, UNFORTUNATELY, IT'S THE LAW!

WELL, YES, XENOCRATES! THE ANTI-MACEDONIANS ARE AFTER ME AND, AS IF THAT WASN'T ENOUGH, MY COLLEAGUES ARE SLANDERING ME!

WELL, THEIR MOTIVES CHANGE...

...THE OLDER PLATO GETS!

I STILL DON'T REALLY THINK THAT I DESERVED IT. I ALMOST WANT TO FORGET IT ALL AND JUST LEAVE.

BE AWARE, IF YOU DO, I'M GOING WITH YOU!

DIRTY MACEDONIAN!

PING!

PONG!

!!!

LEAVE!

GO ON, GO!

YOU CORRUPT OUR YOUTH!

XENOCRATES, GO! QUICK!

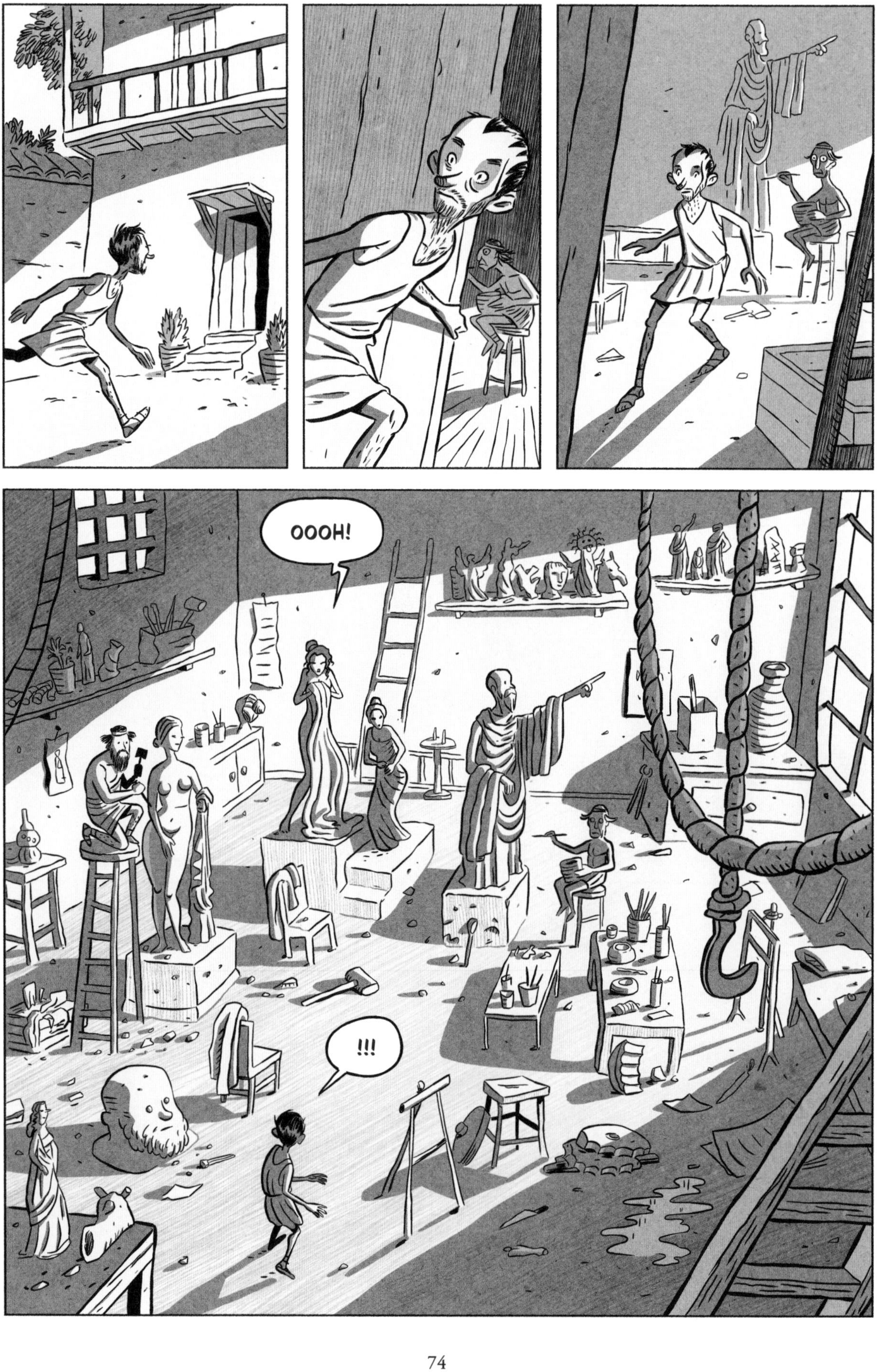
OOOH!
!!!

OOH!

PRAXITELES! I'M SO SORRY! HOW DID I END UP IN YOUR STUDIO?

YOU CAME IN THROUGH THE BACK DOOR!

WHAT'S GOING ON, ARISTOTLE?

THE USUAL. THE ANTI-MACEDONIANS AMBUSHED ME AND THREW ROCKS. I MANAGED TO GET AWAY!

DEMOSTHENES IS AGITATING THEM!

ARE YOU HURT?

NO!

BUT I'VE INTERRUPTED YOU!

DO YOU KNOW PHRYNE?

I'VE SEEN HER!

PHRYNE HAS LENT ME HER BODY AND KRATINE HER HEAD FOR MY STATUE OF APHRODITE.

I SEE!!!

ONE WOMAN WASN'T ENOUGH FOR YOU! OH, YOU SCULPTORS!

HA HA! ALWAYS GOOD FOR A LAUGH, ARISTOTLE!

- A LIFE-SIZE STATUE OF A NAKED GODDESS!
- NICIAS IS GOING TO PAINT IT.
- NICIAS? THE GUY WITH THE BRUSHES?
- YES, HE'S A PAINTER. HE'LL BE USING NATURAL COLORS.

- ISN'T ALL OF THAT SORT OF HERETICAL?
- OF COURSE IT IS! IN GREECE, IT WOULD BE HARD TO ACCEPT. BUT THE STATUE IS FOR THE TEMPLE OF APHRODITE IN KNIDOS, IN CARIA.
- FROM WHAT I WAS ABLE TO SEE, YOUR APHRODITE IS GORGEOUS!
- LIKE A GODDESS! HA HA HA! THE OLD LADY WHO DOES MY CLEANING ASKED ME ONE DAY: "PRAXITELES, WHEN CHIPPING AWAY AT THE MARBLE, DID YOU KNOW APHRODITE WAS HIDING INSIDE?" HA HA HA!

YOU JUST GAVE ME AN IDEA FOR MY CLASS ON THE THEORY OF THE FOUR CAUSES.

I'M GLAD ART COULD BE OF SERVICE TO PHILOSOPHY.

IT'S RECIPROCAL! DON'T LISTEN TO PLATO WHEN HE SAYS THAT ART MOVES US AWAY FROM THE TRUTH!

BE CAREFUL!

THANKS FOR HAVING ME!

GOODBYE, GIRLS!

YOU KNOW, IF I HAD TO PAINT THEM, I'D SHOW PLATO POINTING AT THE SKY AND ARISTOTLE AT THE EARTH!

BE A GOOD BOY AND CONCENTRATE ON YOUR BRUSH!

ENTELECHY IS THE TENDENCY OF BEINGS TO FULFILL THE PURPOSE FOR WHICH THEY WERE CREATED. IN OTHER WORDS, ENTELECHY IS THE ACCOMPLISHMENT OF THE BEING.

ENTELECHY

ARISTOTLE IDENTIFIES FOUR CAUSES. THESE "CAUSES" ACCOUNT FOR THINGS AS THEY ARE. WE ARE AS INTERESTED IN THE DEFINITION OF BEINGS WITHIN THIS FRAMEWORK AS WE ARE IN THE PRODUCTION OF NATURAL PHENOMENA.

THE "MATERIAL CAUSE" IS WHAT THE THING IS MADE OF. THE "EFFICIENT CAUSE" IS HOW THE THING IS PRODUCED.

THE "FORMAL CAUSE" REFERS TO THE SET OF A THING'S ESSENTIAL PROPERTIES, THOSE THAT JUSTIFY ITS NATURE. THE "FINAL CAUSE" IS THE PURPOSE FOR WHICH THE THING IS MADE.

THE FOUR CAUSES
◇ MATERIAL
◇ EFFICIENT
◇ FORMAL
◇ FINAL

THE TERM "CAUSE" CAN BE INTERPRETED AS A SORT OF EXPLANATION, WHICH ALLOWS US TO DETERMINE WHY "THIS" IS "THAT WAY."

I was lucky enough to get to attend his class on the "four causes." I had barely just arrived at the Academy and it was the first time I saw him up close!

I'LL GIVE YOU AN EXAMPLE.

IMAGINE THAT WE ARE IN PRAXITELES'S STUDIO.

THE SCULPTOR WANTS TO CREATE A STATUE OF THE GODDESS APHRODITE.

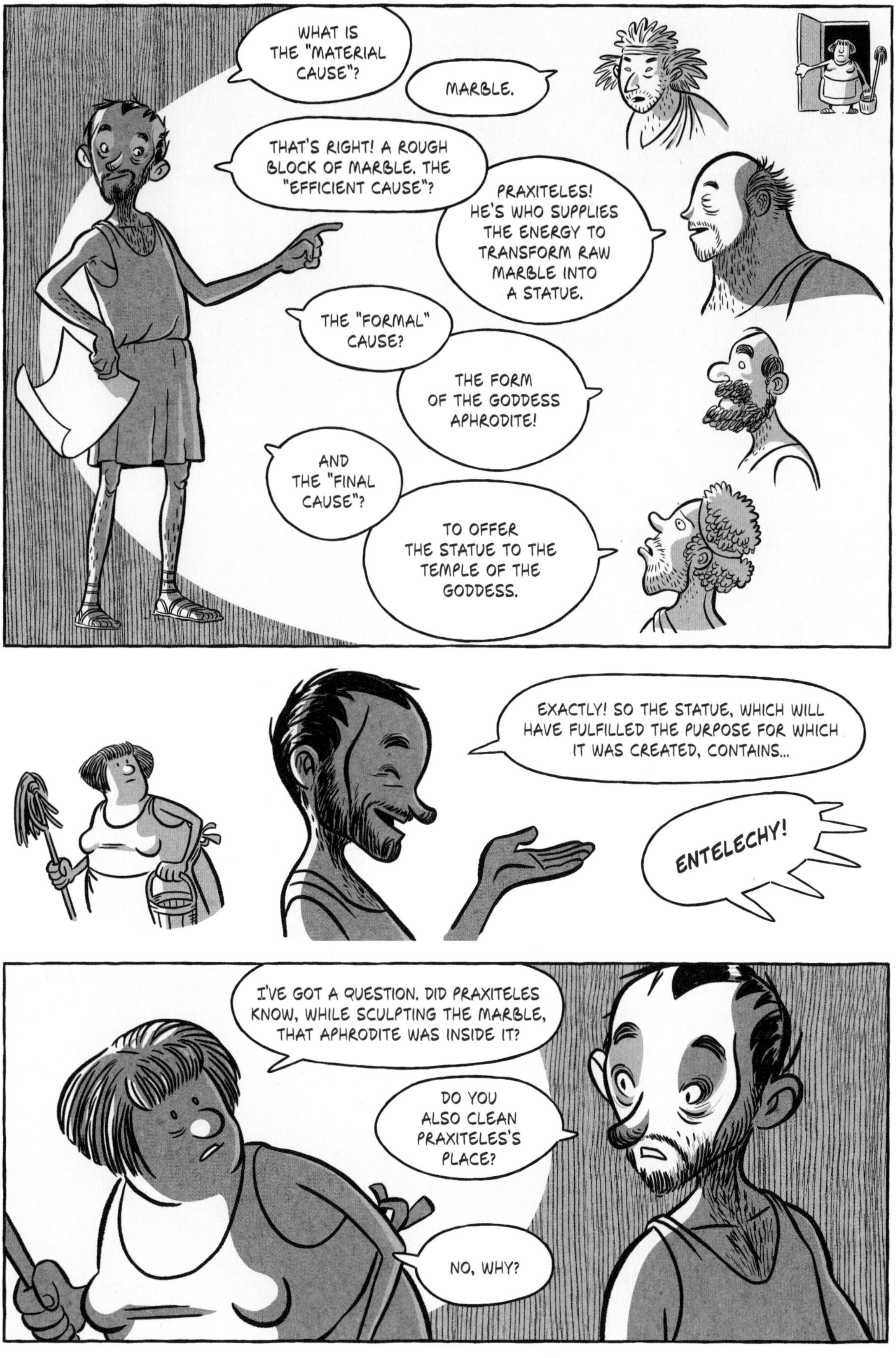

WHAT IS THE "MATERIAL CAUSE"?
MARBLE.
THAT'S RIGHT! A ROUGH BLOCK OF MARBLE. THE "EFFICIENT CAUSE"?
PRAXITELES! HE'S WHO SUPPLIES THE ENERGY TO TRANSFORM RAW MARBLE INTO A STATUE.
THE "FORMAL" CAUSE?
THE FORM OF THE GODDESS APHRODITE!
AND THE "FINAL CAUSE"?
TO OFFER THE STATUE TO THE TEMPLE OF THE GODDESS.
EXACTLY! SO THE STATUE, WHICH WILL HAVE FULFILLED THE PURPOSE FOR WHICH IT WAS CREATED, CONTAINS...
ENTELECHY!
I'VE GOT A QUESTION. DID PRAXITELES KNOW, WHILE SCULPTING THE MARBLE, THAT APHRODITE WAS INSIDE IT?
DO YOU ALSO CLEAN PRAXITELES'S PLACE?
NO, WHY?

I'VE NEVER SEEN YOU BEFORE.

I'M TYRTAMUS. I'M FROM ERESOS, ON THE ISLAND OF LESBOS.

HE'S A NEW STUDENT.

INTELLIGENT, STUDIOUS, AND WELL-SPOKEN.

TRITAMUS. I'LL REMEMBER YOUR NAME!

TYRTAMUS, MASTER, NOT TRITAMUS!

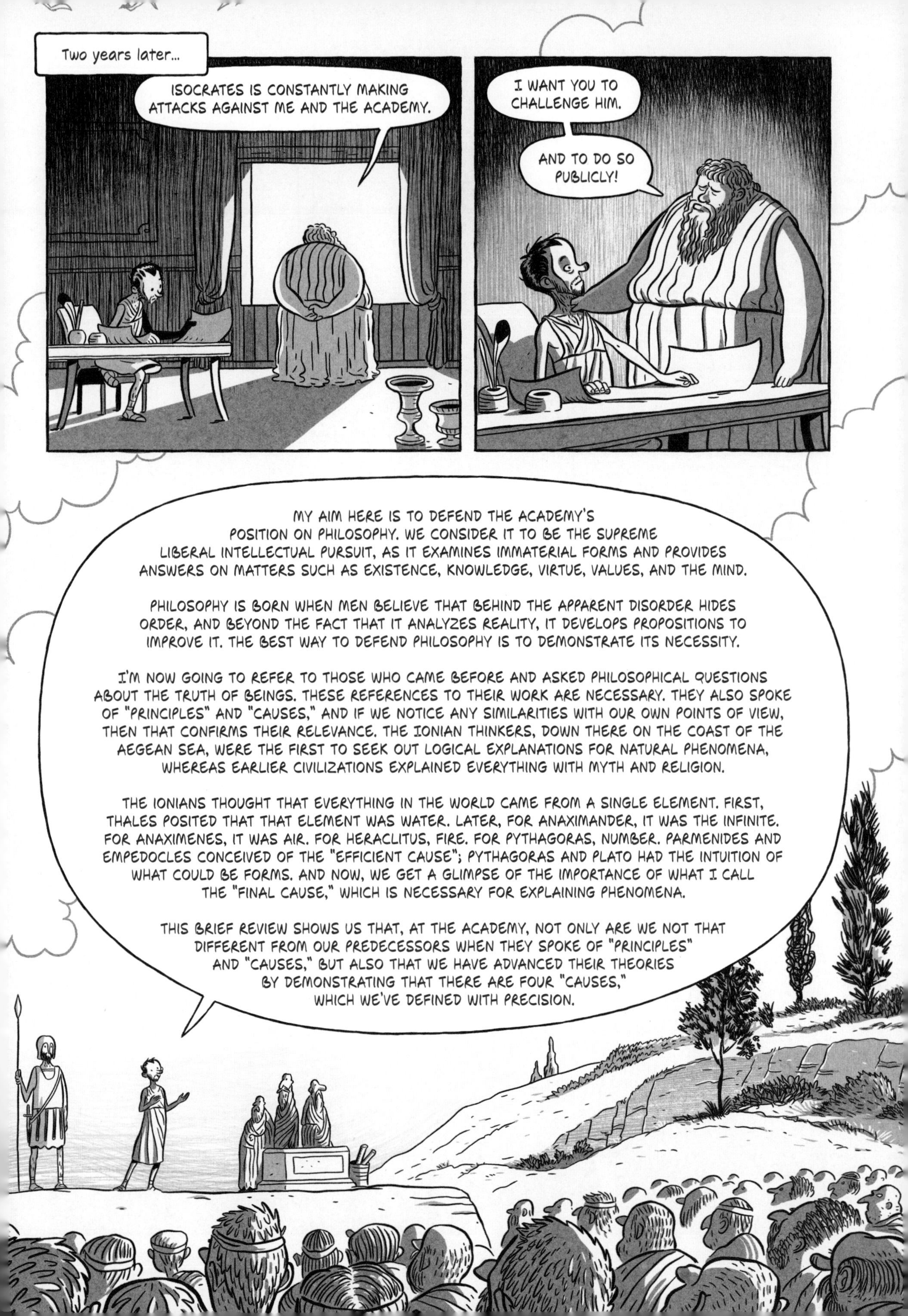
Two years later...
ISOCRATES IS CONSTANTLY MAKING ATTACKS AGAINST ME AND THE ACADEMY.
I WANT YOU TO CHALLENGE HIM.
AND TO DO SO PUBLICLY!
MY AIM HERE IS TO DEFEND THE ACADEMY'S POSITION ON PHILOSOPHY. WE CONSIDER IT TO BE THE SUPREME LIBERAL INTELLECTUAL PURSUIT, AS IT EXAMINES IMMATERIAL FORMS AND PROVIDES ANSWERS ON MATTERS SUCH AS EXISTENCE, KNOWLEDGE, VIRTUE, VALUES, AND THE MIND.
PHILOSOPHY IS BORN WHEN MEN BELIEVE THAT BEHIND THE APPARENT DISORDER HIDES ORDER, AND BEYOND THE FACT THAT IT ANALYZES REALITY, IT DEVELOPS PROPOSITIONS TO IMPROVE IT. THE BEST WAY TO DEFEND PHILOSOPHY IS TO DEMONSTRATE ITS NECESSITY.
I'M NOW GOING TO REFER TO THOSE WHO CAME BEFORE AND ASKED PHILOSOPHICAL QUESTIONS ABOUT THE TRUTH OF BEINGS. THESE REFERENCES TO THEIR WORK ARE NECESSARY. THEY ALSO SPOKE OF "PRINCIPLES" AND "CAUSES," AND IF WE NOTICE ANY SIMILARITIES WITH OUR OWN POINTS OF VIEW, THEN THAT CONFIRMS THEIR RELEVANCE. THE IONIAN THINKERS, DOWN THERE ON THE COAST OF THE AEGEAN SEA, WERE THE FIRST TO SEEK OUT LOGICAL EXPLANATIONS FOR NATURAL PHENOMENA, WHEREAS EARLIER CIVILIZATIONS EXPLAINED EVERYTHING WITH MYTH AND RELIGION.
THE IONIANS THOUGHT THAT EVERYTHING IN THE WORLD CAME FROM A SINGLE ELEMENT. FIRST, THALES POSITED THAT THAT ELEMENT WAS WATER. LATER, FOR ANAXIMANDER, IT WAS THE INFINITE. FOR ANAXIMENES, IT WAS AIR. FOR HERACLITUS, FIRE. FOR PYTHAGORAS, NUMBER. PARMENIDES AND EMPEDOCLES CONCEIVED OF THE "EFFICIENT CAUSE"; PYTHAGORAS AND PLATO HAD THE INTUITION OF WHAT COULD BE FORMS. AND NOW, WE GET A GLIMPSE OF THE IMPORTANCE OF WHAT I CALL THE "FINAL CAUSE," WHICH IS NECESSARY FOR EXPLAINING PHENOMENA.
THIS BRIEF REVIEW SHOWS US THAT, AT THE ACADEMY, NOT ONLY ARE WE NOT THAT DIFFERENT FROM OUR PREDECESSORS WHEN THEY SPOKE OF "PRINCIPLES" AND "CAUSES," BUT ALSO THAT WE HAVE ADVANCED THEIR THEORIES BY DEMONSTRATING THAT THERE ARE FOUR "CAUSES," WHICH WE'VE DEFINED WITH PRECISION.

TO CONCLUDE, I SAY WE MUST ALL MAKE GOOD USE OF THE LOGIC NATURE HAS BESTOWED UPON US AND DEVOTE OURSELVES TO PHILOSOPHY!

WE DO NOT NEED PHILOSOPHY IN ORDER TO LIVE, BUT IN ORDER TO LIVE BETTER.

PHILOSOPHY MAKES US SEE THE WORLD AS IT IS, BUT IT ALSO MAKES US SEE HOW IT COULD OR SHOULD BE.

INTELLECTUAL ACTIVITY AND A VIRTUOUS LIFE LEAD MEN TO HAPPINESS, WHICH IS THE ULTIMATE GOAL OF LIFE!

CLAP

A REMARKABLE SPEECH, ARISTOTLE!

OH! CORISCUS, ERASTUS! I'M SO HAPPY THAT YOU LIKED IT.

82

- WHAT ABOUT THE GUY FROM ERESOS? TERMENUS, I THINK.
- TYRTAMUS! YOU NEVER CAN REMEMBER HIS NAME! HA HA HA!
- THAT'S NOT A NAME!
- HE LEFT IN A HURRY FOR LESBOS ON ACCOUNT OF A FAMILY MATTER. HE DIDN'T HAVE TIME TO SAY GOODBYE.
- I UNDERSTAND!
- WE WON'T BE ABLE TO HEAR ANY MORE OF YOUR SPEECHES. IT'S A SHAME!
- WHY? WHAT'S GOING ON?

- CORISCUS AND I ARE LEAVING FOR ASSOS.
- IT'S A TOWN NEAR ATARNEUS. HERMIAS, WHO IS NOW IN POWER THERE, HAS GRANTED US A LABORATORY TO DO OUR RESEARCH ON FAUNA AND FLORA.
- HE'S FINANCING US, TOO!
- NOW, THAT'S NOT BAD AT ALL!
- AFTER TWENTY YEARS, WE LEARNED ABOUT ALL WE COULD AT THE ACADEMY!
- YOU ALSO CONTRIBUTED A LOT. IT'LL FEEL EMPTY WITHOUT YOU! SAFE TRAVELS!
- YOU'LL ALWAYS BE WELCOME IN ASSOS!
- THANKS!

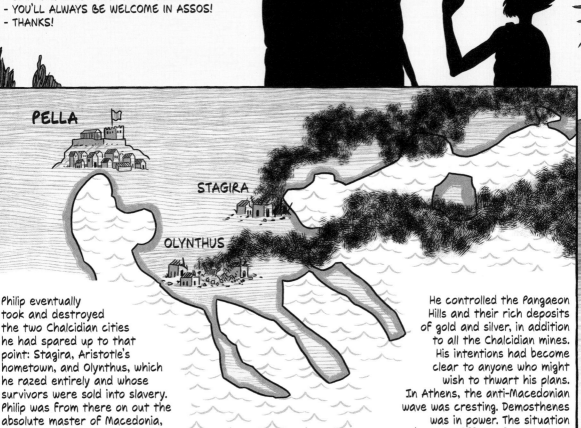

PELLA

STAGIRA

OLYNTHUS

Philip eventually took and destroyed the two Chalcidian cities he had spared up to that point: Stagira, Aristotle's hometown, and Olynthus, which he razed entirely and whose survivors were sold into slavery. Philip was from there on out the absolute master of Macedonia, Thrace, and Thessaly.

He controlled the Pangaeon Hills and their rich deposits of gold and silver, in addition to all the Chalcidian mines. His intentions had become clear to anyone who might wish to thwart his plans. In Athens, the anti-Macedonian wave was cresting. Demosthenes was in power. The situation became difficult for Aristotle.

AND STAGIRA!

I THINK YOU OUGHT TO GET OUT OF ATHENS FOR A WHILE!

MAYBE YOU SHOULD ACCEPT THE INVITATION FROM THE "CIRCLE OF MISSING SCHOLARS" ON SALAMIS.

THEY'D LIKE YOU TO RETURN AND FINISH YOUR TEACHINGS ON NATURE.

ON SALAMIS? YEAH, THOSE PEOPLE ARE A BIT...

THAT'S NOT REALLY THE PROBLEM!

FINE! TELL THEM I'LL COME. LET ATARUS AND THAT NEW ASTRONOMER, CALLIPPUS, KNOW THEY'LL BE COMING WITH ME.

AND WE HAVE A LOT TO TAKE WITH US!

84

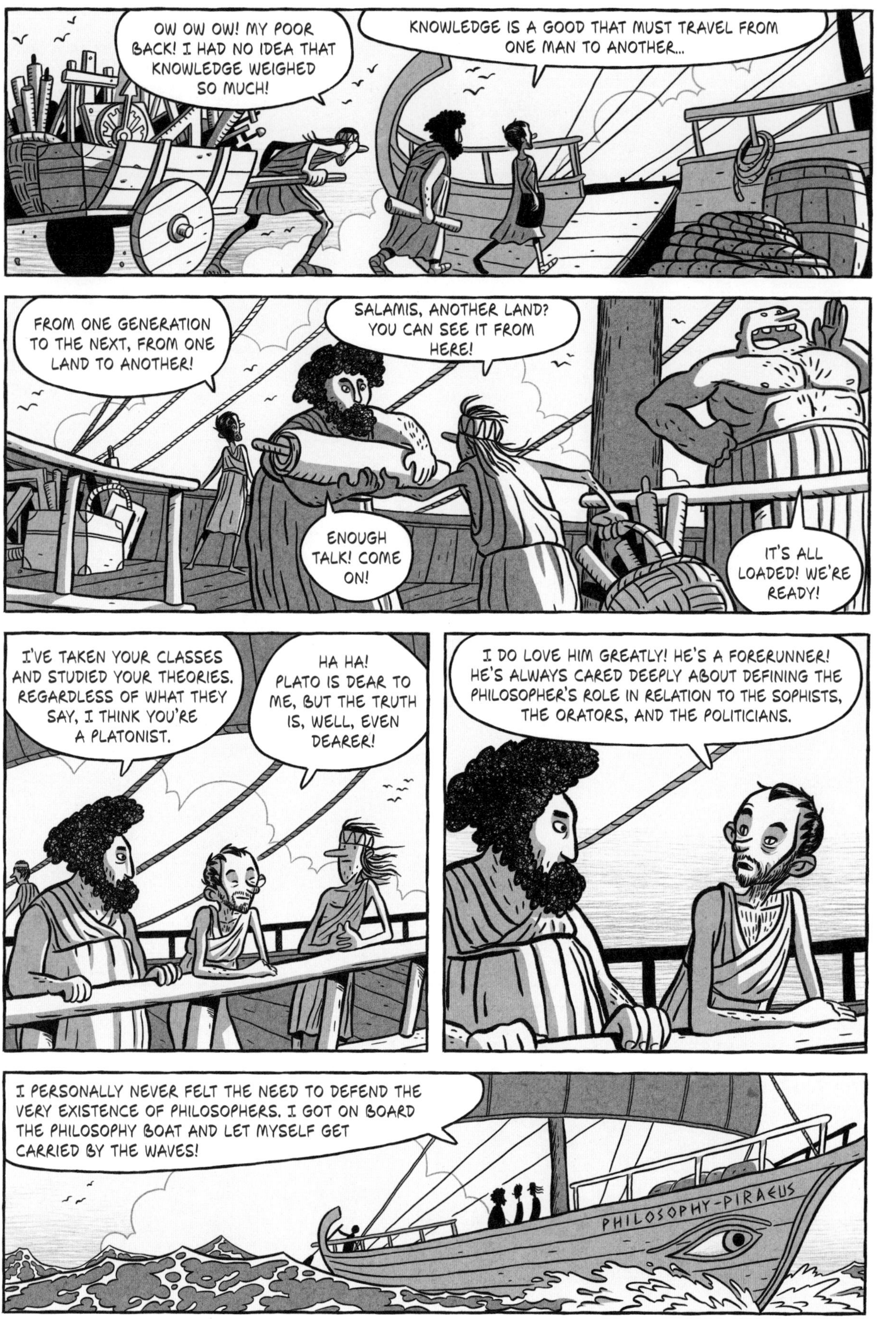
OW OW OW! MY POOR BACK! I HAD NO IDEA THAT KNOWLEDGE WEIGHED SO MUCH!
KNOWLEDGE IS A GOOD THAT MUST TRAVEL FROM ONE MAN TO ANOTHER...
FROM ONE GENERATION TO THE NEXT, FROM ONE LAND TO ANOTHER!
SALAMIS, ANOTHER LAND? YOU CAN SEE IT FROM HERE!
ENOUGH TALK! COME ON!
IT'S ALL LOADED! WE'RE READY!
I'VE TAKEN YOUR CLASSES AND STUDIED YOUR THEORIES. REGARDLESS OF WHAT THEY SAY, I THINK YOU'RE A PLATONIST.
HA HA! PLATO IS DEAR TO ME, BUT THE TRUTH IS, WELL, EVEN DEARER!
I DO LOVE HIM GREATLY! HE'S A FORERUNNER! HE'S ALWAYS CARED DEEPLY ABOUT DEFINING THE PHILOSOPHER'S ROLE IN RELATION TO THE SOPHISTS, THE ORATORS, AND THE POLITICIANS.
I PERSONALLY NEVER FELT THE NEED TO DEFEND THE VERY EXISTENCE OF PHILOSOPHERS. I GOT ON BOARD THE PHILOSOPHY BOAT AND LET MYSELF GET CARRIED BY THE WAVES!
PHILOSOPHY-PIRAEUS

These were the waters where, one hundred and thirty years ago, the "Battle of Salamis" took place. Three hundred Persian ships were sunk there, along with their crews. That battle, and the Battle of Plataea, were confirmation of the Greek victory and put an end to the Persian War.

By a curious coincidence, Aeschylus, the first great tragic poet, took part in the battle, while the young Sophocles, who would become the second great tragic poet, was in Athens, taking part in the victory celebrations... which took place the very same day that Euripides, the third great tragic poet, was born on Salamis!

GET READY TO DISEMBARK! WE'VE ARRIVED.

WELCOME, EVERYONE!

IF I REMEMBER CORRECTLY, THE LAST TIME I CAME HERE, WE TALKED ABOUT MATTER, FORM, AND THE FOUR CAUSES.

IF YOU SAY SO!

DO YOU REMEMBER THAT, TWO?

NO, ONE, I DON'T REMEMBER THAT. ONLY TWELVE REMEMBERS!

HOW ABOUT YOU REMIND ME WHY YOU DESIGNATE YOURSELVES WITH NUMBERS? YOU DON'T HAVE NAMES?

WE DO, BUT WE ALL LOOK A LITTLE BIT ALIKE AND WITH NUMBERS, IT'S EASIER TO DISTINGUISH EACH OTHER!

EACH ONE OF US HAS AN ASSIGNED SEAT, AND ONCE WE SIT DOWN, WE KNOW WHO'S WHO!

IF YOU SAY SO!!!

TEN AND FIVE, TAKE YOUR SEATS! LET'S BEGIN!

FOR THE NEXT THREE DAYS, WE'LL BE TALKING ABOUT NATURE, MOTION, TIME, THE UNIVERSE THAT SURROUNDS US, AND, IF WE HAVE THE TIME, A LITTLE METEOROLOGY.

YES, BUT SIMPLIFY IT A LITTLE, IF POSSIBLE!

DON'T BE RIDICULOUS, THREE!

FINE! NATURE IS THE WHOLE SET OF BEINGS IN MOTION!

A LITTLE SIMPLER, PLEASE!

ATARUS, STOP LAUGHING.

IN NATURE, THERE ARE ANIMATE BEINGS CAPABLE OF MOVING ON THEIR OWN, AND INANIMATE BEINGS MOVED ONLY BY THE INTERVENTION OF AN EXTERNAL CAUSE.

HUH? WHY PROVED?

NOT PROVED, MOVED! LISTEN!

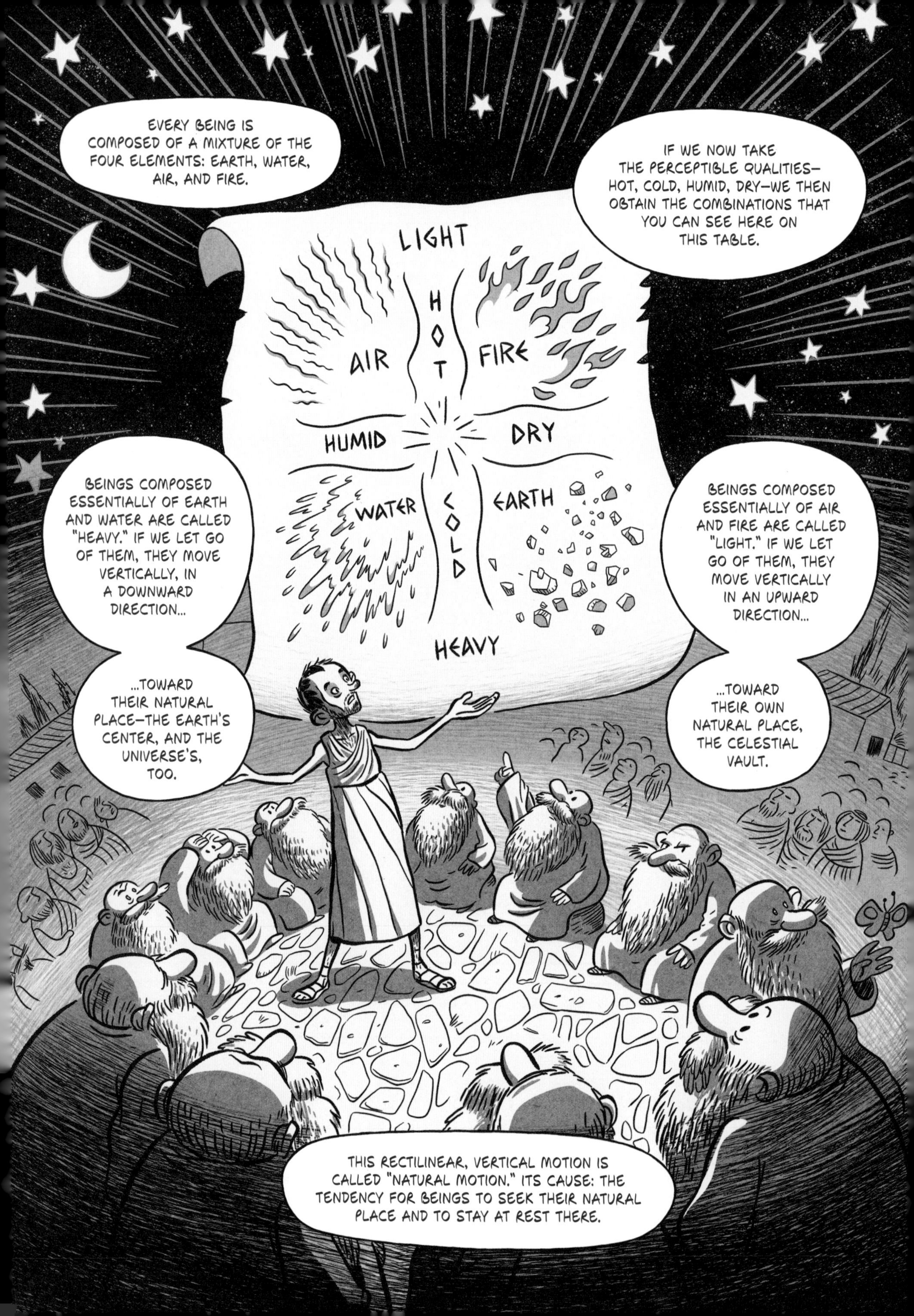
EVERY BEING IS COMPOSED OF A MIXTURE OF THE FOUR ELEMENTS: EARTH, WATER, AIR, AND FIRE.
IF WE NOW TAKE THE PERCEPTIBLE QUALITIES—HOT, COLD, HUMID, DRY—WE THEN OBTAIN THE COMBINATIONS THAT YOU CAN SEE HERE ON THIS TABLE.
LIGHT
HOT
AIR
FIRE
HUMID
DRY
WATER
COLD
EARTH
HEAVY
BEINGS COMPOSED ESSENTIALLY OF EARTH AND WATER ARE CALLED "HEAVY." IF WE LET GO OF THEM, THEY MOVE VERTICALLY, IN A DOWNWARD DIRECTION...
...TOWARD THEIR NATURAL PLACE—THE EARTH'S CENTER, AND THE UNIVERSE'S, TOO.
BEINGS COMPOSED ESSENTIALLY OF AIR AND FIRE ARE CALLED "LIGHT." IF WE LET GO OF THEM, THEY MOVE VERTICALLY IN AN UPWARD DIRECTION...
...TOWARD THEIR OWN NATURAL PLACE, THE CELESTIAL VAULT.
THIS RECTILINEAR, VERTICAL MOTION IS CALLED "NATURAL MOTION." ITS CAUSE: THE TENDENCY FOR BEINGS TO SEEK THEIR NATURAL PLACE AND TO STAY AT REST THERE.

Second day...

THE FUNDAMENTAL TRAIT OF NATURE IS MOTION, WHICH BEGINS SOMEWHERE AND THEN ENDS SOMEWHERE.

AND WHAT WE MEAN BY "MOTION" IS ANY CHANGE OR ANY TRANSFORMATION. BECAUSE, IN A CERTAIN WAY, THOSE ARE "MOTIONS" AS WELL.

TWELVE, YOU SURPRISE ME!

YOU SAID THAT TO ME LAST TIME!

I FEEL TOTALLY, COMPLETELY LOST TODAY!

I HAVE SINCE YESTERDAY!

SO REALLY, WE SHOULD CALL OURSELVES "THE CIRCLE OF LOST SCHOLARS"!

A BEING CAN CHANGE IN TERMS OF PLACE, BY MOVING.

HEY, YOU! SCRAM!

OR IN TERMS OF SUBSTANCE, BY BEING BORN, GROWING OLD, AND DYING.

DON'T SAY THAT!

OR DEPENDING ON QUALITY, MEANING IF IT CHANGES COLOR, APPEARANCE...

OR, LASTLY, DEPENDING ON QUANTITY, FOR EXAMPLE, A CHILD OR A PLANT THAT GROWS!

MY DEAR NINE, YOU'VE GOTTEN EVEN BALDER!

CORINA'S REALLY GROWN! LOOK AT THAT LOVELY YOUNG LADY.

WANT TO TAKE OVER, CALLIPPUS?

UH... YES, SURE! BEINGS, AS WE KNOW, ARE COMPOSED OF MATTER AND FORM. MATTER CONTAINS THE POTENTIAL BEING. WHAT THAT MEANS IS THAT IT'S PREDISPOSED TO RECEIVING A CERTAIN FORM.

FORM IS THE ACTUAL BEING, MEANING THAT IT'S THE BEING FULLY ACTUALIZED IN MATTER. FORM IS THAT WHICH DETERMINES MATTER.

OOO! CORINA'S BACK!

WHO COULD HAVE DETERMINED HER MATTER?

WE CAN THEREFORE ASSERT THAT MOTION IS THE CHANGE FROM POTENTIAL BEING TO ACTUAL BEINGS, AND FROM MATTER TO FORM.

THE ACTUALIZATION OF FORM CORRESPONDS TO ENTELECHY.

SO CORINA HAS AN "ENTELECHY"!

DEFINITELY!

I'D ALSO ADD...

...ONE CAN DEFINE THE MOTION OF A BEING AS A PROCESS DETERMINED BY ENTELECHY, THE FULFILLED BEING.

HE'S IMPROVED HIS THEORY. HE TOLD GLYKERA, "MOTION IS ENTELECHY, OR THE ACT OF MOVING IN AND OF ITSELF!"

THAT'S JUST A DIFFERENT WAY OF SAYING IT! SO, WHO'S GLYKERA?

NEVER MIND!

Third day...

YESTERDAY, WE SPOKE ABOUT "NATURAL" MOTION, WHICH IS ALWAYS RECTILINEAR AND VERTICAL. TODAY, WE'RE GOING TO TALK ABOUT "UNNATURAL MOTION."

COULD WE MAKE IT SIMPLE?

FOR EXAMPLE, IF YOU THROW A STONE, YOU IMPOSE UPON IT A MOTION THAT IS NOT NATURAL TO IT.

SPLASH

THE VIOLENT MOTION CAN ONLY TAKE PLACE WHEN AN EXTERNAL CAUSE, AN EXTERNAL FORCE, INTERVENES...

...WHICH BENDS THE NATURAL MOTION OF THE STONE AND MAKES IT MOVE ON A CURVE.

SPLISH

STOP THROWING STONES!!!

IT'S TO OBSERVE THE CURVE!

CALLIPPUS, TAKE OVER, PLEASE!

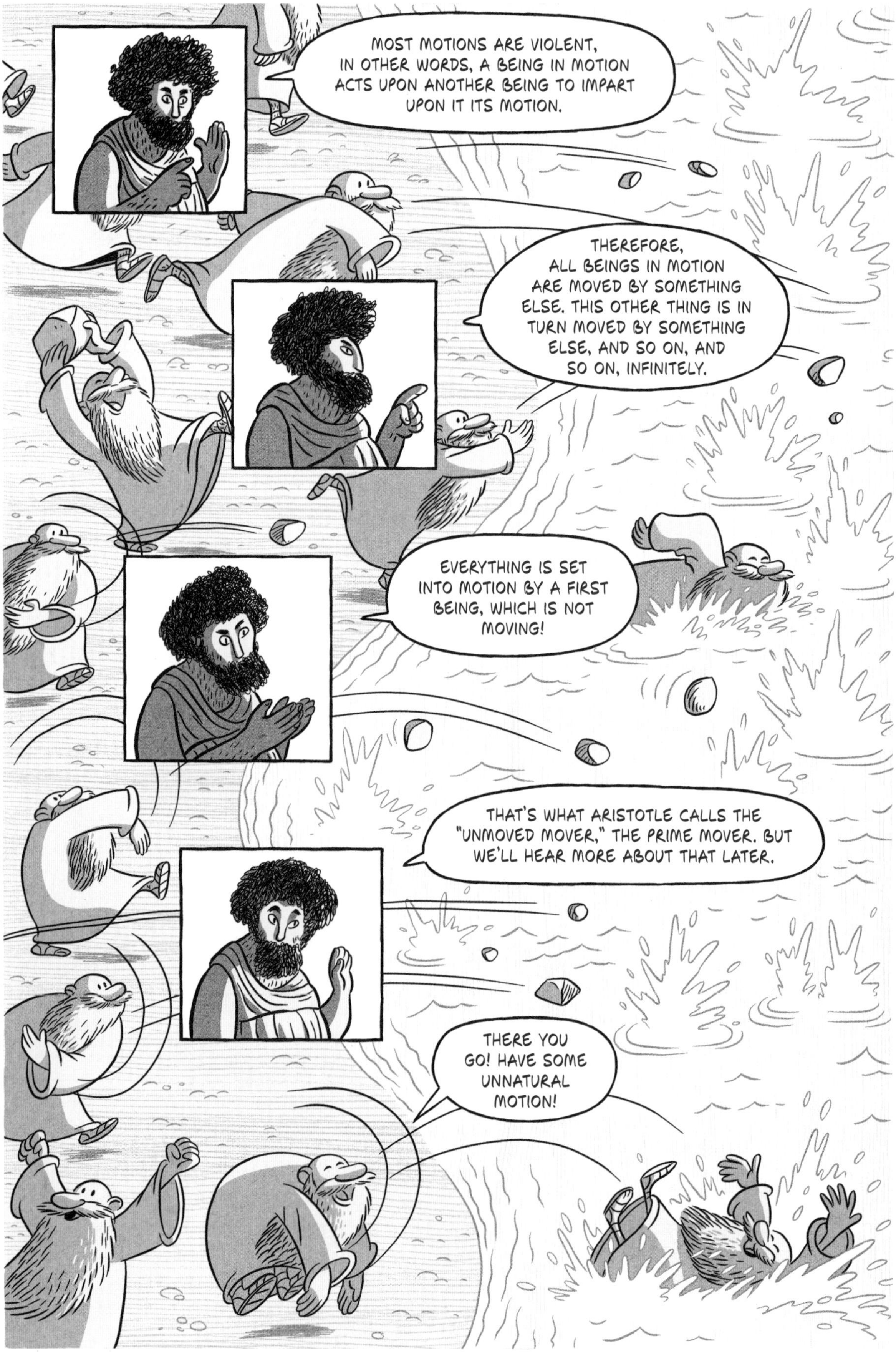
MOST MOTIONS ARE VIOLENT, IN OTHER WORDS, A BEING IN MOTION ACTS UPON ANOTHER BEING TO IMPART UPON IT ITS MOTION.
THEREFORE, ALL BEINGS IN MOTION ARE MOVED BY SOMETHING ELSE. THIS OTHER THING IS IN TURN MOVED BY SOMETHING ELSE, AND SO ON, AND SO ON, INFINITELY.
EVERYTHING IS SET INTO MOTION BY A FIRST BEING, WHICH IS NOT MOVING!
THAT'S WHAT ARISTOTLE CALLS THE "UNMOVED MOVER," THE PRIME MOVER. BUT WE'LL HEAR MORE ABOUT THAT LATER.
THERE YOU GO! HAVE SOME UNNATURAL MOTION!

ATARUS, CALL THEM! IF THEY REFUSE TO COME, HAVE THEIR WIVES CALL THEM.

ENOUGH GOOFING OFF! PLAYTIME'S OVER! SIT DOWN! WE'RE GOING TO TALK ABOUT TIME.

ALL MOTION IS MEASURED BY ITS DURATION, MEANING, ACCORDING TO THE TIME IT NEEDS TO BE COMPLETED.

FROM THIS YOU CAN INFER THAT MOTION DOESN'T EXIST WITHOUT TIME AND THAT TIME DOESN'T EXIST WITHOUT MOTION.

EVERY BEING THAT IS BORN DIES AFTER A CERTAIN TIME.

WHY ARE YOU LOOKING AT ME?

TELL ME, EIGHT. IF I'D CLAPPED MY HANDS WHEN YOUR HAIR WAS DARK, WHAT WOULD YOU SAY?

THAT YOU WERE A BABY BACK THEN!

AND IF I CLAP MY HANDS WHEN I SEE YOUR WHITE HAIR, WHAT CAN YOU SAY ABOUT THE CHANGE?

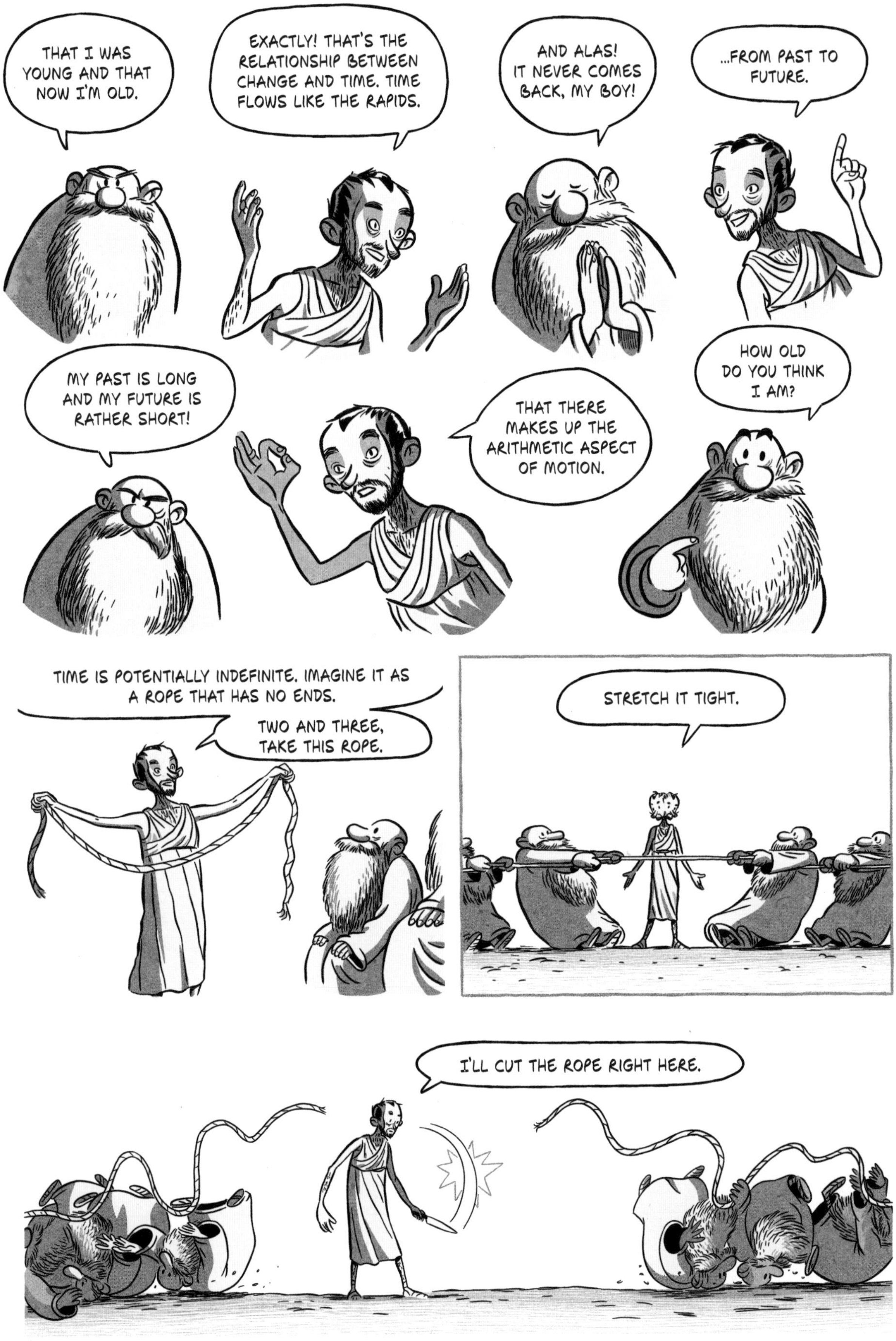
THAT I WAS YOUNG AND THAT NOW I'M OLD.
EXACTLY! THAT'S THE RELATIONSHIP BETWEEN CHANGE AND TIME. TIME FLOWS LIKE THE RAPIDS.
AND ALAS! IT NEVER COMES BACK, MY BOY!
...FROM PAST TO FUTURE.
MY PAST IS LONG AND MY FUTURE IS RATHER SHORT!
THAT THERE MAKES UP THE ARITHMETIC ASPECT OF MOTION.
HOW OLD DO YOU THINK I AM?
TIME IS POTENTIALLY INDEFINITE. IMAGINE IT AS A ROPE THAT HAS NO ENDS.
TWO AND THREE, TAKE THIS ROPE.
STRETCH IT TIGHT.
I'LL CUT THE ROPE RIGHT HERE.

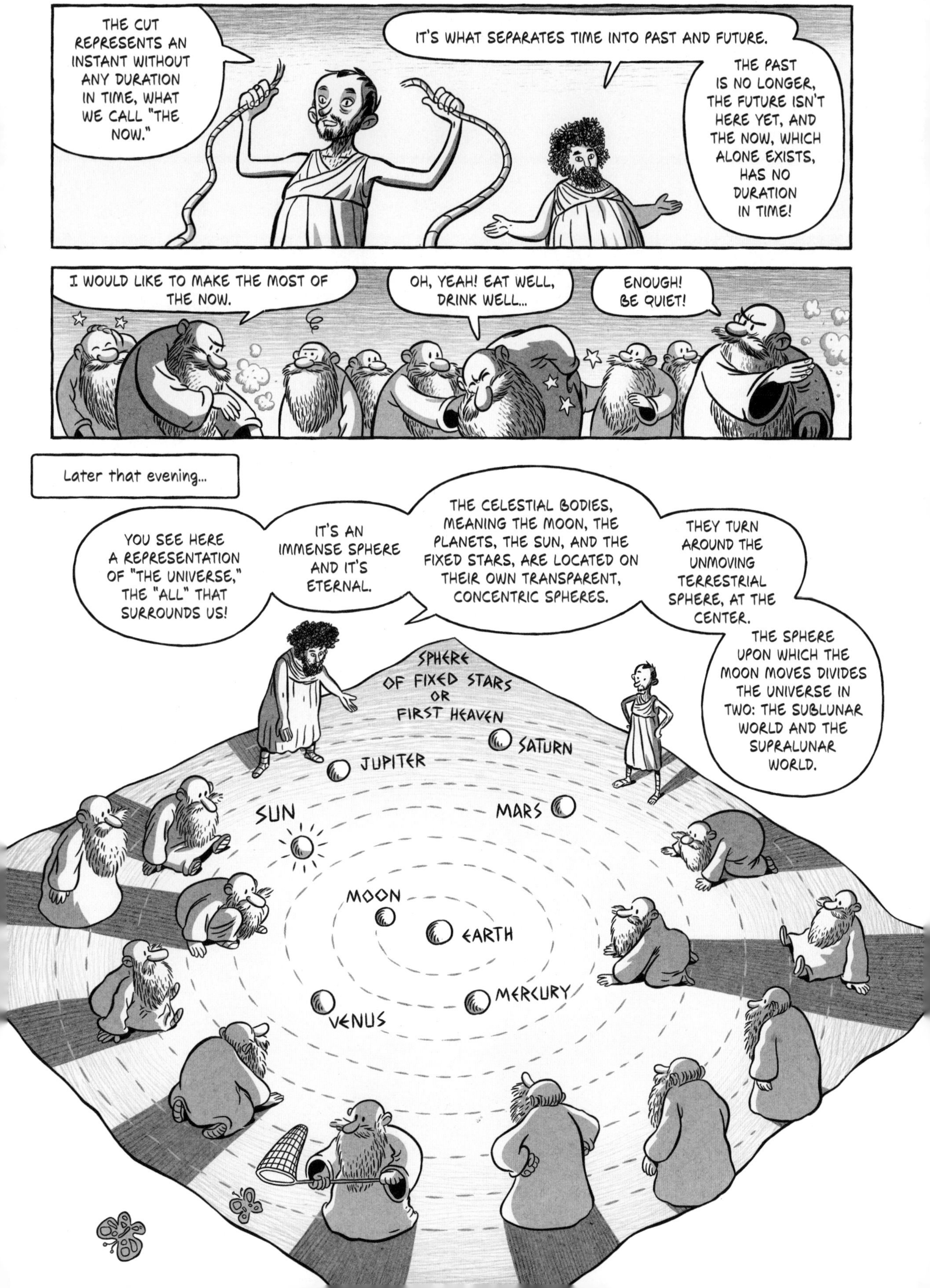

THE CUT REPRESENTS AN INSTANT WITHOUT ANY DURATION IN TIME, WHAT WE CALL "THE NOW."
IT'S WHAT SEPARATES TIME INTO PAST AND FUTURE.
THE PAST IS NO LONGER, THE FUTURE ISN'T HERE YET, AND THE NOW, WHICH ALONE EXISTS, HAS NO DURATION IN TIME!
I WOULD LIKE TO MAKE THE MOST OF THE NOW.
OH, YEAH! EAT WELL, DRINK WELL...
ENOUGH! BE QUIET!
Later that evening...
YOU SEE HERE A REPRESENTATION OF "THE UNIVERSE," THE "ALL" THAT SURROUNDS US!
IT'S AN IMMENSE SPHERE AND IT'S ETERNAL.
THE CELESTIAL BODIES, MEANING THE MOON, THE PLANETS, THE SUN, AND THE FIXED STARS, ARE LOCATED ON THEIR OWN TRANSPARENT, CONCENTRIC SPHERES.
THEY TURN AROUND THE UNMOVING TERRESTRIAL SPHERE, AT THE CENTER.
THE SPHERE UPON WHICH THE MOON MOVES DIVIDES THE UNIVERSE IN TWO: THE SUBLUNAR WORLD AND THE SUPRALUNAR WORLD.
SPHERE OF FIXED STARS OR FIRST HEAVEN
SATURN
JUPITER
SUN
MARS
MOON
EARTH
MERCURY
VENUS

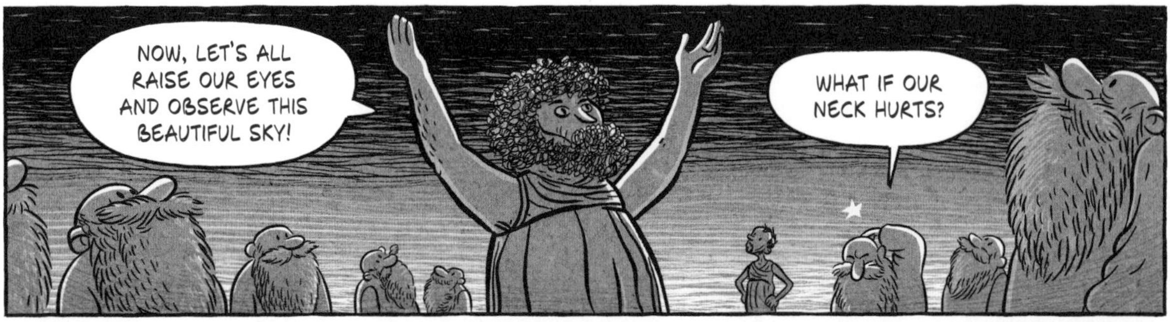
NOW, LET'S ALL RAISE OUR EYES AND OBSERVE THIS BEAUTIFUL SKY!
WHAT IF OUR NECK HURTS?

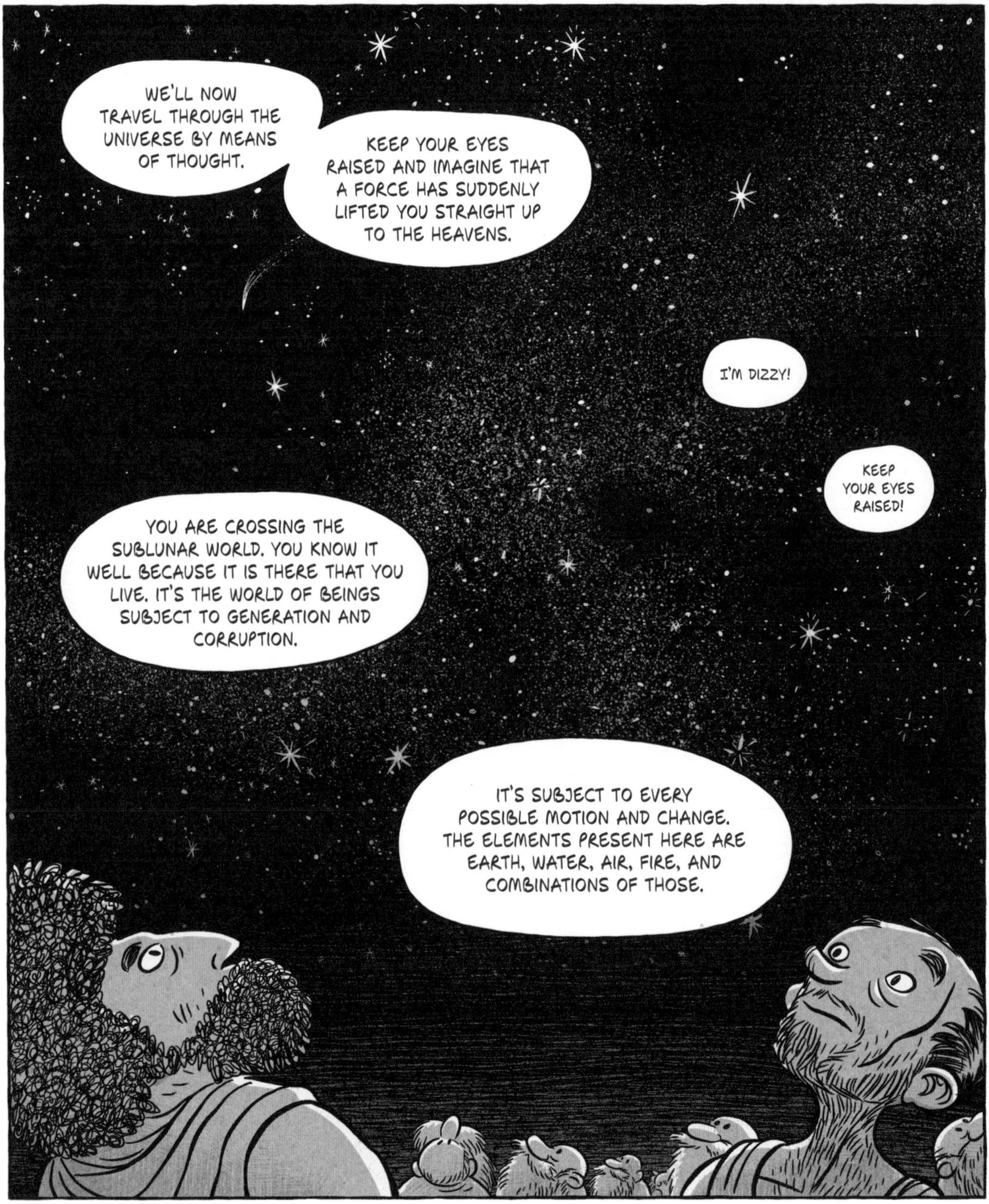
WE'LL NOW TRAVEL THROUGH THE UNIVERSE BY MEANS OF THOUGHT.
KEEP YOUR EYES RAISED AND IMAGINE THAT A FORCE HAS SUDDENLY LIFTED YOU STRAIGHT UP TO THE HEAVENS.
I'M DIZZY!
KEEP YOUR EYES RAISED!
YOU ARE CROSSING THE SUBLUNAR WORLD. YOU KNOW IT WELL BECAUSE IT IS THERE THAT YOU LIVE. IT'S THE WORLD OF BEINGS SUBJECT TO GENERATION AND CORRUPTION.
IT'S SUBJECT TO EVERY POSSIBLE MOTION AND CHANGE. THE ELEMENTS PRESENT HERE ARE EARTH, WATER, AIR, FIRE, AND COMBINATIONS OF THOSE.

YOU RISE HIGHER AND HIGHER, AND YOU MOVE BEYOND THE SPHERE CARRYING THE MOON. LOOK! THERE, IN THE SUPRALUNAR REGION: EVERYTHING IS DIFFERENT!

THERE'S ABSOLUTE SILENCE, ORDER, AND HARMONY. NOTHING BUT THE REGULAR, ETERNAL, CIRCULAR MOTION OF THE CELESTIAL BODIES, DRAWN BY THEIR SPHERES!

ZZZZZ!

WAKE UP! THIS IS A ONE-OF-A-KIND SHOW!

AND HERE'S THE FINAL SPHERE, THE ONE WITH THE FIXED STARS, THE "FIRST HEAVEN." IT MAKES ONE FULL ROTATION UPON ITSELF IN A DAY AND A NIGHT, AND IT DRAWS ALONG THE OTHER SPHERES.

WE SAY THAT THE STARS ARE "FIXED" BECAUSE IN THEIR MOTION AROUND THE EARTH, THE SPACES BETWEEN THEM NEVER CHANGE.

I CAN'T SEE VENUS!

OBVIOUSLY! YOU'RE LOOKING AT THE SEA, NOT THE SKY!

IT'S NIGHT, SO WE DO NOT SEE THE SUN. ITS SPHERE IS LOCATED JUST BEYOND THE SPHERE OF VENUS.

THE MOTION OF THE SUN DETERMINES THE SEASONS AND VEGETATION, BUT ALSO LIFE ON EARTH. SINCE THE MOTION OF THE CELESTIAL BODIES IS CIRCULAR AND ETERNAL, THERE CAN BE NO "UNNATURAL" MOTION. "UNNATURAL" MOTIONS DON'T HAVE THESE CHARACTERISTICS. SO THIS IS A "NATURAL" MOTION. BUT WE DO KNOW THAT THE NATURAL MOTION OF THE FOUR TERRESTRIAL ELEMENTS, WHICH ARE EARTH, WATER, AIR, AND FIRE, IS RECTILINEAR AND VERTICAL. THUS, THE CELESTIAL BODIES ARE MADE OF ANOTHER ELEMENT, A FIFTH ELEMENT WHOSE NATURAL MOTION IS CIRCULAR, UNIFORM, AND ETERNAL. ARISTOTLE CALLS THIS FIFTH ELEMENT "AETHER."

The next morning...

WE'LL COVER THE REST NEXT TIME.

WE'RE COUNTING ON YOU!

I'LL LEAVE YOU THESE PAPYRI SO YOU CAN STUDY METEOROLOGY!

THANK YOU SO MUCH! THESE WILL BE THE FIRST PAPYRI IN OUR PAPYROTHEQUE, INAUGURATED TWO YEARS AGO!

SAFE TRAVELS!

THANKS FOR EVERYTHING!

I HOPE THINGS HAVE CALMED DOWN A LITTLE IN ATHENS.

I'M GETTING THE IMPRESSION THAT THEY HAVE!

- WHAT?
- HIS NEPHEW SPEUSIPPUS HAS BEEN MADE HEAD OF THE SCHOOL.
- I EXPECTED THAT!
- THE LAW STATES THAT THE CLOSEST RELATIVE IS THE HEIR. PLATO HAD NO CHILDREN.
- HEIR TO THE PROPERTY, FINE, BUT THE CLASSES AS WELL?

XENOCRATES, YOU TOLD ME ONE DAY THAT IF I EVER LEFT ATHENS, YOU'D GO WITH ME. DOES THAT STILL STAND?
- OF COURSE!
- THEN PACK YOUR BAGS. WE'RE GOING TO JOIN ERASTUS AND CORISCUS IN ASSOS. LET HERMIAS KNOW.

The next morning...

ASSOS

ATHENS

LESBOS

In Assos...

YES, HERMIAS! IT'S NOT JUST SPEUSIPPUS AND THE POLITICAL SITUATION IN ATHENS. I REALLY WANTED TO LEAVE THE ACADEMY.

I NO LONGER HAD TIME TO SPEND WRITING OR WORKING ON ALL THE SUBJECTS THAT I'M INTERESTED IN, SUCH AS MY RESEARCH INTO FAUNA AND FLORA.

YOU'RE IN THE RIGHT PLACE AT THE RIGHT TIME. THAT'S WHAT CORISCUS AND ERASTUS ARE WORKING ON.

THANKS TO HERMIAS'S GENEROUS SUPPORT, WE'VE SET UP A LABORATORY.

WE'RE COLLECTING PLANTS AND ANIMALS FROM THE REGION AND RECORDING OUR OBSERVATIONS.

AND PYTHIAS ORGANIZES THEM.

PYTHIAS?

MY NIECE. THOSE SUBJECTS ARE HER PASSION. TAKE A LOOK AT HER BOOK OF HERBS, YOU'LL SEE.

HELLO, PYTHIAS!

WELCOME! MY UNCLE AND HIS FRIENDS CAN'T STOP TALKING ABOUT YOU!

YOUR UNCLE HOLDS A SPECIAL PLACE IN MY HEART, ALONG WITH MY PARENTS AND MY GUARDIAN.

AS FOR MY FRIENDS, I'VE MISSED THEM A LOT.

100

SPEAKING OF WHICH, HOW'S MY GUARDIAN PROXENUS? IS HE STILL HARANGUING CROWDS IN THE SQUARES OF ATARNEUS? HA HA!

WHAT IS IT?

HIS WIFE DIED TWO YEARS AGO, JUST AFTER GIVING BIRTH TO A BOY. PROXENUS DIED LAST MONTH OUT OF GRIEF.

AND THE BOY?

I'M GOING TO ATARNEUS!

DON'T YOU WANT TO SETTLE IN FIRST?

XENOCRATES CAN DO IT.

HOLD ON! I'LL GO WITH YOU!

Assos, a colony of people from the island of Lesbos, just across from it in the Aegean Sea, was a Mysian city. Mysia was under Persian control, and its capital was Atarneus.

Hermias, who succeeded Eubulus as ruler, maintained relations with the Academy, but with the Macedonian court as well.

He often advised Philip on his great plan for a campaign against the Persians and provided him with intel on their troop movements.

At this time, utter confusion reigned over Athens. Demosthenes was in power, and in his speeches he constantly ranted about Philip and the threat of an invasion into Greece, in order to provoke an uprising of the people against him. Aeschines, the head of the pro-Macedonian party, defended the opposite position.

Isocrates, the old orator, tried to use his speeches and letters to convince Philip to lead his campaign against the Persians as king of all Greeks, knowing that Athens could oversee such a conflict.

Aristotle's only wish was to forget all that!
The political situation in Athens, the Academy, Speusippus and his philosophical subjects, the sophists and their fancy talk, the droning of orators...
In Assos, things changed with the arrival of Nicanor in his life.

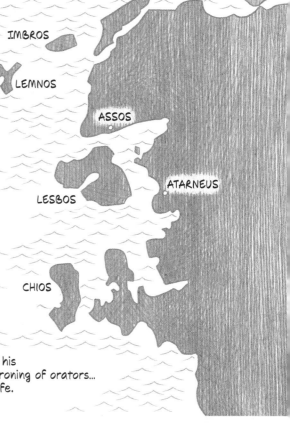

HIS NAME IS NICANOR.

WHEN MY PARENTS DIED, HIS FATHER TOOK ME UNDER HIS WING. I WAS THIRTEEN.

I KNOW. XENOCRATES TOLD US EVERYTHING.

ORPHANED SO YOUNG. HE STILL NEEDS TO BE LAVISHED WITH ATTENTION.

DON'T YOU WORRY! EVERYONE HERE WILL LOOK AFTER HIM!

THANKS!

I'VE BEEN TOLD SO MUCH ABOUT YOU, BUT NO ONE MENTIONED HOW SENSITIVE YOU WERE!

MAYBE THAT'S BECAUSE I DON'T SHOW IT!

♡

YOU'VE ALREADY COLLECTED QUITE A LOT OF STUFF!

THE LOCALS HAVE HELPED US OUT A LOT.

OF COURSE, IT'S ALL A BIT OF A JUMBLE!

WE'LL HAVE TO GET ORGANIZED!

LOOK AT MY HERBARIUM.

COLLECTING AND DESCRIBING ARE ONLY THE FIRST STEP!

WITH PLANTS, IT'S FAIRLY SIMPLE.

IT'S BEAUTIFUL!

THANKS!

NOW, AS FOR ANIMALS...

WE HAVE TO STUDY THEIR LIFE, THEIR EATING HABITS, THEIR HABITAT, THEIR ENEMIES....

BUT WE ALSO HAVE TO DISSECT DEAD ANIMALS TO EXAMINE THEIR LIMBS, BONES, TISSUES...

WATER, SALT, AND HONEY WILL HELP US PRESERVE ALL THAT.

IN ANY CASE, WE'LL HAVE TO MAKE PRECISE DRAWINGS OF WHAT WE SEE AND CLASSIFY OUR RESULTS.

I CAN HANDLE THAT.

PERFECT! YOU'LL ALSO TAKE DICTATION!

I THINK THAT PLAYTIME IS OVER!

ARISTOTLE'S CHANGED!

COME! I'LL READ YOU ODYSSEUS'S ADVENTURES ON CALYPSO'S ISLAND!

YOU PROMISED TO TAKE ME TO THE TEMPLE OF ATHENA.

SO I DID. WELL, LET'S GO THERE NOW!

THE TEMPLE AND THE ACROPOLIS ARE OUR LOCAL SIGHTS.

I NOTICED THAT, FOR A WOMAN, YOU POSSESS A GREAT DEAL OF KNOWLEDGE.

WHEN YOU'RE HERMIAS'S NIECE, YOU CAN'T REALLY REMAIN IGNORANT!

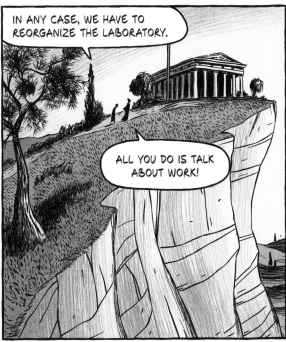

IN ANY CASE, WE HAVE TO REORGANIZE THE LABORATORY.

ALL YOU DO IS TALK ABOUT WORK!

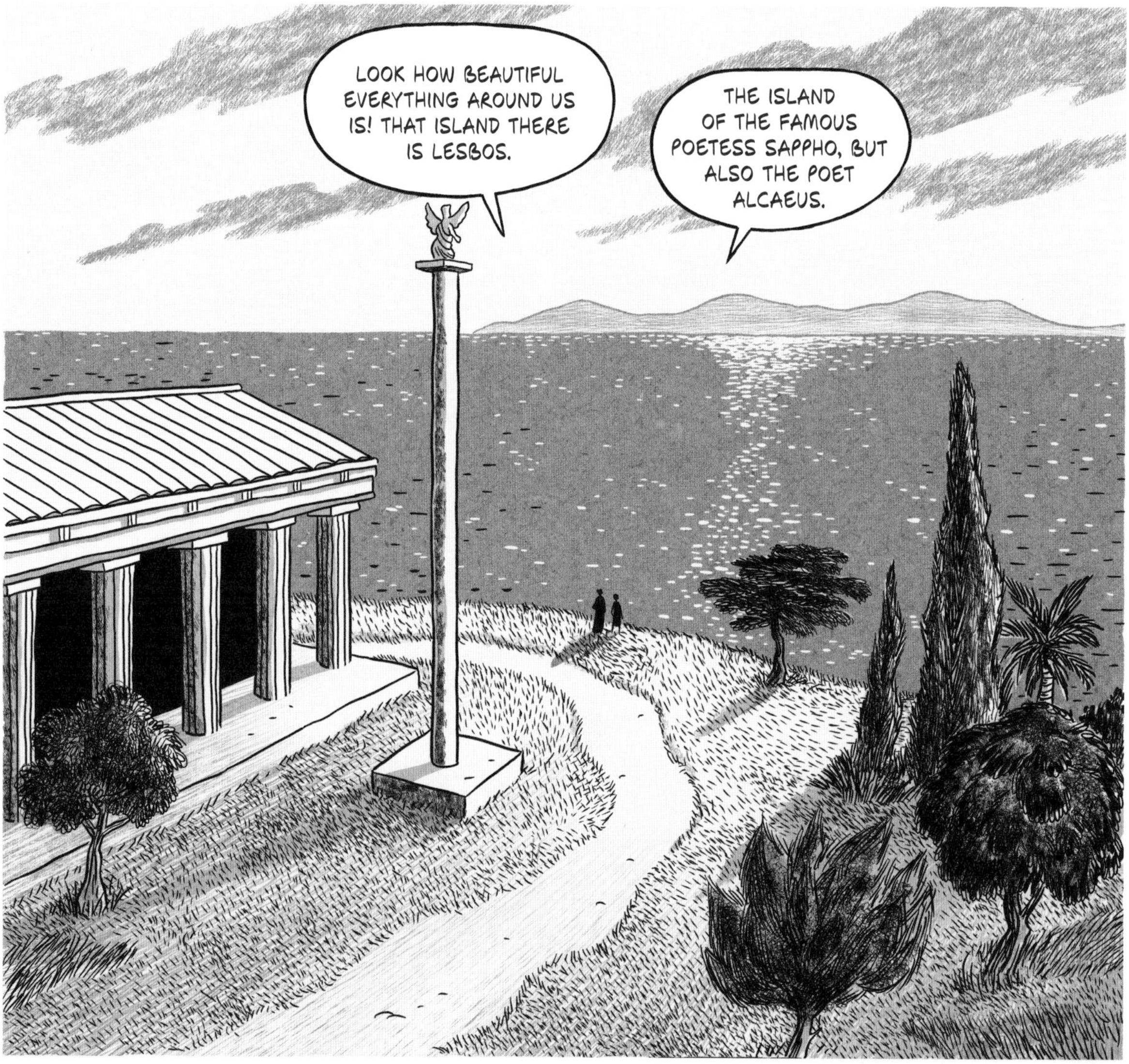
LOOK HOW BEAUTIFUL EVERYTHING AROUND US IS! THAT ISLAND THERE IS LESBOS.
THE ISLAND OF THE FAMOUS POETESS SAPPHO, BUT ALSO THE POET ALCAEUS.

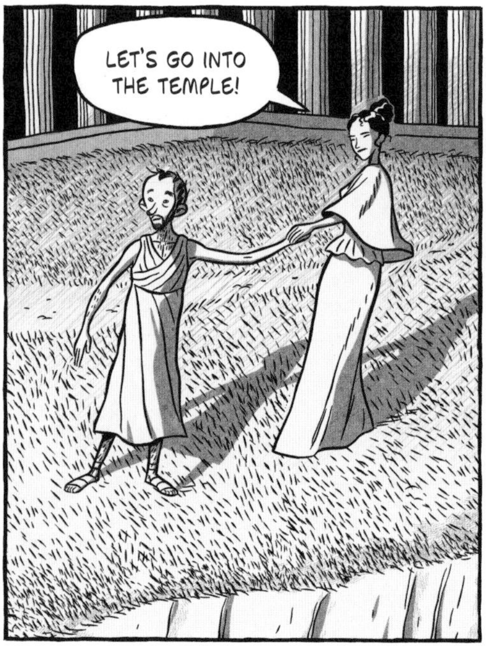
LET'S GO INTO THE TEMPLE!

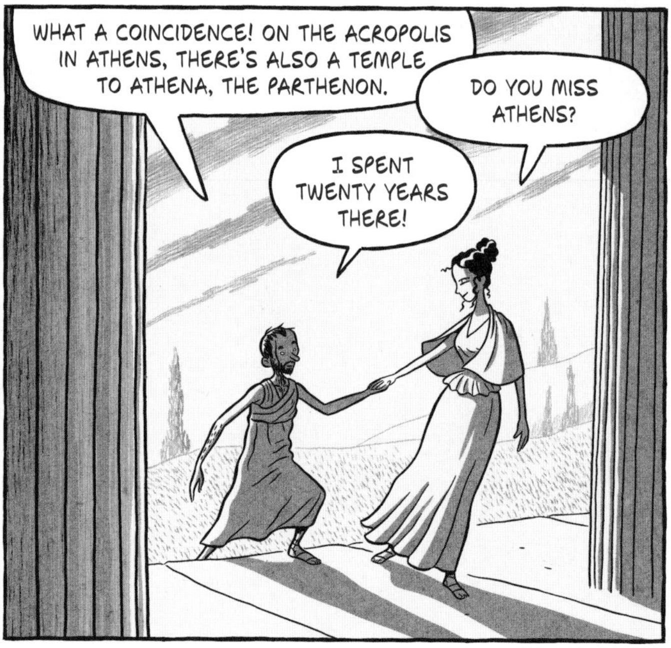
WHAT A COINCIDENCE! ON THE ACROPOLIS IN ATHENS, THERE'S ALSO A TEMPLE TO ATHENA, THE PARTHENON.
DO YOU MISS ATHENS?
I SPENT TWENTY YEARS THERE!

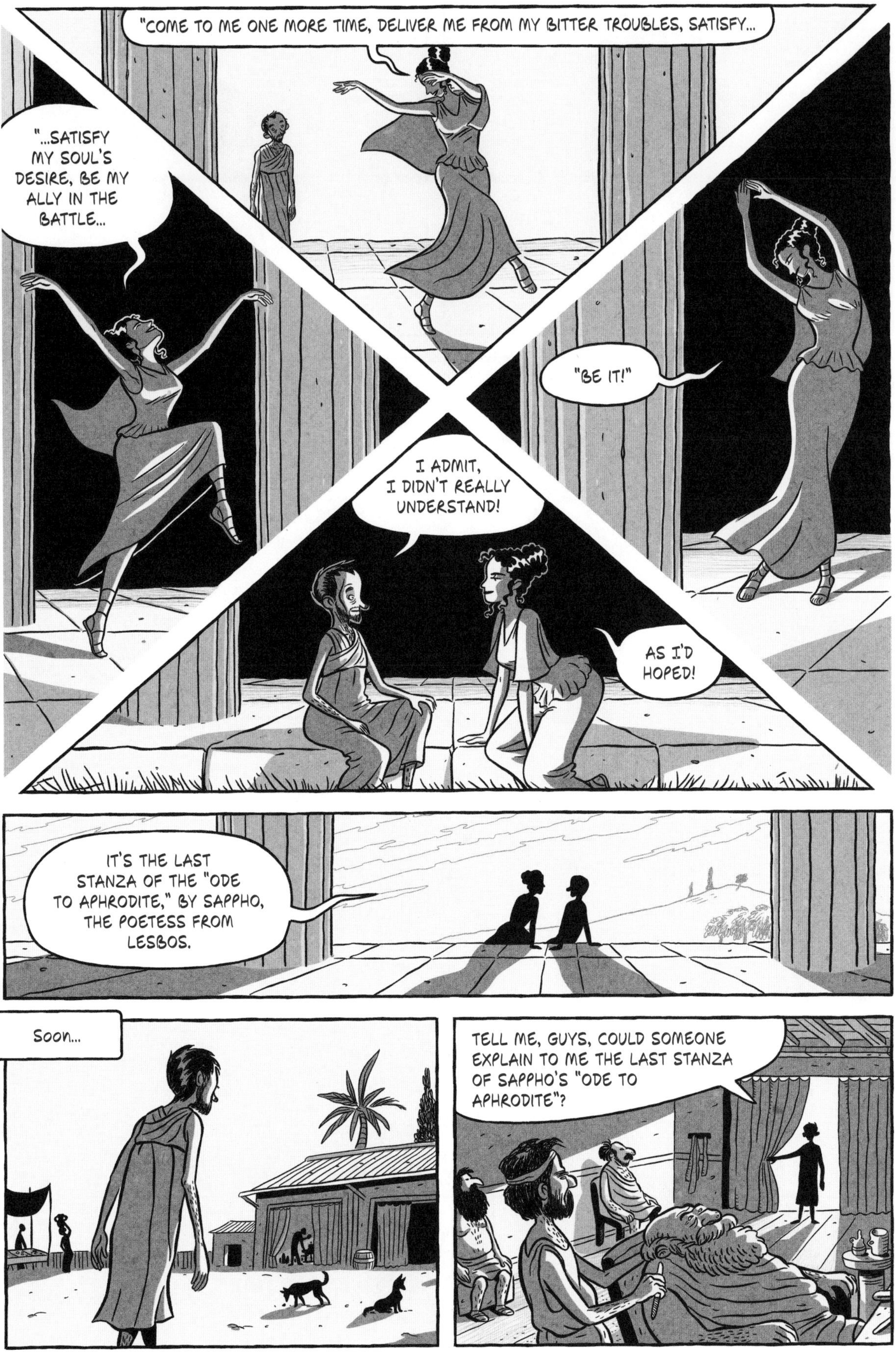
"COME TO ME ONE MORE TIME, DELIVER ME FROM MY BITTER TROUBLES, SATISFY...
"...SATISFY MY SOUL'S DESIRE, BE MY ALLY IN THE BATTLE...
"BE IT!"
I ADMIT, I DIDN'T REALLY UNDERSTAND!
AS I'D HOPED!
IT'S THE LAST STANZA OF THE "ODE TO APHRODITE," BY SAPPHO, THE POETESS FROM LESBOS.
Soon...
TELL ME, GUYS, COULD SOMEONE EXPLAIN TO ME THE LAST STANZA OF SAPPHO'S "ODE TO APHRODITE"?

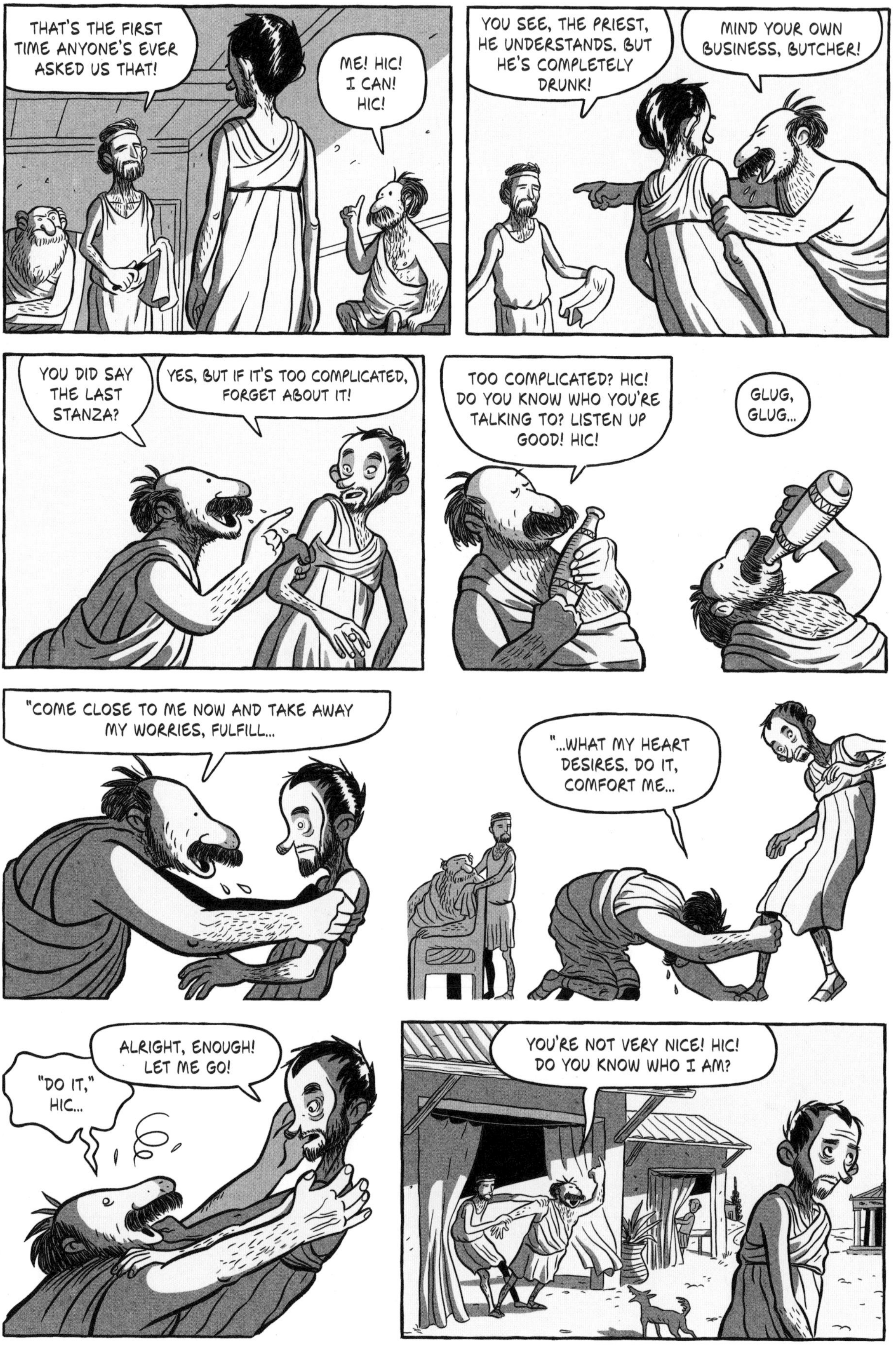
THAT'S THE FIRST TIME ANYONE'S EVER ASKED US THAT!
ME! HIC! I CAN! HIC!
YOU SEE, THE PRIEST, HE UNDERSTANDS. BUT HE'S COMPLETELY DRUNK!
MIND YOUR OWN BUSINESS, BUTCHER!
YOU DID SAY THE LAST STANZA?
YES, BUT IF IT'S TOO COMPLICATED, FORGET ABOUT IT!
TOO COMPLICATED? HIC! DO YOU KNOW WHO YOU'RE TALKING TO? LISTEN UP GOOD! HIC!
GLUG, GLUG...
"COME CLOSE TO ME NOW AND TAKE AWAY MY WORRIES, FULFILL...
"...WHAT MY HEART DESIRES. DO IT, COMFORT ME...
ALRIGHT, ENOUGH! LET ME GO!
"DO IT," HIC...
YOU'RE NOT VERY NICE! HIC! DO YOU KNOW WHO I AM?

WE CALL "BEINGS" THE REALITIES WE PERCEIVE AROUND US WITH OUR SENSES. THERE ARE ANIMATE BEINGS AND INANIMATE BEINGS.

PLANTS, ANIMALS, AND HUMANS ARE ANIMATE BEINGS!

WE CALL "LIFE" THE FACULTY OF EACH ANIMATE BEING TO FEED, DEVELOP, AND REPRODUCE ITSELF.

THE MATTER OF THE ANIMATED BEING IS ITS BODY, ITS FORM IS ITS SOUL. SOUL IS THE PRINCIPLE OF MOTION AND THE CAUSE OF LIFE. IT DEFINES THE NATURE OF THE LIVING BEING.

THE SOUL AND THE BODY ARE INSEPARABLE. THE BODY IS POTENTIAL LIFE BUT THIS POTENTIAL IS ONLY ACTUALIZED IF THE SOUL ANIMATES THE BODY. THE SOUL IS THUS THE BODY'S ENTELECHY.

IN THIS SENSE, WE CAN CONSIDER THE SOUL THE SET OF FACULTIES OF EVERY ANIMATE BEING.

THE HEART IS THE ORGAN WHERE THE MOTIONS OF THE SOUL COME TO A HEAD. THERE, STIMULATIONS OF THE SENSES MIX WITH DESIRES AND SET OFF ACTIONS.

IF ONLY YOU COULD FEEL MY HEART BEAT AND SENSE WHAT IT DESIRES AT THIS MOMENT!

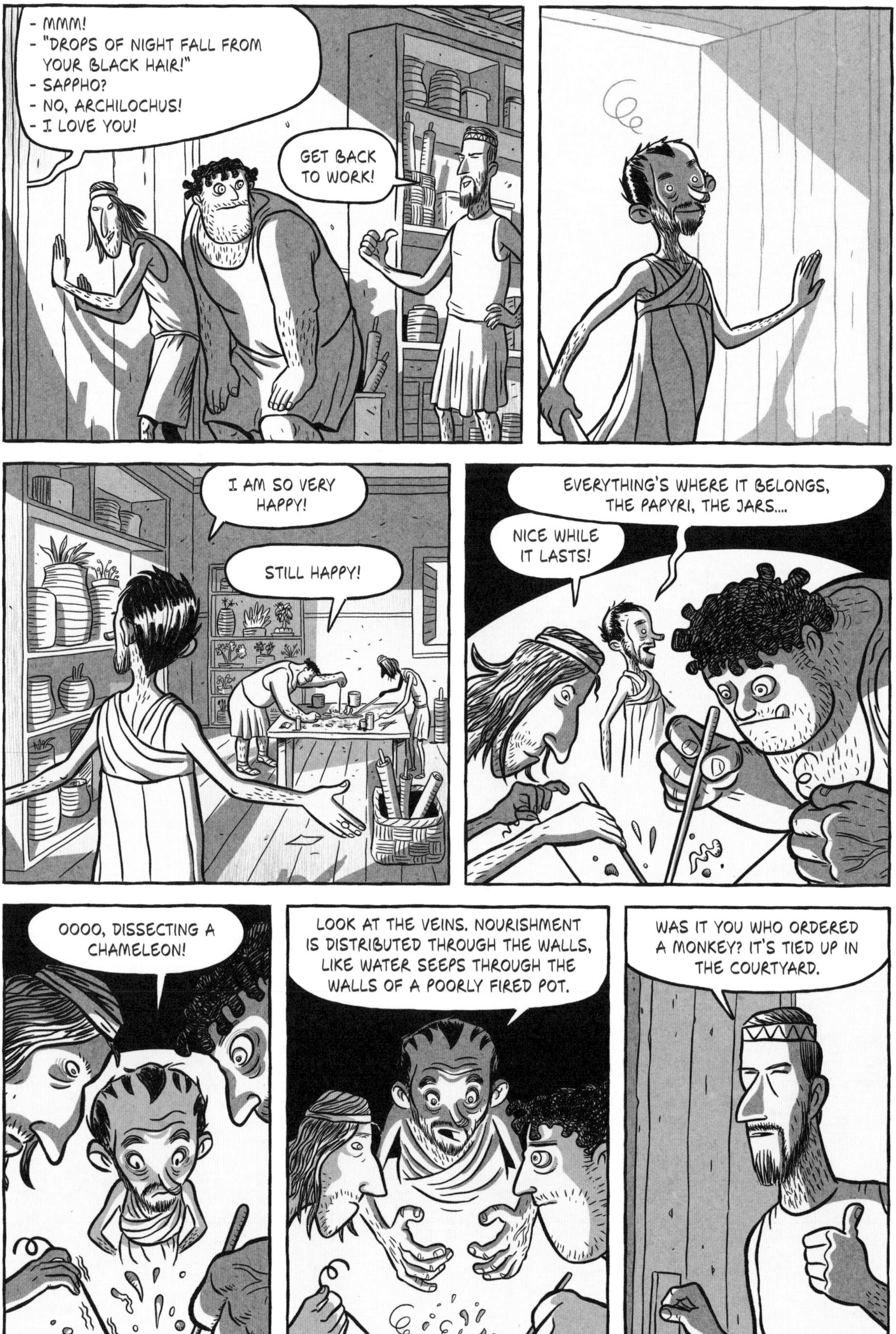
- MMM!
- "DROPS OF NIGHT FALL FROM YOUR BLACK HAIR!"
- SAPPHO?
- NO, ARCHILOCHUS!
- I LOVE YOU!
GET BACK TO WORK!
I AM SO VERY HAPPY!
STILL HAPPY!
EVERYTHING'S WHERE IT BELONGS, THE PAPYRI, THE JARS....
NICE WHILE IT LASTS!
OOOO, DISSECTING A CHAMELEON!
LOOK AT THE VEINS. NOURISHMENT IS DISTRIBUTED THROUGH THE WALLS, LIKE WATER SEEPS THROUGH THE WALLS OF A POORLY FIRED POT.
WAS IT YOU WHO ORDERED A MONKEY? IT'S TIED UP IN THE COURTYARD.

His need to gather material was limitless. Not content with having devoured all that was written on a particular subject, he would go question hunters, peasants, or fishermen. What they taught him didn't always turn out to be true.

It was in this period that he formulated the theory stating that "by their very nature, all men wish to learn." To which he added that, if men love all of their senses, sight is the one they prefer, because with it the most knowledge is acquired.

GIVE ARISTOTLE A KISS. IT'S TIME FOR YOU TO GO TO BED.

NO! I WANNA HEAR THE STORY OF ODYSSEUS AND CALYPSO.

BUT I'VE TOLD YOU IT SO MANY TIMES!

I WANNA HEAR IT AGAIN!

I WANT ODYSSEUS!

WHAT DO WE DO WITH THE MONKEY?

OBSERVE ITS CHARACTERISTICS!

A few months later...

BY YOUR SIDE, THE WORLD SEEMS MORE BEAUTIFUL TO ME, THE STARS BRIGHTER, THE MOON CLOSER!

SAPPHO?

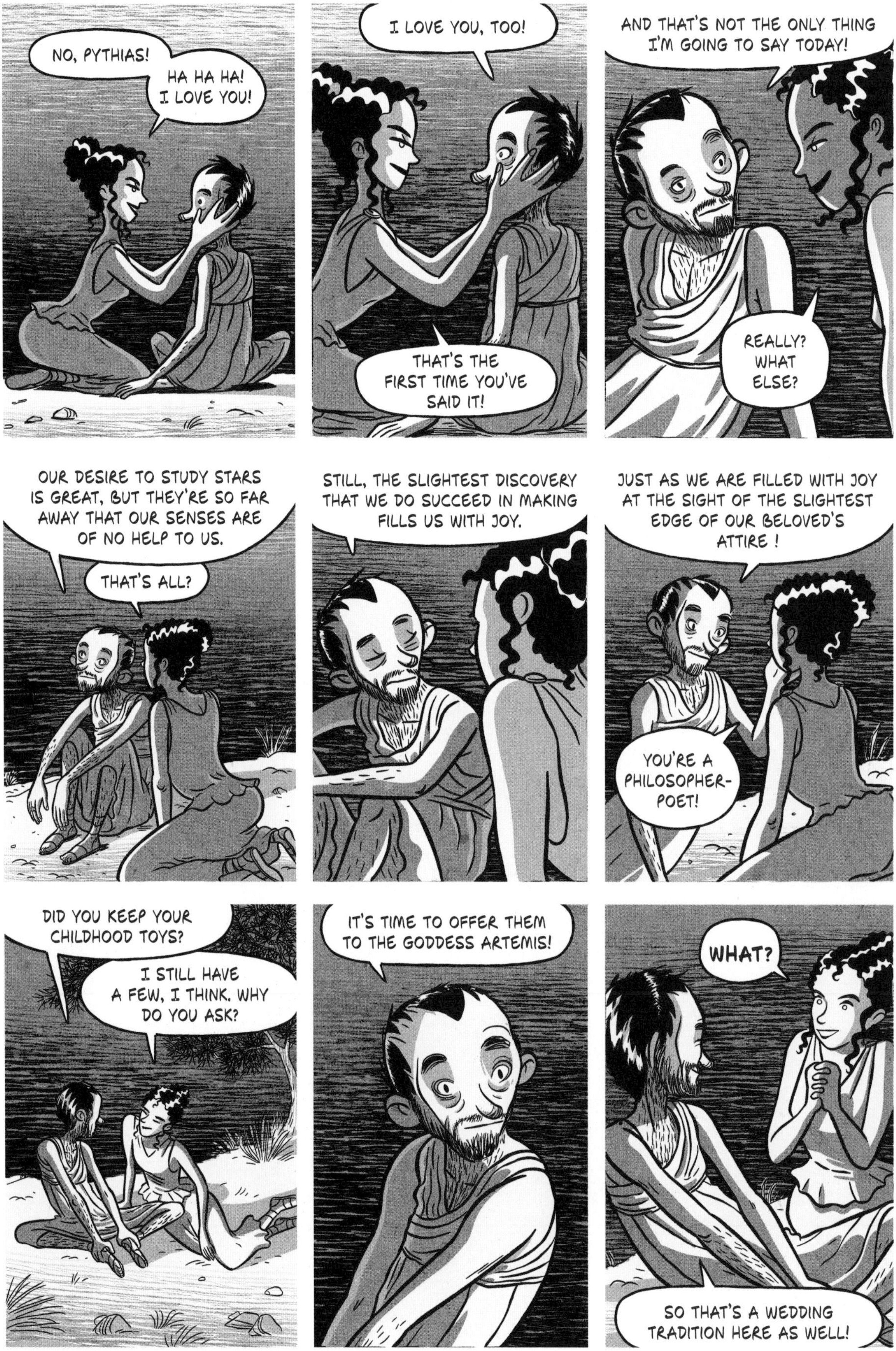
NO, PYTHIAS!
HA HA HA! I LOVE YOU!
I LOVE YOU, TOO!
THAT'S THE FIRST TIME YOU'VE SAID IT!
AND THAT'S NOT THE ONLY THING I'M GOING TO SAY TODAY!
REALLY? WHAT ELSE?
OUR DESIRE TO STUDY STARS IS GREAT, BUT THEY'RE SO FAR AWAY THAT OUR SENSES ARE OF NO HELP TO US.
THAT'S ALL?
STILL, THE SLIGHTEST DISCOVERY THAT WE DO SUCCEED IN MAKING FILLS US WITH JOY.
JUST AS WE ARE FILLED WITH JOY AT THE SIGHT OF THE SLIGHTEST EDGE OF OUR BELOVED'S ATTIRE !
YOU'RE A PHILOSOPHER-POET!
DID YOU KEEP YOUR CHILDHOOD TOYS?
I STILL HAVE A FEW, I THINK. WHY DO YOU ASK?
IT'S TIME TO OFFER THEM TO THE GODDESS ARTEMIS!
WHAT?
SO THAT'S A WEDDING TRADITION HERE AS WELL!

HERMIAS, MY MASTER, YOU HAVE A LETTER FROM ASSOS. THERE ARE ALSO TWO OF PHILIP'S OFFICERS WAITING.

SHOW THEM IN!

HA HA HA, I HAD A FEELING! AND I WAS HOPING!

HA HA.

EH-HEM.

HEM.

RESEARCH DOES REQUIRE GREAT EFFORT, BUT WE ARE COMPENSATED FOR IT BY THE JOY OF DISCOVERING WONDER IN EVERY ONE OF NATURE'S CREATIONS!

EVER SINCE HE DECIDED TO GET MARRIED, IT'S ALL JOY THIS, JOY THAT!

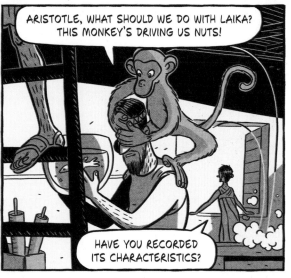

ARISTOTLE, WHAT SHOULD WE DO WITH LAIKA? THIS MONKEY'S DRIVING US NUTS!

HAVE YOU RECORDED ITS CHARACTERISTICS?

YESH, IT'SH DONE!

THEN EVERYTHING'S GOOD! BE HAPPY, MY FRIENDS!

SMACK!

The wedding took place, honoring the traditions.

"HER LOVELY WASHED BODY, HER NEW BRIDAL GOWN..."

BY ZEUS AND HERA! MAY THEY GRANT THEM A LONG LIFE, FULL OF HAPPINESS AND CHILDREN!

FRIENDS, THIS IS A GREAT DAY FOR ME! MY ADORED NIECE IS MARRYING MY DEAREST FRIEND. LET US DRINK TO THEIR HAPPINESS!

CONGRATULATIONS!

BEST WISHES!

DEMOSTHENES SAID: "WE HAVE MISTRESSES FOR PLEASURE, CONCUBINES FOR DAILY LIFE, AND WIVES TO RUN THE HOUSEHOLD AND TO GIVE US CHILDREN."

HA HA HA

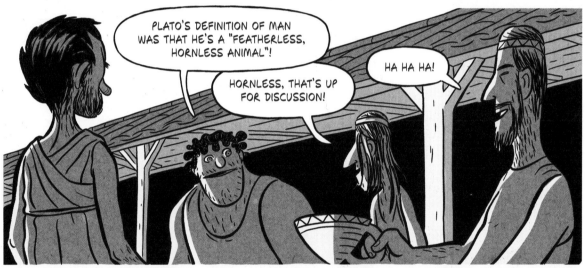

PLATO'S DEFINITION OF MAN WAS THAT HE'S A "FEATHERLESS, HORNLESS ANIMAL"!

HORNLESS, THAT'S UP FOR DISCUSSION!

HA HA HA!

Two years had gone by, but I had only just learned of his arrival.

Aristotle was in Assos, I in Eresos on the neighboring island of Lesbos.

I couldn't wait to see him again!

ALL RESEARCH HAS TO BEGIN BY OBSERVING THE BEINGS WE KNOW BEST BEFORE PURSUING THE STUDY OF LESSER-KNOWN ONES. IT IS THEREFORE JUDICIOUS, IN THE STUDY OF THE PARTS OF THE BODY, TO BEGIN WITH THOSE OF THE HUMAN BEING.

STAND UP, CORISCUS!

WHAT ARE YOU GOING TO DO?

THE MAIN PARTS OF THE HUMAN BODY ARE THE HEAD, THE NECK, THE THORAX, THE TWO ARMS, AND THE TWO LEGS.

OPENING A HUMAN BODY UP TO FIND OUT ABOUT THE INTERNAL ORGANS IS REPUGNANT.

CAN I SIT DOWN?

I FEAR THE WORST!

SO, IN ORDER TO STUDY THOSE ORGANS, WE MUST PROCEED BY ANALOGY WITH ANIMALS THAT ARE CLOSE TO MAN.

NO! HE'S WORKING!

I WANT TO ASK HIM A QUESTION!

HOW LONG DID ODYSSEUS STAY WITH CALYPSO, AND ON WHAT ISLAND?

!

SEVEN YEARS, ON OGYGIA! I'VE TOLD YOU THAT A NUMBER OF TIMES!

I WANT TO HEAR IT AGAIN!

SORRY TO INTERRUPT, ARISTOTLE, BUT YOU'LL BE HAPPY TO SEE WHO'S JUST ARRIVED!

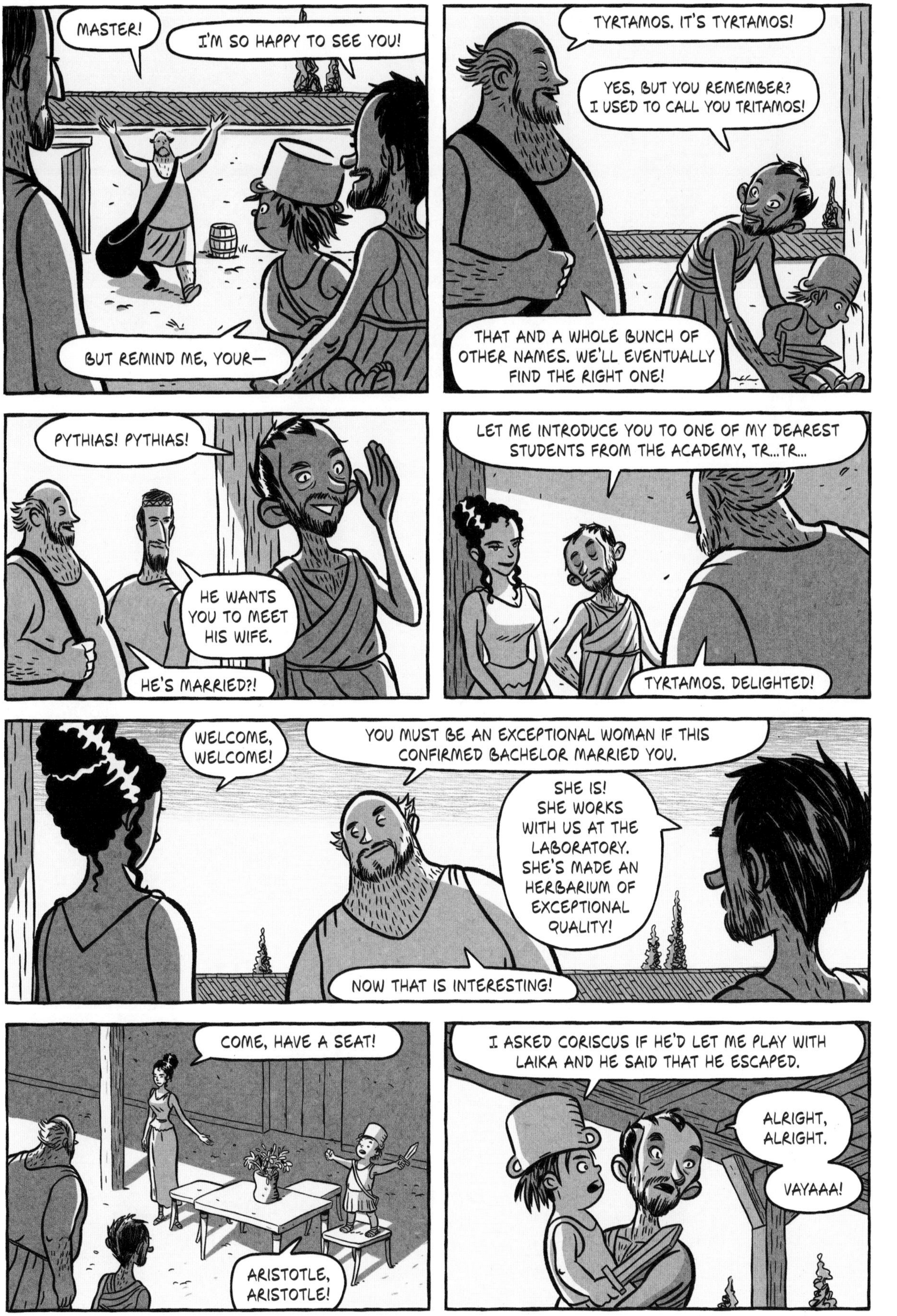
MASTER!
I'M SO HAPPY TO SEE YOU!
BUT REMIND ME, YOUR—
TYRTAMOS. IT'S TYRTAMOS!
YES, BUT YOU REMEMBER? I USED TO CALL YOU TRITAMOS!
THAT AND A WHOLE BUNCH OF OTHER NAMES. WE'LL EVENTUALLY FIND THE RIGHT ONE!
PYTHIAS! PYTHIAS!
HE WANTS YOU TO MEET HIS WIFE.
HE'S MARRIED?!
LET ME INTRODUCE YOU TO ONE OF MY DEAREST STUDENTS FROM THE ACADEMY, TR...TR...
TYRTAMOS. DELIGHTED!
WELCOME, WELCOME!
YOU MUST BE AN EXCEPTIONAL WOMAN IF THIS CONFIRMED BACHELOR MARRIED YOU.
SHE IS! SHE WORKS WITH US AT THE LABORATORY. SHE'S MADE AN HERBARIUM OF EXCEPTIONAL QUALITY!
NOW THAT IS INTERESTING!
COME, HAVE A SEAT!
ARISTOTLE, ARISTOTLE!
I ASKED CORISCUS IF HE'D LET ME PLAY WITH LAIKA AND HE SAID THAT HE ESCAPED.
ALRIGHT, ALRIGHT.
VAYAAA!

HERMIAS HAS SENT A MESSENGER.

EVERYONE'S DROPPING BY TODAY! SHOW HIM IN!

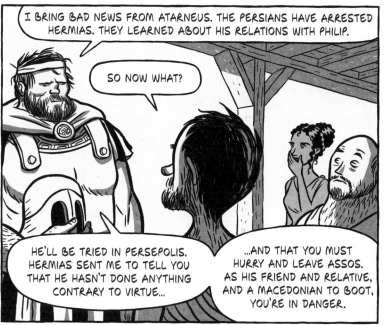

I BRING BAD NEWS FROM ATARNEUS. THE PERSIANS HAVE ARRESTED HERMIAS. THEY LEARNED ABOUT HIS RELATIONS WITH PHILIP.

SO NOW WHAT?

HE'LL BE TRIED IN PERSEPOLIS. HERMIAS SENT ME TO TELL YOU THAT HE HASN'T DONE ANYTHING CONTRARY TO VIRTUE...

...AND THAT YOU MUST HURRY AND LEAVE ASSOS. AS HIS FRIEND AND RELATIVE, AND A MACEDONIAN TO BOOT, YOU'RE IN DANGER.

OH, NO!

COME WITH ME TO LESBOS! YOU'LL BE SAFE THERE. I HAVE A LABORATORY ON THE GULF OF PYRRHA WHERE THERE'S ENOUGH WORK FOR EVERYONE.

PYTHIAS, WE'RE MOVING! GATHER OUR BELONGINGS AND THE PAPYRI. QUICKLY! AND GET THE BOY READY!

WE'RE GOING TO STAY PUT. HOW CAN WE ABANDON THE FRUIT OF OUR LONG YEARS OF LABOR? YOU DO UNDERSTAND...!

I UNDERSTAND!

I THINK I'M GOING TO RETURN TO ATHENS. DO YOU UNDERSTAND?

I UNDERSTAND!

I'VE DECIDED THAT I'LL CALL YOU THEOPHRASTUS!

- THEOPHRASTUS? WHY NOT, AS LONG AS YOU'RE ABLE TO REMEMBER!

HA HA HA!

- THANK YOU, THEOPHRASTUS!

- DON'T MENTION IT!

On Lesbos, Aristotle was a happy man! He lived peacefully in a beautiful setting, surrounded by his family, without fear, and far from any threats.

He had wanted to stay in Pyrrha, a city amongst olive trees, on the coast of the lagoon of the same name.

YOU REMEMBER HOW I LEFT ATHENS IN A RUSH ON ACCOUNT OF MY FATHER'S DEATH.

HE WAS A MERCHANT AND ALSO HAD A LAUNDRY BUSINESS. FOR A WHILE, I TOOK OVER HIS WORK, BUT PLANTS AND PHILOSOPHY ARE MY TRUE PASSIONS.

THAT'S PERFECT!

YOU WILL DEVOTE YOURSELF TO PLANTS, AND I TO ANIMALS, AND BOTH OF US TO PHILOSOPHY!

We built an even bigger laboratory in Pyrrha, but the true laboratory, bigger still, was the natural life on the island.
     Aristotle's main center of interest at this time was the animate world. Every being, every phenomenon, had to be observed and described in order to understand its "truth," that is, the cause that had brought it into existence.
     Aristotle spent his days observing the animate beings on the hill, on the shores, in the swamps, and in the lagoon. He often brought along Pythias, Nicanor, or myself.

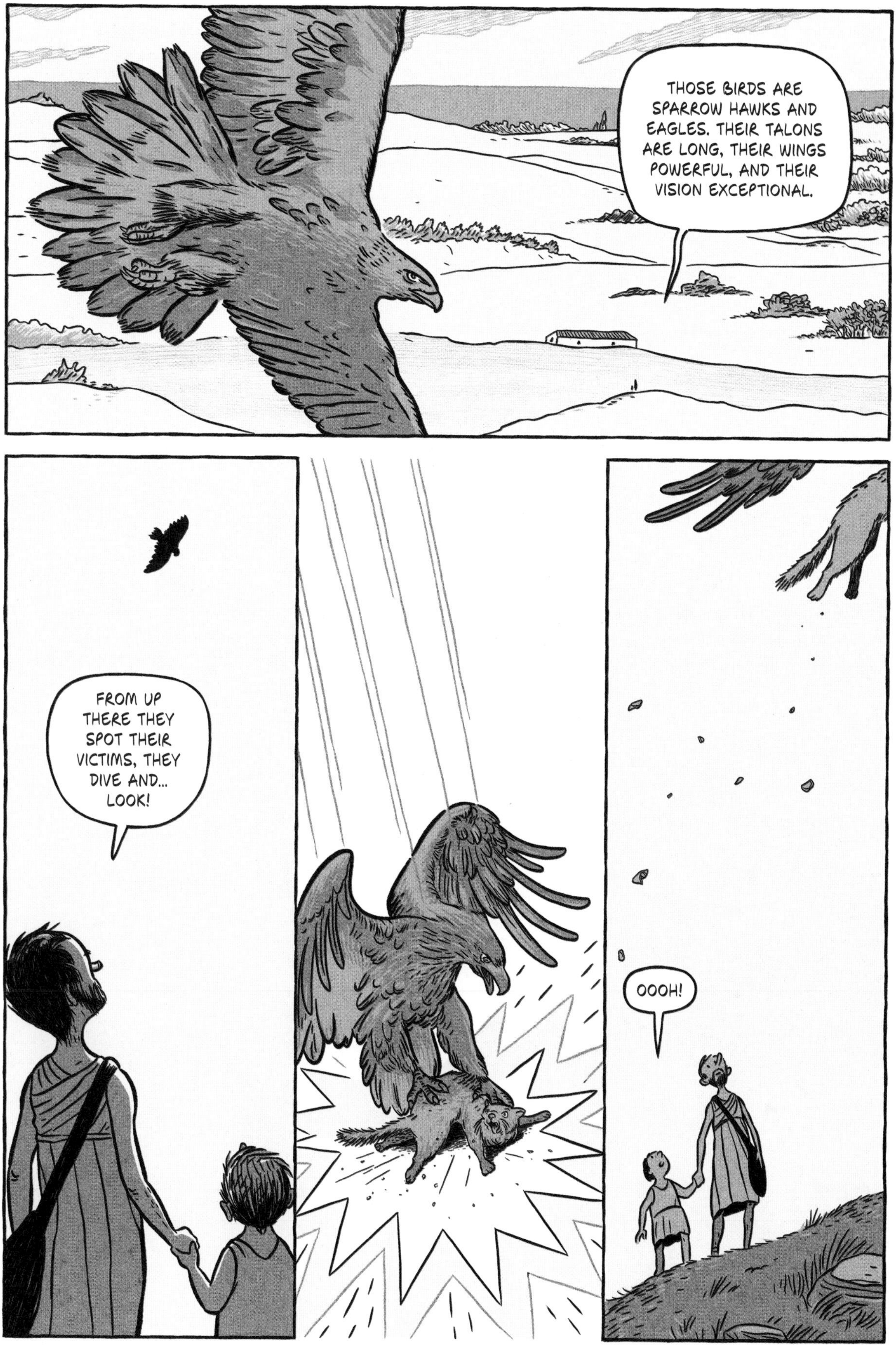
THOSE BIRDS ARE SPARROW HAWKS AND EAGLES. THEIR TALONS ARE LONG, THEIR WINGS POWERFUL, AND THEIR VISION EXCEPTIONAL.
FROM UP THERE THEY SPOT THEIR VICTIMS, THEY DIVE AND... LOOK!
OOOH!

WE KNOW THAT ANIMATE BEINGS OF THE SAME SPECIES REPRODUCE BY COUPLING.

STILL, SOME APPEAR TO REPRODUCE ON THEIR OWN.

I'VE NOTICED THE SAME THING WITH CERTAIN PLANTS.

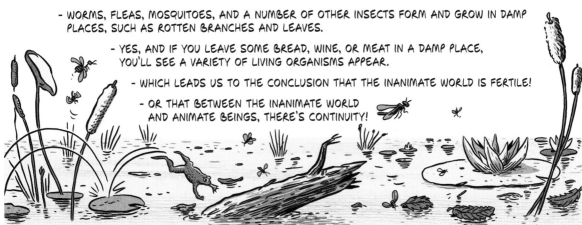

- WORMS, FLEAS, MOSQUITOES, AND A NUMBER OF OTHER INSECTS FORM AND GROW IN DAMP PLACES, SUCH AS ROTTEN BRANCHES AND LEAVES.

- YES, AND IF YOU LEAVE SOME BREAD, WINE, OR MEAT IN A DAMP PLACE, YOU'LL SEE A VARIETY OF LIVING ORGANISMS APPEAR.

- WHICH LEADS US TO THE CONCLUSION THAT THE INANIMATE WORLD IS FERTILE!

- OR THAT BETWEEN THE INANIMATE WORLD AND ANIMATE BEINGS, THERE'S CONTINUITY!

I had two good reasons to be happy.
First, my invitation to the island had nothing but a beneficial effect on him. And, more importantly,
I was by his side—associate, friend, and student all at once, something I'd never dared to hope for.

DOLPHINS ARE FISH, AND YET, BY POSEIDON, THEY DO NOT HAVE GILLS BUT LUNGS!

THE YOUNG THAT THEY GIVE BIRTH TO ARE NURSED BY THE MOTHER.

I'M GOING TO CLASSIFY THEM ALONG WITH WHALES AND SEALS IN A NEW CATEGORY WHICH I'LL CALL "CETACEANS."

?

?

OBSERVING THE SPECIFIC CHARACTERISTICS OF BEINGS HAS MADE ME CLASSIFY THEM INTO DIFFERENT CATEGORIES.

I'VE PREPARED ALL THE INFORMATION FOR YOU. I WANT YOU TO STUDY IT AND PUT TOGETHER A SORT OF TABLE!

GOT IT!

He would note down his observations, as well as information provided by the inhabitants.
Pythias would record them, and Nicanor, who was growing up, would always ask questions.

WHAT'S THIS "NOSTOS" THAT CALYPSO REFUSED ODYSSEUS?

"NOSTOS" IS A RETURN TO THE HOMELAND.

OH!

SO, DO MIGRATORY BIRDS DO THEIR "NOSTOS" WHEN THEY LEAVE OR WHEN THEY COME BACK?

ER...

IN A WAY, PHILOSOPHY IS A RESPONSE TO THE QUESTIONS THAT CHILDREN ASK.

IT SEEMS YOU'VE BEEN WITH NICANOR!

HOW'S THE CLASSIFICATION COMING?

I'M MAKING PROGRESS. IT'S FASCINATING!

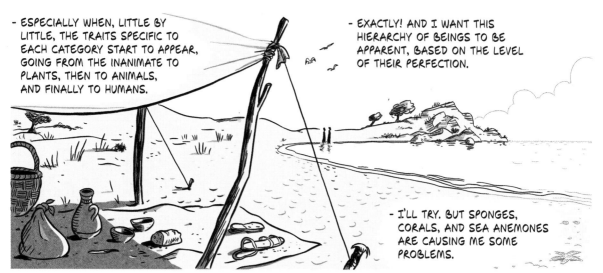

- ESPECIALLY WHEN, LITTLE BY LITTLE, THE TRAITS SPECIFIC TO EACH CATEGORY START TO APPEAR, GOING FROM THE INANIMATE TO PLANTS, THEN TO ANIMALS, AND FINALLY TO HUMANS.

- EXACTLY! AND I WANT THIS HIERARCHY OF BEINGS TO BE APPARENT, BASED ON THE LEVEL OF THEIR PERFECTION.

- I'LL TRY. BUT SPONGES, CORALS, AND SEA ANEMONES ARE CAUSING ME SOME PROBLEMS.

THEY'RE PLANTS, BUT YOU WRITE THAT THEY HAVE SENSES BECAUSE THEY REACT WHEN TOUCHED.

UH... I'VE GOT IT! PUT THEM INTO AN INTERMEDIARY CATEGORY. LET'S CALL THEM ANTHOZOA, "FLOWER-ANIMALS."

SOMETIMES IT'S HARD TO SET A CLEAR BOUNDARY BETWEEN DIFFERENT SPECIES.

He'd analyze with precision the problems he encountered.

The solutions he proposed were proof of his genius, his foresight, and his insight.

According to Aristotle, the natural world isn't harmless. It's the scene of nonstop battles for survival.

Not long after...

I'VE FINALLY FINISHED THE TABLE YOU ASKED ME FOR. IF IT'S WHAT YOU WANTED, I'LL MAKE A NICE COPY.

!!!

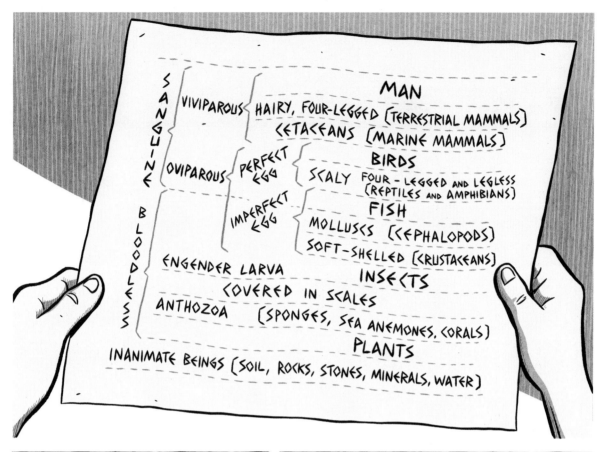

EXCELLENT! PERFECT! IT'S EXACTLY WHAT I WANTED! YOU'RE AMAZING!

BEYOND CLASSIFYING THEM, YOU'VE PERFECTLY REPRESENTED CONTINUITY AND GRADATION BETWEEN NATURAL BEINGS, FROM THE INANIMATE TO THE MOST PERFECT, MAN.

For Aristotle, continuity was inseparable from the reality of nature.

We've already seen, by the way, continuity as an element of motion, change, and time.

But sometimes it so happens that continuity is generated by a letter.

A LETTER?

IT ARRIVED JUST NOW!

"HERMIAS HAS SPOKEN VERY HIGHLY OF YOU. THAT IS WHY I WANT TO ENTRUST YOU WITH THE EDUCATION OF MY SON, ALEXANDER. PHILIP II OF MACEDONIA."

ARE WE MOVING AGAIN?

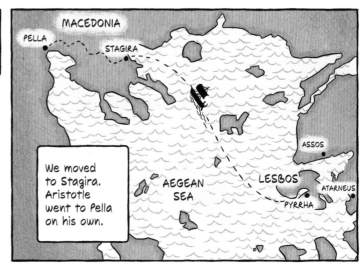

We moved to Stagira. Aristotle went to Pella on his own.

WELCOME, MACEDONIAN PHILOSOPHER!

HAPPY TO BE HERE, MY KING!

I TOLD MY GENERALS YESTERDAY THAT ARISTOTLE WOULD BE HERE SOON! I KNEW IT! HA HA HA!

ANTIPATER.

PARMENION.

A PLEASURE!

COME ADMIRE YOUR NEW STUDENT!

HE'S TRYING TO MOUNT A WILD HORSE THAT NO ONE'S YET BEEN ABLE TO TAME.

HE ONLY TAKES ON THINGS THAT ARE UNDOABLE! A DIFFICULT CHILD!

A GLASS OF WINE?

AND YET, HE'S DONE IT!

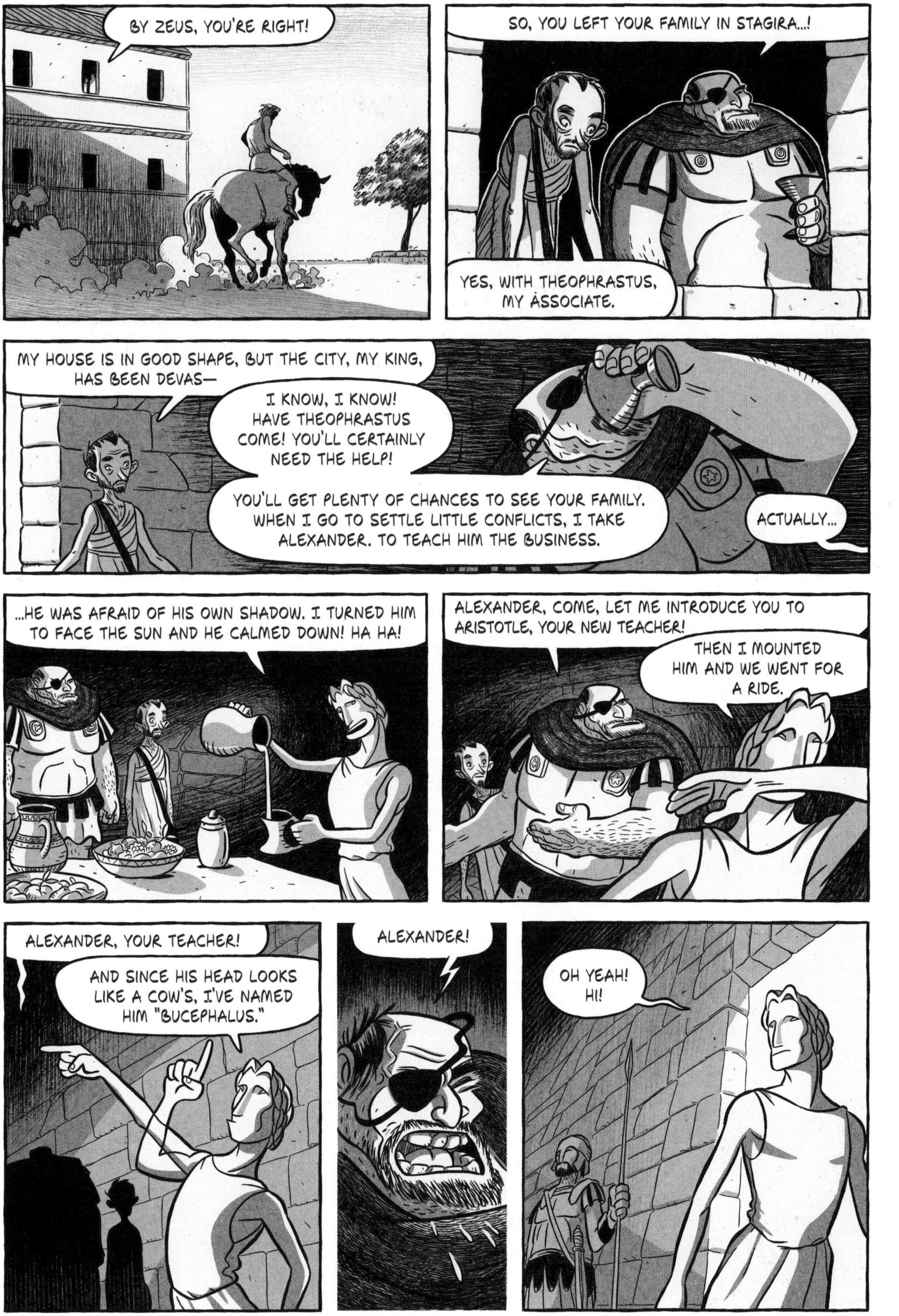
BY ZEUS, YOU'RE RIGHT!
SO, YOU LEFT YOUR FAMILY IN STAGIRA...!
YES, WITH THEOPHRASTUS, MY ASSOCIATE.
MY HOUSE IS IN GOOD SHAPE, BUT THE CITY, MY KING, HAS BEEN DEVAS—
I KNOW, I KNOW! HAVE THEOPHRASTUS COME! YOU'LL CERTAINLY NEED THE HELP!
YOU'LL GET PLENTY OF CHANCES TO SEE YOUR FAMILY. WHEN I GO TO SETTLE LITTLE CONFLICTS, I TAKE ALEXANDER. TO TEACH HIM THE BUSINESS.
ACTUALLY...
...HE WAS AFRAID OF HIS OWN SHADOW. I TURNED HIM TO FACE THE SUN AND HE CALMED DOWN! HA HA!
ALEXANDER, COME, LET ME INTRODUCE YOU TO ARISTOTLE, YOUR NEW TEACHER!
THEN I MOUNTED HIM AND WE WENT FOR A RIDE.
ALEXANDER, YOUR TEACHER!
AND SINCE HIS HEAD LOOKS LIKE A COW'S, I'VE NAMED HIM "BUCEPHALUS."
ALEXANDER!
OH YEAH! HI!

THE DINNER IS OBVIOUSLY IN YOUR HONOR. HIC!

THANKS!

IF YOU ASK ME, HERMIAS IS A HERO. DESPITE WHAT THE PERSIANS ARE PUTTING HIM THROUGH, I KNOW HE HASN'T REVEALED MY PLANS.

- I HOPE WE GET THERE IN TIME TO SAVE HIM... HEY, YOU'RE NOT DRINKING! HIC!

- I AM! I'M DRINKING!

- YOU KNOW, MY CAPTIVITY IN THEBES TURNED OUT TO BE USEFUL. EPAMINONDAS, PELOPIDAS, HIC! SOME GREAT GENERALS WERE MY MASTERS! I CAME BACK FULL OF IDEAS!

- I CREATED THE "COMPANION CORPS," CAREFULLY CHOSEN OFFICERS WHO SWORE LIFELONG LOYALTY TO ME.

- I HEARD THAT—

- I ALSO CREATED, AND THIS CONCERNS YOU, THE "ROYAL CHILDREN." HIC! ALL THE CHILDREN FROM ILLUSTRIOUS FAMILIES ARE RAISED AND EDUCATED WITH MY OWN HEIR. LIVING TOGETHER CREATES BONDS. THOSE KIDS ARE THE OFFICERS OF TOMORROW.

- VERY CLEVER!

- AT THE SAME TIME, THEY'RE HOSTAGES. THAT WAY THEIR FATHERS WON'T THINK OF PLOTTING OR REBELLING AGAINST ME. HIC!

- HOW DIABOLICAL!

I KNOW. YOU'RE QUIET.

I'M LISTENING CLOSELY AND ENJOYING THE SHOW!

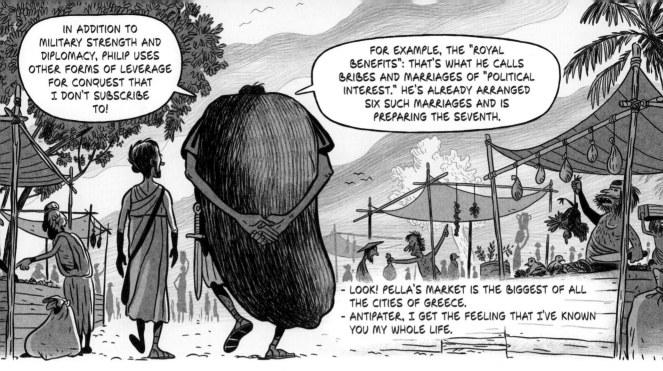

IN ADDITION TO MILITARY STRENGTH AND DIPLOMACY, PHILIP USES OTHER FORMS OF LEVERAGE FOR CONQUEST THAT I DON'T SUBSCRIBE TO!

FOR EXAMPLE, THE "ROYAL BENEFITS": THAT'S WHAT HE CALLS BRIBES AND MARRIAGES OF "POLITICAL INTEREST." HE'S ALREADY ARRANGED SIX SUCH MARRIAGES AND IS PREPARING THE SEVENTH.

- LOOK! PELLA'S MARKET IS THE BIGGEST OF ALL THE CITIES OF GREECE.
- ANTIPATER, I GET THE FEELING THAT I'VE KNOWN YOU MY WHOLE LIFE.

HIS PREVIOUS TEACHERS, AND HIS MOTHER OLYMPIAS MOST OF ALL, HAVE MADE HIM AN EGOTISTICAL MONSTER!

I PERSONALLY WANT MY SON TO HAVE A CLASSICAL GREEK EDUCATION, TO SHAPE HIS CHARACTER AND PREPARE HIM FOR HIS FUTURE ROLE AS LEADER.

WE'VE COME TO MIEZA, IN THE "GARDEN OF THE NYMPHS." THIS IDYLLIC SETTING IS PERFECT FOR STUDY. THERE ARE BUILDINGS, A GYMNASIUM, AND A THEATER.

- HIS COURSES WILL TAKE PLACE HERE. THAT WAY ALEXANDER WILL BE FAR FROM HIS MOTHER, ALL OF WHOSE FAULTS HE'S INHERITED. HIC! HE'S VERY ATTACHED TO HER, INFLUENCED BY HER... WHY SO QUIET?
- I'M LISTENING CLOSELY!
- GET SETTLED IN! THE GUARDS WILL HELP YOU. LATER, WE'LL HAVE A DRINK! ON THE SUBJECT OF STAGIRA, I'LL DO IT! I'LL HAVE IT REBUILT AND ALL YOUR BANISHED FELLOW CITIZENS CAN COME BACK! AS FOR YOU, YOU'LL HAVE A ROYAL SALARY!
- I'M LISTENING CLOSELY!

I DESCEND FROM ACHILLES BY MY MOTHER, AND HERACLES BY MY FATHER.

WHICH OF THE HEROES IS YOUR FAVORITE?

ACHILLES! I WANT TO BE LIKE HIM. AND HEPHAESTION WILL BE MY PATROCLUS.

HEPHAESTION?

MY BEST FRIEND. YOU'LL MEET HIM TOMORROW WITH THE OTHERS.

- TELL ME ABOUT YOUR PREVIOUS TEACHERS!
- THOSE WHO TAUGHT ME TO READ AND WRITE, AND MATHEMATICS AND MUSIC, WERE UNINTERESTING. MY TRUE MASTERS WERE LEONIDAS AND LYSIMACHUS.
- GO ON!
- THE FIRST, A RELATIVE OF MY MOTHER, WAS VERY STRICT. ALL DAY LONG IT WAS WEAPONS TRAINING, LONG RUNS, AND LONG HORSE RIDES.
- AND WHAT DID YOU LEARN FROM HIM?
- HE HARDENED ME. I EAT LITTLE, AND I'M OPINIONATED.
- AND THE SECOND?
- LYSIMACHUS? HE TAUGHT ME TO BE AMBITIOUS. HE UNDERSTOOD MY LOVE OF THE "ILIAD" AND ENCOURAGED ME TO TAKE ACHILLES AS A ROLE MODEL.
- WHAT ELSE WOULD YOU LIKE TO LEARN?
- I LIKE GEOGRAPHY, PHILOSOPHY, RHETORIC, AND POETRY.
- POETRY? INTERESTING!
- THREE YEARS AGO, WHEN AMBASSADORS FROM ATHENS CAME TO ASK FOR PEACE, MY FATHER MADE ME RECITE THEM A POEM!
- DO YOU REMEMBER IT?
- OF COURSE! IT WAS QUITE LONG, BUT DO YOU WANT TO HEAR AN EXCERPT?
- GLADLY!

"WHAT MORTAL KNOWS THE DAY OF HIS DEATH? WHO KNOWS IF TODAY WILL BE PEACEFUL AND HAPPY? EVERYTHING IS ENDLESSLY CHANGING AND TRANSFORMING, BRINGING US NOW JOY, NOW SORROW."

PINDAR!

I LOVE PINDAR!

"EVERYTHING IS ENDLESSLY CHANGING AND TRANSFORMING" IS THE BASIS FOR MY PHILOSOPHICAL THEORY OF NATURE.

OH, IS THAT SO?

ALTHOUGH THIS IS A VERY PLEASANT CONVERSATION, I MUST GO PREPARE MY CLASSES. WE START TOMORROW!

YOU KNOW WHAT? I'M ACTUALLY STARTING TO LIKE YOU!

THAT'S GOOD. AND THE FEELING IS MUTUAL.

BYE!

The next day...

MY NAME IS SELEUCUS. I WANT TO BE A GENERAL.

MY NAME IS HARPALUS. I'M INTERESTED IN ECONOMICS.

HEPHAESTION. I WANT TO GO WHERE ALEXANDER GOES.

I'M PTOLEMY. I'M MAD ABOUT EGYPTIAN HISTORY.

NEARCHUS. I'LL BE AN ADMIRAL.

MY NAME IS PHILOTAS AND I DON'T KNOW WHAT I WANT TO BE.

DELIGHTED.

THE ROOTS OF EDUCATION ARE BITTER, BUT ITS FRUIT IS SWEET!

IN ORDER TO ACQUIRE A GOOD EDUCATION, THREE CONDITIONS MUST BE FULFILLED: ONE'S INNATE FACULTIES, THE PROCESS OF LEARNING, AND PRACTICE.

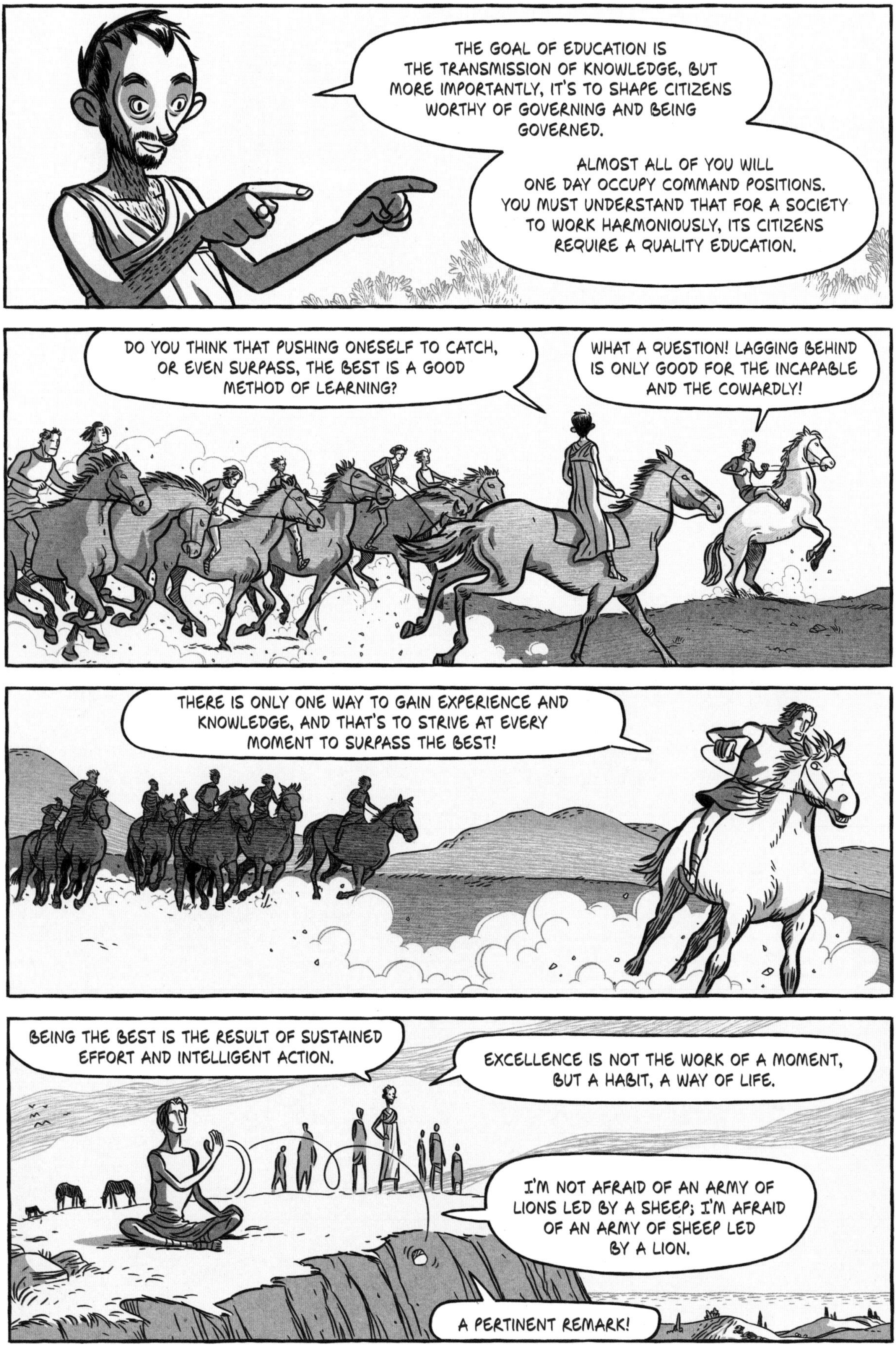
THE GOAL OF EDUCATION IS THE TRANSMISSION OF KNOWLEDGE, BUT MORE IMPORTANTLY, IT'S TO SHAPE CITIZENS WORTHY OF GOVERNING AND BEING GOVERNED.
ALMOST ALL OF YOU WILL ONE DAY OCCUPY COMMAND POSITIONS. YOU MUST UNDERSTAND THAT FOR A SOCIETY TO WORK HARMONIOUSLY, ITS CITIZENS REQUIRE A QUALITY EDUCATION.
DO YOU THINK THAT PUSHING ONESELF TO CATCH, OR EVEN SURPASS, THE BEST IS A GOOD METHOD OF LEARNING?
WHAT A QUESTION! LAGGING BEHIND IS ONLY GOOD FOR THE INCAPABLE AND THE COWARDLY!
THERE IS ONLY ONE WAY TO GAIN EXPERIENCE AND KNOWLEDGE, AND THAT'S TO STRIVE AT EVERY MOMENT TO SURPASS THE BEST!
BEING THE BEST IS THE RESULT OF SUSTAINED EFFORT AND INTELLIGENT ACTION.
EXCELLENCE IS NOT THE WORK OF A MOMENT, BUT A HABIT, A WAY OF LIFE.
I'M NOT AFRAID OF AN ARMY OF LIONS LED BY A SHEEP; I'M AFRAID OF AN ARMY OF SHEEP LED BY A LION.
A PERTINENT REMARK!

One year later...

HUMAN NATURE IMPROVES THROUGH EDUCATION. BUT NEITHER WOMEN NOR SLAVES NOR BARBARIANS CAN ENJOY ITS BENEFITS. THAT IS WHY IT IS SAID THAT...

...BARBARIANS ARE INFERIOR TO GREEKS.

I DON'T AGREE WITH THAT!

I DON'T SEE GREEKS AND BARBARIANS AS OPPOSITES, BUT AS MEN WHO ARE VIRTUOUS AND MEN WHO AREN'T!

DON'T BE SO QUICK TO PHILOSOPHIZE! TAKE MY ADVICE: WITH GREEKS, BEHAVE LIKE A LEADER; WITH BARBARIANS, BEHAVE LIKE A MASTER!

STOP! YOU'RE MAKING ME CRAZY!

DON'T FORGET THE ANCIENT SAYING: "ANYTHING THAT'S NOT GREEK IS BARBARIAN!"

CLAP CLAP CLAP

I FOR ONE KNOW YOU'RE RIGHT! HIC!

YOU HEARD, MY KING?

CLAP CLAP

I'VE COME TO TAKE THEM ON A LITTLE CAMPAIGN IN THE NORTH! AND I KNOW THAT YOU WOULD LIKE TO SEE YOUR FAMILY.

IT'S TRUE THAT I MISS THEM.

In Stagira...

I SEE THAT PHILIP KEPT HIS WORD.

THE WHOLE CITY'S BEING REBUILT.

THAT LOOKS LIKE ARISTOTLE!

WHY, IT IS HIM!

PYTHIAS!

ARISTOTLE!

I THOUGHT YOU'D COME HOME MORE OFTEN!

SO DID I, BUT—

ARISTOTLE!

MY, HOW YOU'VE GROWN!

TAKE ME TO PELLA WITH YOU!

NEXT TIME, I PROMISE. AND IF YOU WANT...

YOU CAN STAY THERE FOR YOUR STUDIES.

YES, I WANT TO!

AND THEOPHRASTUS?

NEXT DOOR, IN THE LABORATORY. HE SPENDS HIS DAYS THERE!

I'LL GO SEE HIM AND THEN COME BACK.

WHAT'S GOING ON HERE?

WE'VE COME TO SHOW OUR THANKS.

THE EXILED CITIZENS HAVE RETURNED.

PHILIP IS REBUILDING THE CITY. WE KNOW THAT YOU ASKED HIM TO.

YOU'RE OUR SAVIOR!

YOU ARE THE BENEFACTOR AND FOUNDER OF OUR CITY.

YES, THE FOUNDER!

THANK YOU!

Several days later...

THIS QUESTION'S BEEN BOTHERING ME SINCE LESBOS. NEITHER THE WORKERS NOR THE DRONES ENGENDER A KING! SO...

IT MUST BE A KING THAT ENGENDERS A KING!

HA HA.

WHY EVEN ACKNOWLEDGE THAT THEY REPRODUCE IF YOU CONTINUE TO THINK THE HEAD OF THE BEES IS A MALE? YOU SAY "KING"!

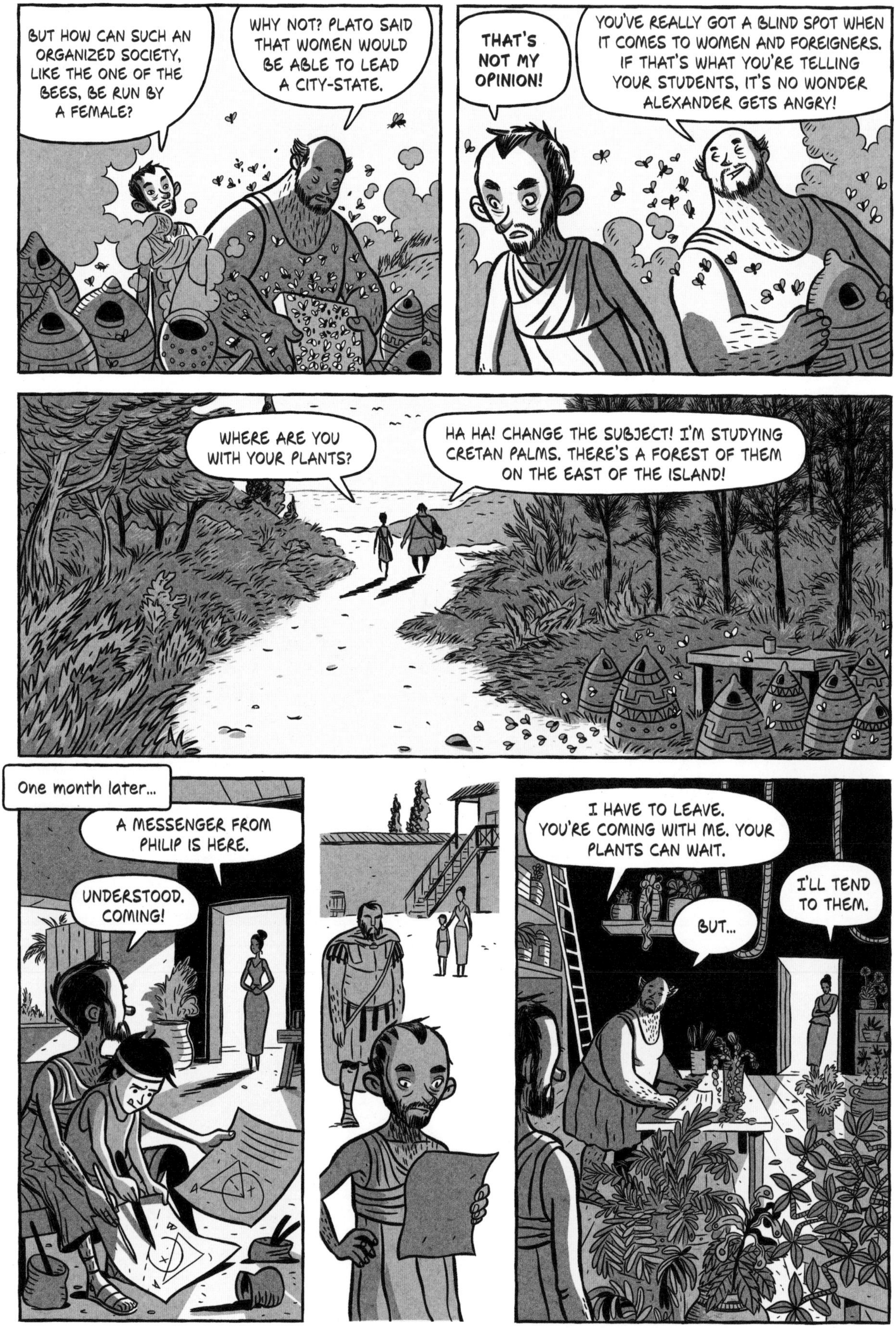
BUT HOW CAN SUCH AN ORGANIZED SOCIETY, LIKE THE ONE OF THE BEES, BE RUN BY A FEMALE?
WHY NOT? PLATO SAID THAT WOMEN WOULD BE ABLE TO LEAD A CITY-STATE.
THAT'S NOT MY OPINION!
YOU'VE REALLY GOT A BLIND SPOT WHEN IT COMES TO WOMEN AND FOREIGNERS. IF THAT'S WHAT YOU'RE TELLING YOUR STUDENTS, IT'S NO WONDER ALEXANDER GETS ANGRY!
WHERE ARE YOU WITH YOUR PLANTS?
HA HA! CHANGE THE SUBJECT! I'M STUDYING CRETAN PALMS. THERE'S A FOREST OF THEM ON THE EAST OF THE ISLAND!
One month later...
A MESSENGER FROM PHILIP IS HERE.
UNDERSTOOD. COMING!
I HAVE TO LEAVE. YOU'RE COMING WITH ME. YOUR PLANTS CAN WAIT.
BUT...
I'LL TEND TO THEM.

- THIS IS THEOPHRASTUS, MY ASSOCIATE.

- I KNOW, I KNOW. GOOD THINKING, BRINGING HIM HERE TO HELP YOU TAME OUR LITTLE SAVAGES! HIC!

COME HAVE A DRINK!

- SO, HOW DID THE EXPEDITION GO?

- HOW DID IT GO? WE WENT, WE SAW, WE CONQUERED! BUT... UM...

ARISTOTLE, I'VE GOT SOME BAD NEWS.

THEY KILLED HERMIAS.

O VIRTUE, O BEAUTY, O STRIVING, LIFELONG PURSUIT IN GREECE...

ARISTOTLE SAID FRIENDSHIP IS ONE SOUL INHABITING TWO BODIES.

NO ONE CAN LIVE WITHOUT FRIENDS.

SEEK OUT YOUR FRIENDS AND KEEP THEM CLOSE!

!

IN LIFE, YOU MUST AVOID EXTREMES AND STICK TO THE MIDDLE GROUND.

YOU MUST BE NEITHER COWARDLY NOR RECKLESS. YOU MUST BE COURAGEOUS!

One year later...

PHILIP HAS NAMED ME VICEROY AND I'LL HAVE TO GO INTO BATTLE MORE OFTEN. I HOPE HE'LL LET ME HAVE A CHANCE TO DISTINGUISH MYSELF.

TELL US ONE LAST TIME WHAT IT MEANS, THE LIFE OF A WARRIOR!

YOU'LL HAVE MANY SUCH CHANCES!

FOR OUR STUDIES NOW MUST END.

YES, I GOT THAT.

TO ME, HE WHO CONQUERS HIS DESIRES IS MORE COURAGEOUS THAN HE WHO CONQUERS HIS ENEMIES.

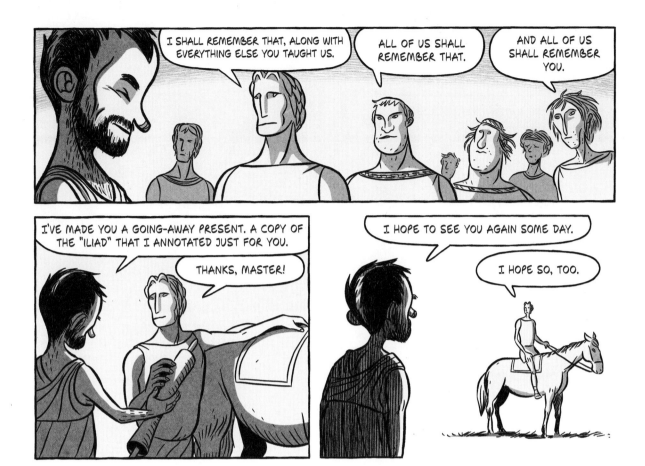

Philip and Alexander had to go face several of Macedonia's border populations, in order to consolidate the territory before undertaking the great campaign. During one of these battles Philip's right knee was wounded by a spear. Thereafter, he walked with a limp.

In Athens, the situation remained the same. The pro-Macedonians fought for a campaign against the Persians, one led by a Greek coalition with Philip at its head. The anti-Macedonians wanted, with the financial support of the Persians, to attack Philip, whom they considered a dictatorial tyrant. Their view won out.

The great battle pitting Athenians and Thebans against the Macedonians took place at Chaeronea, in Boeotia. The Macedonians were victorious. Alexander distinguished himself as commander of the cavalry and decimated the "Sacred Band." Philip then called together a Panhellenic congress in Corinth and formed the "League of Corinth," with himself at the head and, for the first time, officially declared his intention to wage a Panhellenic campaign against the Persians.

He went off to finish preparations in Macedonia and decided to get married "out of political interest" to Cleopatra, his general Attalus's niece.

We were invited to the wedding, but we stayed in Stagira and followed the events from there.

We learned, of course, that Xenocrates had taken over as head of the Academy after the death of Speusippus. Aristotle said nothing about it. He wrote a lot and continued his research.

The great campaign began. Parmenion was in the Hellespont with 10,000 Macedonians in order to prepare the landing of the majority of Greek troops on the Asian shore.

Philip, leaving nothing to chance, even in his family, arranged another "marriage of convenience" between his daughter, also called Cleopatra, and the king of Epirus, who was the brother of Olympias. In other words, her uncle.

The wedding celebration was to be in Aegae and we, of course, were invited...

In Stagira...

WHY DO YOU CARE SO MUCH ABOUT GOING TO THIS WEDDING, WHEN WE REFUSED TO GO TO PHILIP'S OWN WEDDING?

I HAVE MY REASONS.

SO, ON OGYGIA, ODYSSEUS WAS THE ONLY MAN, DESIRED NOT ONLY BY THE NYMPH CALYPSO BUT BY HUNDREDS OF GORGEOUS, HALF-NAKED MAIDSERVANTS?

HEE HEE!

THAT'S WHY! NICANOR IS ENTERING ADOLESCENCE. I WANT TO BE SEEN AT THE COURT IN ORDER TO GET HIM ENLISTED INTO THE ARMY IN PELLA.

I'VE SPOKEN TO ANTIPATER.

DO AS YOU LIKE.

OH, AND THE INVITATION TO DELPHI!

WHAT INVITATION?

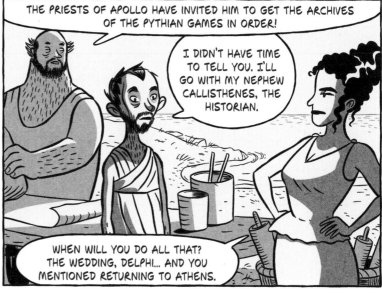

THE PRIESTS OF APOLLO HAVE INVITED HIM TO GET THE ARCHIVES OF THE PYTHIAN GAMES IN ORDER!

I DIDN'T HAVE TIME TO TELL YOU. I'LL GO WITH MY NEPHEW CALLISTHENES, THE HISTORIAN.

WHEN WILL YOU DO ALL THAT? THE WEDDING, DELPHI... AND YOU MENTIONED RETURNING TO ATHENS.

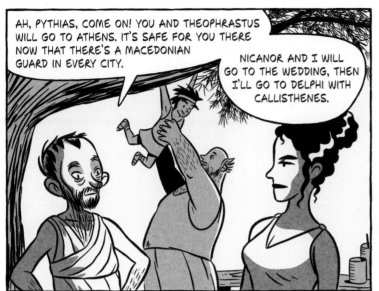

AH, PYTHIAS, COME ON! YOU AND THEOPHRASTUS WILL GO TO ATHENS. IT'S SAFE FOR YOU THERE NOW THAT THERE'S A MACEDONIAN GUARD IN EVERY CITY.

NICANOR AND I WILL GO TO THE WEDDING, THEN I'LL GO TO DELPHI WITH CALLISTHENES.

AND WHEN WE'RE DONE, I'LL COME JOIN YOU IN ATHENS.

DO SOME SCOUTING, SEE IF THERE'S ANY CHANCE OF OPENING A SCHOOL...

...OF FINDING BUILDINGS AND TEACHERS.

GOT IT!

VAYA SAYS THAT SINCE WE NO LONGER NEED HER, SHE WOULD PREFER TO RETURN TO ATARNEUS.

SURE, BUT GIVE HER A NICE PARTING BONUS!

ALSO, PICK OUT ONE OF YOUR SLAVES TO GO WITH YOU TO ATHENS!

ALREADY DONE. I'M TAKING HERPYLLIS.

141

HE'S OBSESSED WITH ODYSSEUS AND CALYPSO, BUT HE'S KIND AND SMART.

TOOT TOOT
TOOT TOOT — TOOT
TOOT

I'M AWARE OF ALL THAT. HERE, HE'LL CONTINUE HIS EDUCATION, HE'LL TRAIN. I'LL BE BY HIS SIDE. I'M TOO OLD TO TAKE PART IN THE CAMPAIGN.

THANKS, ANTIPATER! YOU'RE MORE THAN JUST A FRIEND.

I FEEL THE SAME. WE'LL WRITE EACH OTHER. BUT COME, LET'S SIT DOWN!

LEAVE ME! I'LL GO INTO THE THEATER ALONE, WITHOUT GUARDS.

TOOT
TOOT
TOOT

Around the theater's "orchestra," Philip had thirteen statues erected representing the twelve Olympian gods and himself!

HURRAH THE KING HURRAH

As soon as he ascended the throne, Alexander severely punished those he judged to be responsible for Philip's death, as well as those who sought to usurp power. He then convened a Panhellenic assembly in Corinth and, as his father had done before him, took official control of the war against the Persians, proclaiming all Greeks as allies, with the exception of the Spartans. Once back in Macedonia, he had to deal with small skirmishes on the northern border.

At that time a rumor was circulating throughout Greece that Alexander had died. The Thebans, spurred on by the anti-Macedonians in Athens, immediately broke the alliance, exterminated the Macedonian guard occupying the acropolis, and retook control of their city.

When Alexander learned of this, his anger drove him without delay to Thebes, which he razed. He only spared the temples and Pindar's home. The result: six thousand dead and thirty thousand prisoners sold into slavery. After that, no other city dared risk contesting Alexander's power and opposing his plans. There were, however, no reprisals against Athens for encouraging Thebes to rebel: Alexander knew that he would soon need the Athenian fleet for his campaign against the Persians, and besides, Aristotle had taught him to respect Athens for its cultural role.

Before leaving for Asia, Alexander nevertheless felt the need to seek forgiveness from the priests at Delphi for his actions in Thebes.

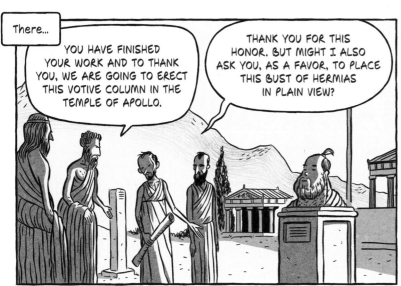

There...

YOU HAVE FINISHED YOUR WORK AND TO THANK YOU, WE ARE GOING TO ERECT THIS VOTIVE COLUMN IN THE TEMPLE OF APOLLO.

THANK YOU FOR THIS HONOR. BUT MIGHT I ALSO ASK YOU, AS A FAVOR, TO PLACE THIS BUST OF HERMIAS IN PLAIN VIEW?

SURE, WITH PLEASURE!

ALEXANDER. ALEXANDER'S COMING.

WHO?

FORGIVEN AND INVINCIBLE!

I SALUTE YOU, MY KING!

I KNEW THAT I'D FIND YOU HERE.

NICE TO SEE YOU! HOW ARE YOU?

I'M FINISHING UP THE FINAL PREPARATIONS. I'M TAKING WITH ME ADVISORS AND SPECIALISTS FROM EVERY FIELD.

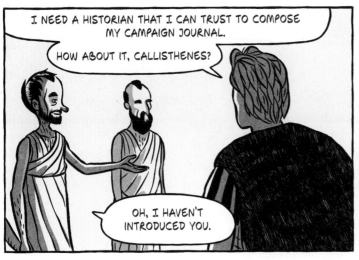

- I ALSO KNOW WHAT YOU THINK OF THIS CAMPAIGN, ARISTOTLE. OUR POLITICAL VIEWS ARE DIAMETRICALLY OPPOSED.

- NOW'S NOT THE MOMENT TO—

- IT IS MY DREAM TO CREATE A HELLENO-ASIAN KINGDOM FOUNDED ON THE COLLABORATION OF EQUALS, BETWEEN PERSIANS AND GREEKS, WITH A COMMON LANGUAGE—GREEK—AND A COMMON CURRENCY, AND THE FREE CIRCULATION OF MEN AND GOODS. WITHOUT DISTINCTION BASED ON NATIONALITY, COLOR, OR SEX.

ALL PEOPLE WILL HAVE THE SAME LAWS AND THE SAME RIGHTS. I WILL FOUND NEW CITIES, I'LL BUILD ROADS, THEATERS, PORTS, AQUEDUCTS, BRIDGES, AND EVERYTHING ELSE THAT WILL MAKE THE INHABITANTS' LIVES EASIER AND MORE COMFORTABLE. I'LL PROPAGATE POETRY, PHILOSOPHY, AND THE GREEK ARTS.

BY SUBJUGATING FOREIGN NATIONS, I ALSO COMMIT MYSELF TO INSURING THEIR PROSPERITY THROUGH EDUCATION, THE ECONOMY, AND PEACE. THIS SENSE OF RESPONSIBILITY DISTINGUISHES CONQUERORS FROM THE MASTERS OF THE WORLD!

- IT'S A DREAM WITHOUT LIMITS. IT ALL CORRESPONDS TO A DEEP DESIRE YOU HAVE, TO A LIFE'S WORK. I HOPE IT COMES TRUE.

- THANKS, ARISTOTLE!

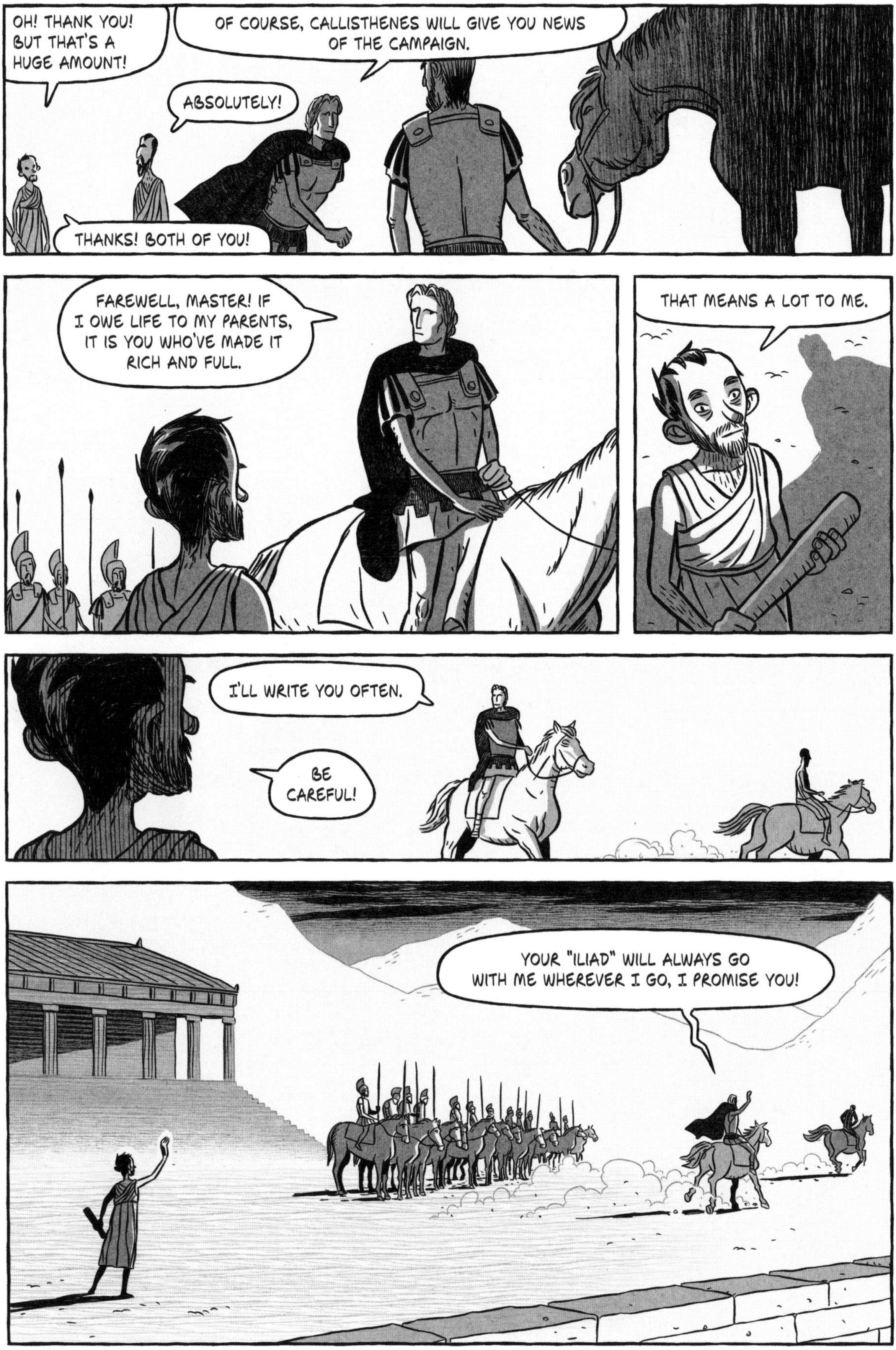
OH! THANK YOU! BUT THAT'S A HUGE AMOUNT!
OF COURSE, CALLISTHENES WILL GIVE YOU NEWS OF THE CAMPAIGN.
ABSOLUTELY!
THANKS! BOTH OF YOU!
FAREWELL, MASTER! IF I OWE LIFE TO MY PARENTS, IT IS YOU WHO'VE MADE IT RICH AND FULL.
THAT MEANS A LOT TO ME.
I'LL WRITE YOU OFTEN.
BE CAREFUL!
YOUR "ILIAD" WILL ALWAYS GO WITH ME WHEREVER I GO, I PROMISE YOU!

Alexander showed himself to be a true genius as a strategist and politician, far beyond what anyone, even Aristotle, could have imagined. The student had acquired, thanks to his master, a mind open to new challenges and new conquests. He was ready to put his own limits to the test and was passionate about sharing his knowledge of literature and the arts!

The Persians wanted to have a trade monopoly on raw materials, precious metals, spices, and silk between China, India, and the countries of the West. The Greek presence, however, made it difficult for them to expand their influence.

That is why they waged a campaign against Greece a hundred and fifty years ago. The Persians killed, pillaged, and razed, but in the end, they were beaten! Afterward, the city-states of southern Greece found themselves weakened by internal wars.

In the north, the rapid transformation of the kingdom of Macedonia into a great commercial, economic, and military power, combined with the desire for a unified Greece, made a clash with the Persians inevitable.

Philip and, after him, Alexander gave priority to their own interests. And so the war that took place was not so much a war of reprisals in response to the horrors that the Persians had inflicted upon the Greeks, but rather a war of conquest, for access to trade with the East was a gauge of power, wealth, and glory. It was also a "war of infiltration" of Greek culture into the culture of the Persians.

- THERE WE GO! THE MONEY SENT BY ALEXANDER MADE IT TO ATHENS BEFORE ME!

- EIGHT HUNDRED TALENTS IS A GREAT SUM!

- IF THE LAW DIDN'T FORBID METICS FROM OWNING PROPERTY, WE COULD BUY OUR INSTALLATIONS OR HAVE THEM BUILT. BUT ALL WE CAN DO IS RENT THEM.

- I'VE ALREADY RENTED FOUR BUILDINGS...

...THE ONE WHERE YOU AND PYTHIAS WILL LIVE, AND THREE OTHERS FOR CLASSROOMS AND LABORATORIES. WE'RE GOING TO HAVE TO RENT MORE, BUT I WANTED TO WAIT FOR YOU TO GET HERE.

- WELL DONE, THEOPHRASTUS. WHAT'S THE SITUATION LIKE HERE?

- THE CITY IS DIVIDED. THE DEMOCRATS LED BY DEMOSTHENES HAVE CALMED DOWN A LITTLE SINCE ALEXANDER'S CAMPAIGN BEGAN. AESCHINES AND THE ARISTOCRATS WHO ARE STILL PRO-MACEDONIAN ARE ENTHUSIASTIC.

OH! HI, ARISTOTLE! WELCOME BACK!

HI THERE!

YOU'RE POPULAR! IT SEEMS THEY WERE AWAITING YOUR RETURN.

WOODS OF LYCIAN APOLLO

"LYCEUM"!

I'M THRILLED YOU'RE JOINING US, CALLIPPUS!

THERE'LL BE OTHERS FROM THE ACADEMY. EUDEMUS AND HIPPARCHUS, FOR EXAMPLE!

I TALKED TO DIOTELES THE PHILOSOPHER, AND THE MATHEMATICIAN AND MUSICIAN ARISTOXENES.

THAT'S WHY I TOLD YOU TO RENT EVEN MORE BUILDINGS.

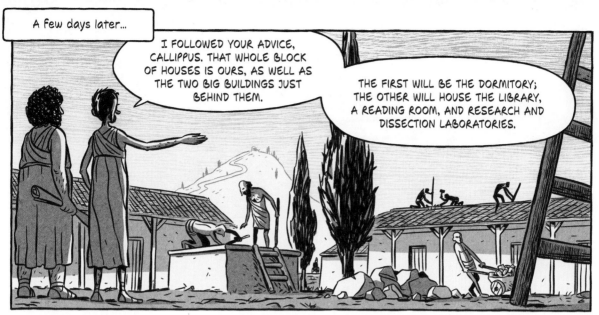

A few days later...

I FOLLOWED YOUR ADVICE, CALLIPPUS. THAT WHOLE BLOCK OF HOUSES IS OURS, AS WELL AS THE TWO BIG BUILDINGS JUST BEHIND THEM.

THE FIRST WILL BE THE DORMITORY; THE OTHER WILL HOUSE THE LIBRARY, A READING ROOM, AND RESEARCH AND DISSECTION LABORATORIES.

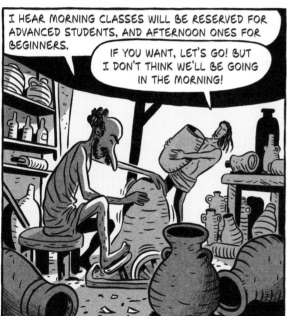

I HEAR MORNING CLASSES WILL BE RESERVED FOR ADVANCED STUDENTS, AND AFTERNOON ONES FOR BEGINNERS.

IF YOU WANT, LET'S GO! BUT I DON'T THINK WE'LL BE GOING IN THE MORNING!

THROUGH HIS TEACHING, ARISTOTLE HOPES TO HAVE A POSITIVE INFLUENCE ON THE DAILY LIFE OF ATHENIANS.

THAT'S AN AMBITIOUS DESIRE!

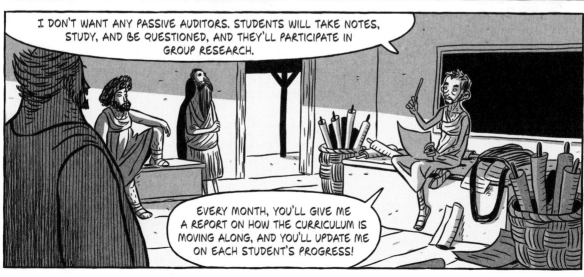

I DON'T WANT ANY PASSIVE AUDITORS. STUDENTS WILL TAKE NOTES, STUDY, AND BE QUESTIONED, AND THEY'LL PARTICIPATE IN GROUP RESEARCH.

EVERY MONTH, YOU'LL GIVE ME A REPORT ON HOW THE CURRICULUM IS MOVING ALONG, AND YOU'LL UPDATE ME ON EACH STUDENT'S PROGRESS!

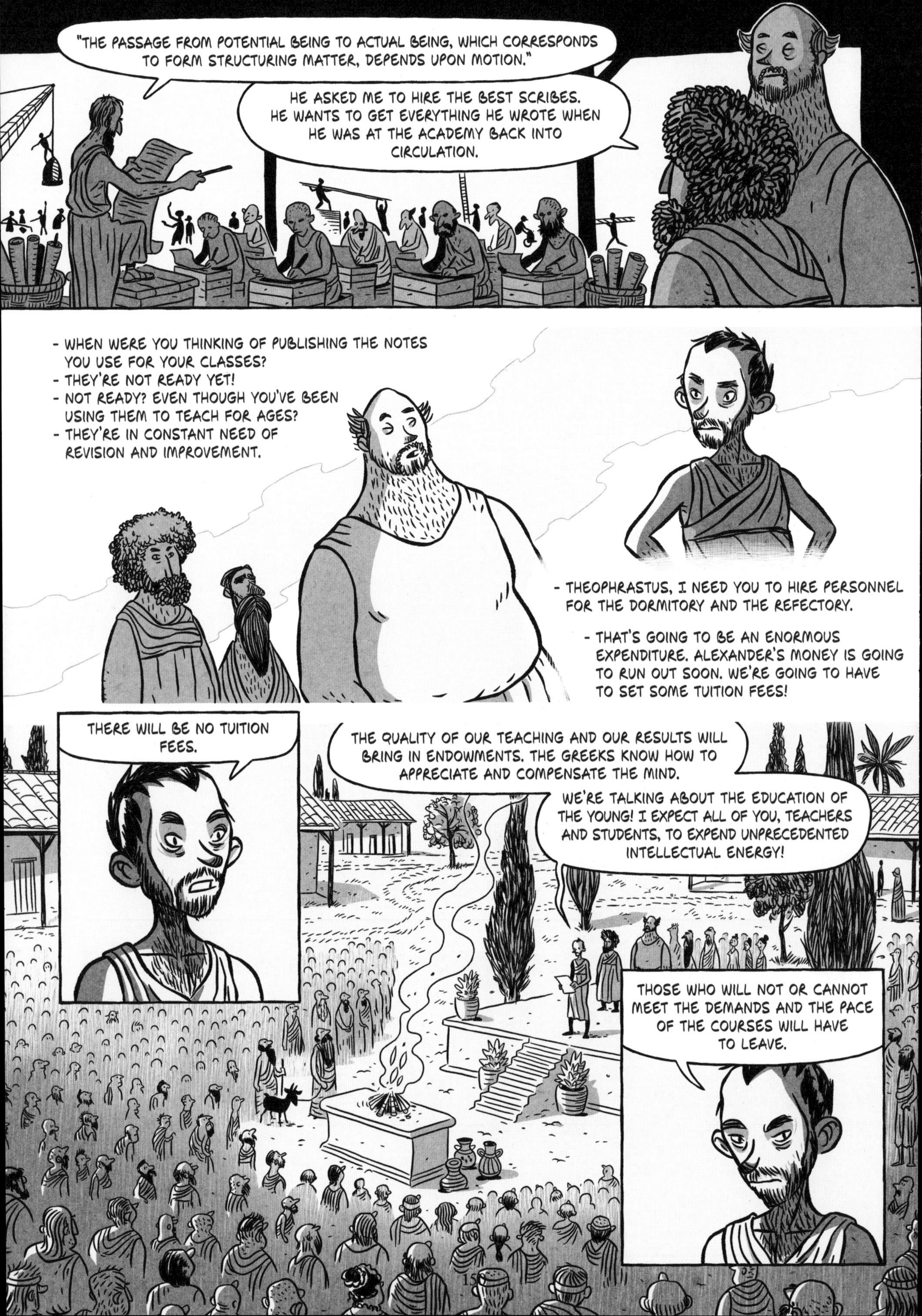
"THE PASSAGE FROM POTENTIAL BEING TO ACTUAL BEING, WHICH CORRESPONDS TO FORM STRUCTURING MATTER, DEPENDS UPON MOTION."
HE ASKED ME TO HIRE THE BEST SCRIBES. HE WANTS TO GET EVERYTHING HE WROTE WHEN HE WAS AT THE ACADEMY BACK INTO CIRCULATION.
- WHEN WERE YOU THINKING OF PUBLISHING THE NOTES YOU USE FOR YOUR CLASSES?
- THEY'RE NOT READY YET!
- NOT READY? EVEN THOUGH YOU'VE BEEN USING THEM TO TEACH FOR AGES?
- THEY'RE IN CONSTANT NEED OF REVISION AND IMPROVEMENT.
- THEOPHRASTUS, I NEED YOU TO HIRE PERSONNEL FOR THE DORMITORY AND THE REFECTORY.
- THAT'S GOING TO BE AN ENORMOUS EXPENDITURE. ALEXANDER'S MONEY IS GOING TO RUN OUT SOON. WE'RE GOING TO HAVE TO SET SOME TUITION FEES!
THERE WILL BE NO TUITION FEES.
THE QUALITY OF OUR TEACHING AND OUR RESULTS WILL BRING IN ENDOWMENTS. THE GREEKS KNOW HOW TO APPRECIATE AND COMPENSATE THE MIND.
WE'RE TALKING ABOUT THE EDUCATION OF THE YOUNG! I EXPECT ALL OF YOU, TEACHERS AND STUDENTS, TO EXPEND UNPRECEDENTED INTELLECTUAL ENERGY!
THOSE WHO WILL NOT OR CANNOT MEET THE DEMANDS AND THE PACE OF THE COURSES WILL HAVE TO LEAVE.

IN THREE MONTHS, THE LANDSCAPE'S TOTALLY CHANGED!

THERE ARE SO MANY PEOPLE ABOUT!

I LOVE HOW SOME CLASSES ARE HELD IN THE WALKWAYS.

- DID YOU KNOW THAT STUDENTS ARE CALLING MORNING CLASSES "MORNING WALK" AND THOSE IN THE EVENING "EVENING WALK"?

- THAT'S WHAT I HEARD! AND I LOVE SEEING STUDENTS USING THE PAPYROTHEQUE, STUDYING IN THE READING ROOM, AND WORKING SO EAGERLY ON RESEARCH AND IN THE LABORATORY!

- YOUR HELP IS PRECIOUS. THANKS!

- BUT OF COURSE!

THIS IS WHAT I DREAMT OF WHEN I WAS AT THE ACADEMY!

AND SINCE GOOD THINGS COME IN PAIRS, I HAVE SOME GOOD NEWS!

I'M LISTENING!

I'M EXPECTING!

WHAT?! HOW?!

A BABY?

HERPYLLIS, PYTHIAS IS EXPECT—

I KNOW!

LOOK AFTER HER! DON'T LET HER OUT OF YOUR SIGHT!

YOU CAN REST EASY!

HERE YOU'LL SEE THE FACULTIES OF THE SOUL OF THE THREE CATEGORIES OF ANIMATE BEINGS WE DISCUSSED YESTERDAY.

ANIMATE BEINGS

PLANTS : NUTRITIVE

ANIMALS : NUTRITIVE
PERCEPTIVE

MAN : NUTRITIVE
PERCEPTIVE
INTELLECT

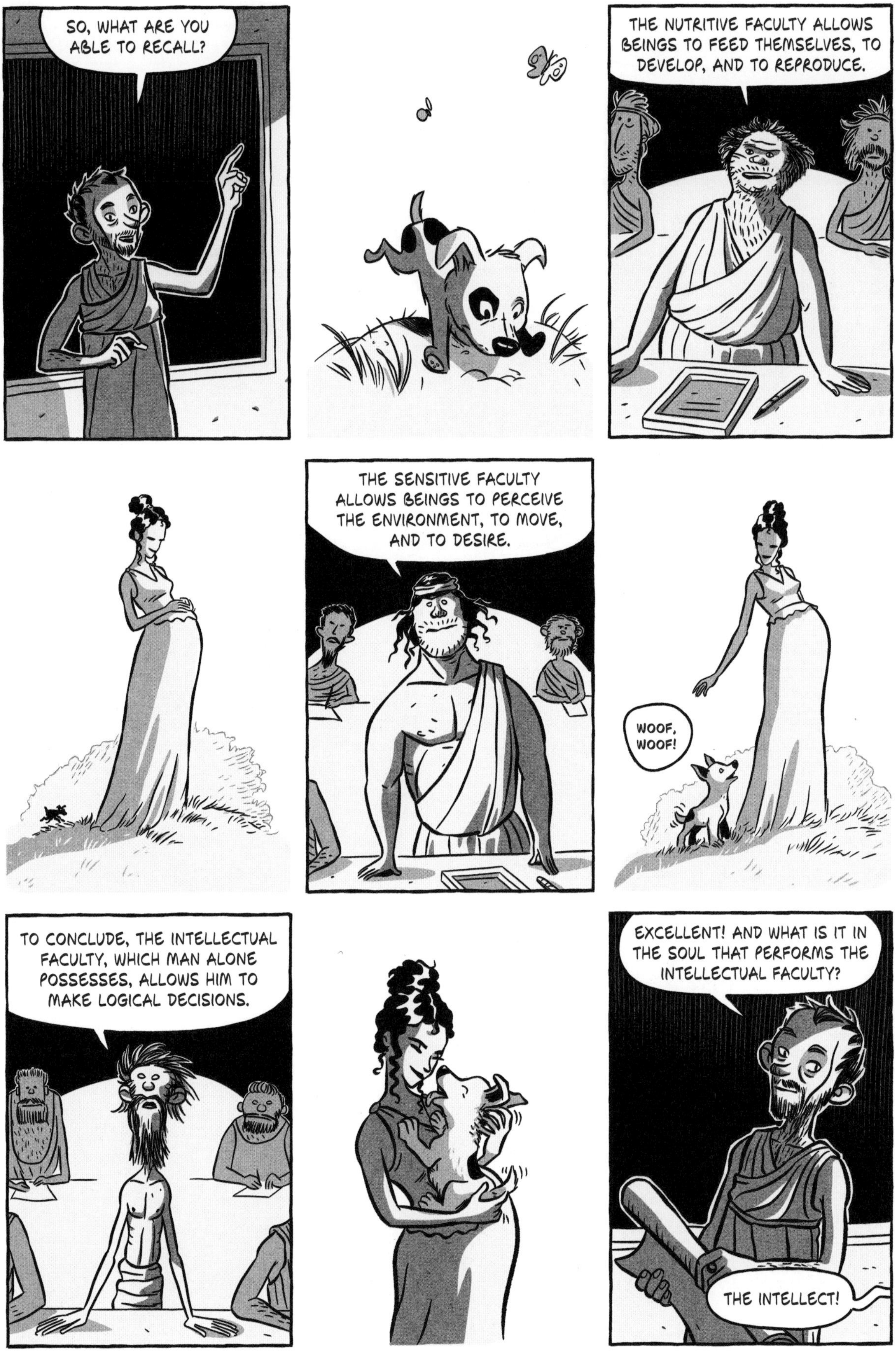
SO, WHAT ARE YOU ABLE TO RECALL?
THE NUTRITIVE FACULTY ALLOWS BEINGS TO FEED THEMSELVES, TO DEVELOP, AND TO REPRODUCE.
THE SENSITIVE FACULTY ALLOWS BEINGS TO PERCEIVE THE ENVIRONMENT, TO MOVE, AND TO DESIRE.
WOOF, WOOF!
TO CONCLUDE, THE INTELLECTUAL FACULTY, WHICH MAN ALONE POSSESSES, ALLOWS HIM TO MAKE LOGICAL DECISIONS.
EXCELLENT! AND WHAT IS IT IN THE SOUL THAT PERFORMS THE INTELLECTUAL FACULTY?
THE INTELLECT!

WHICH, ALONG WITH LANGUAGE, IS MAN'S MOST PRECIOUS GIFT.

AND THEY BOTH MAKE MAN A BEING SUPERIOR TO ALL THE OTHER ANIMATE BEINGS!

ANIMALS USE THEIR VOICES IN ORDER TO EXPRESS PLEASURE OR PAIN.

WOOF, WOOF!

MEN, THANKS TO SPEECH, EXPRESS THEIR THOUGHTS, SHARE THEIR IDEAS, AND DISCUSS JUSTICE AND INJUSTICE WITHIN THE POLITICAL COMMUNITY.

WHAT DO YOU THINK? WILL IT BE A GIRL OR BOY?

OH! THEY'VE STARTED! I CAN HEAR HIPPARCHUS'S VOICE.

WE'RE LATE AND THERE WON'T BE ANY ROOM!

THE INTELLECT ALLOWS MAN TO UNDERSTAND REALITY AND TO PROCESS INFORMATION.

WE HAVE TWO DISTINCT INTELLECTS: THE "PASSIVE" ONE, WHICH NOTICES AND CLASSIFIES REPRESENTATIONS OF THE EXTERNAL WORLD THAT ARRIVE VIA OUR SENSES...

INTELLECT

PASSIVE.

ACTIVE

...AND THE "ACTIVE" ONE, THE MOST DIVINE PART OF US. THERE, THOUGHT REVEALS IDEAS JUST AS LIGHT REVEALS TO US OBJECTS OUTSIDE OURSELVES THAT ARE VISIBLE.

SPLAT

YUCK!!

THAT'S GOOD LUCK!

KNOWLEDGE THAT COMES FROM OBSERVATION BY MEANS OF THE SENSES OR EXPERIENCE IS ASSIMILATED BY THE INTELLECT.

LLECT

PASSIVE.

TIVE

PLATO ALSO SPOKE OF KNOWLEDGE THAT COMES TO US BY INDETERMINATE MEANS, INTUITIVELY, WITH NO CONNECTION TO THE SENSES.

ELLECT

PASSIVE.

TIVE

OH, NO! NOT AGAIN!

155

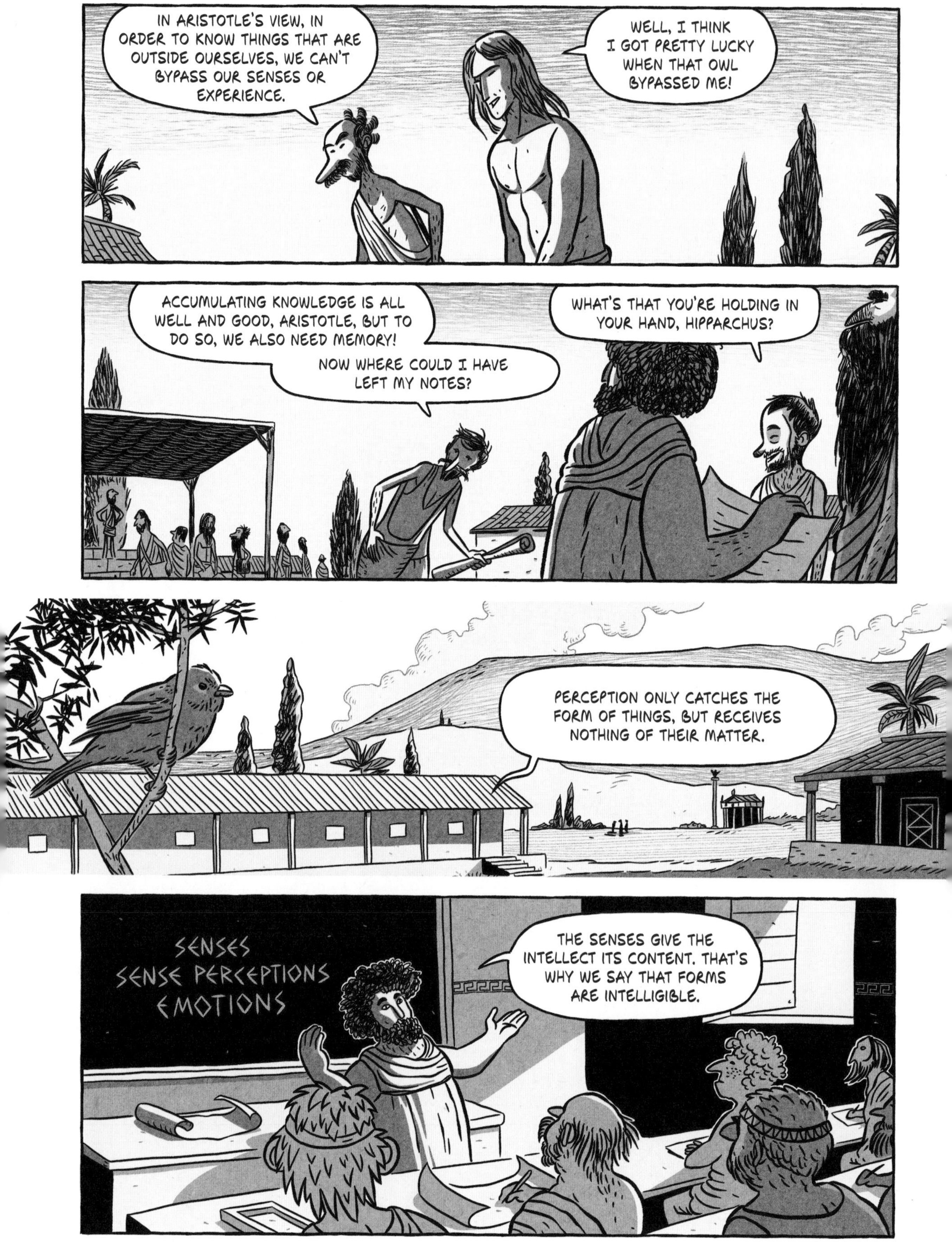
IN ARISTOTLE'S VIEW, IN ORDER TO KNOW THINGS THAT ARE OUTSIDE OURSELVES, WE CAN'T BYPASS OUR SENSES OR EXPERIENCE.
WELL, I THINK I GOT PRETTY LUCKY WHEN THAT OWL BYPASSED ME!
ACCUMULATING KNOWLEDGE IS ALL WELL AND GOOD, ARISTOTLE, BUT TO DO SO, WE ALSO NEED MEMORY!
NOW WHERE COULD I HAVE LEFT MY NOTES?
WHAT'S THAT YOU'RE HOLDING IN YOUR HAND, HIPPARCHUS?
PERCEPTION ONLY CATCHES THE FORM OF THINGS, BUT RECEIVES NOTHING OF THEIR MATTER.
SENSES
SENSE PERCEPTIONS
EMOTIONS
THE SENSES GIVE THE INTELLECT ITS CONTENT. THAT'S WHY WE SAY THAT FORMS ARE INTELLIGIBLE.

WITH THE HELP OF ALL HIS SENSES, MAN PERCEIVES THINGS AND FORMS IMPRESSIONS.

WITHIN THE SOUL, IMPRESSIONS CREATE EMOTIONS. FOR EXAMPLE, JOY, SADNESS, ANGER, FEAR, PASSION, FRIENDSHIP, LOVE... AND THESE DRIVE US INTO ACTION.

THUS, THEY INFLUENCE OUR BEHAVIOR. FOR THIS REASON, IN ORDER TO AVOID POTENTIALLY UNPLEASANT CONSEQUENCES, WE MUST LEARN TO MASTER OUR EMOTIONS!

EASY TO SAY!

AND TO DO! THAT'S WHY YOU ARE GOING TO ORGANIZE AN "ADVICE DEMONSTRATION"!

WHAT'S THAT?

EACH ONE OF YOU IS GOING TO TAKE A SIGN THAT YOU'LL HOLD WHILE WALKING AROUND, SO THAT ALL THE OTHER STUDENTS CAN SEE IT!

?

?

?

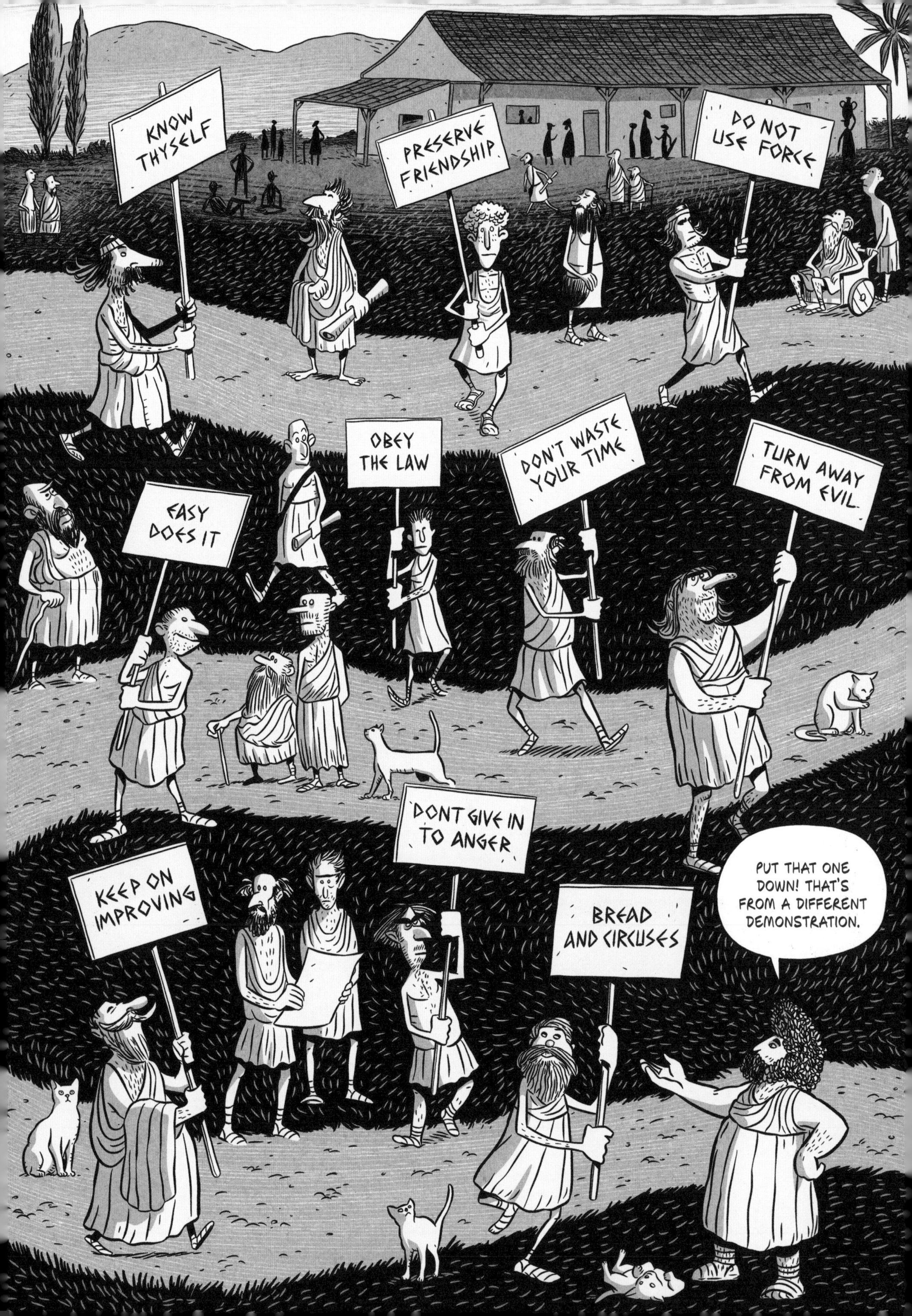
KNOW THYSELF
PRESERVE FRIENDSHIP
DO NOT USE FORCE
OBEY THE LAW
DON'T WASTE YOUR TIME
TURN AWAY FROM EVIL
EASY DOES IT
DONT GIVE IN TO ANGER
KEEP ON IMPROVING
BREAD AND CIRCUSES
PUT THAT ONE DOWN! THAT'S FROM A DIFFERENT DEMONSTRATION.

Men have always contemplated what's happening around them, and they've wondered about it. That's why they've always been hungry for knowledge—knowledge that had been considered up to then to be an overall set of information.

Aristotle was the first to divide knowledge into three distinct scientific disciplines depending on which subject they pertained to.

He defined "science" as the set of propositions that concern a precise subject and that we consider to be true after a process of demonstration resulting from deductive reasoning.

THEORETICAL SCIENCES:
- METAPHYSICS,
  MATHEMATICS, PHYSICS
PRACTICAL SCIENCES:
ETHICS, POLITICS
PRODUCTIVE SCIENCES:
THE ARTS, RHETORIC

THIS TABLE SHOWS YOU THE DIFFERENT SCIENTIFIC DISCIPLINES.

THE THEORETICAL SCIENCES ARE CONCERNED WITH KNOWLEDGE ITSELF AND THE WAYS IT'S ACQUIRED.

THEORETICAL
METAPHYSICS,
MATHEMATICS,
PRACTICAL SCIE
ETHICS POLITICS
PROD
THE ARTS

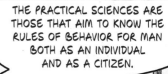

THE PRACTICAL SCIENCES ARE THOSE THAT AIM TO KNOW THE RULES OF BEHAVIOR FOR MAN BOTH AS AN INDIVIDUAL AND AS A CITIZEN.

THE SUBJECT OF THE PRODUCTIVE SCIENCES IS KNOWLEDGE AS A TOOL FOR CREATING USEFUL THINGS, SEEKING TO COMPLEMENT NATURE AND TO IMPROVE OUR LIVES.

CAL SCIENCES:
SICS,
TICS, PHYSICS

L SCIENCES:
OLITICS

IT'S TIME?

EUDEMUS WILL NOW TAKE OVER FOR ME.

MEET YOUR DAUGHTER.

YOU'LL BE CALLED PYTHIAS, LIKE YOUR MOTHER.

BECAUSE I COULD NEVER LOVE A WOMAN WHO HAD A DIFFERENT NAME!

LET HER GET SOME REST! IT WAS A DIFFICULT LABOR.

As you know, each science studies similar subjects. Metaphysics, in its general part, identifies the "principles" and "causes" of beings. In other words, it determines what the basis of each thing's existence is, which is its principle, in order to then explain its cause, why each thing is such as it is. The specific part of metaphysics deals with the "unmoving prime mover."

THE GENERAL PART OF METAPHYSICS CONCERNS ITSELF WITH BEINGS AND CAN BE SUMMARIZED BY THE QUESTION, "WHAT EXISTS?"

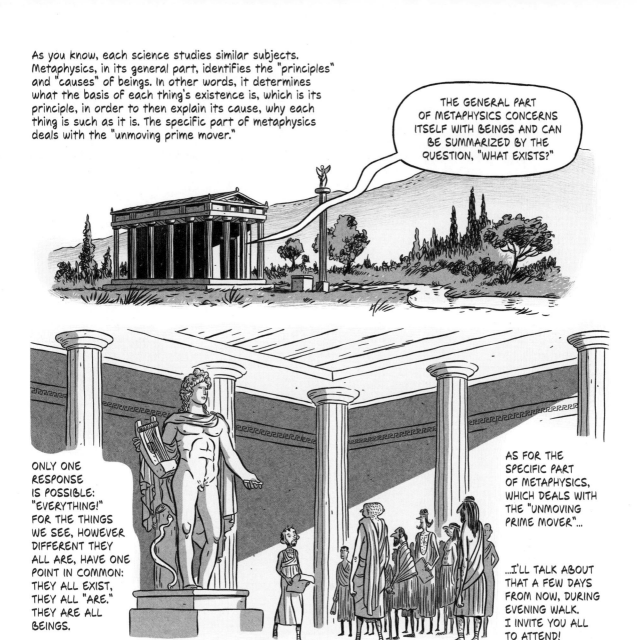

ONLY ONE RESPONSE IS POSSIBLE: "EVERYTHING!" FOR THE THINGS WE SEE, HOWEVER DIFFERENT THEY ALL ARE, HAVE ONE POINT IN COMMON: THEY ALL EXIST, THEY ALL "ARE." THEY ARE ALL BEINGS.

AS FOR THE SPECIFIC PART OF METAPHYSICS, WHICH DEALS WITH THE "UNMOVING PRIME MOVER"...

...I'LL TALK ABOUT THAT A FEW DAYS FROM NOW, DURING EVENING WALK. I INVITE YOU ALL TO ATTEND!

Several days later...

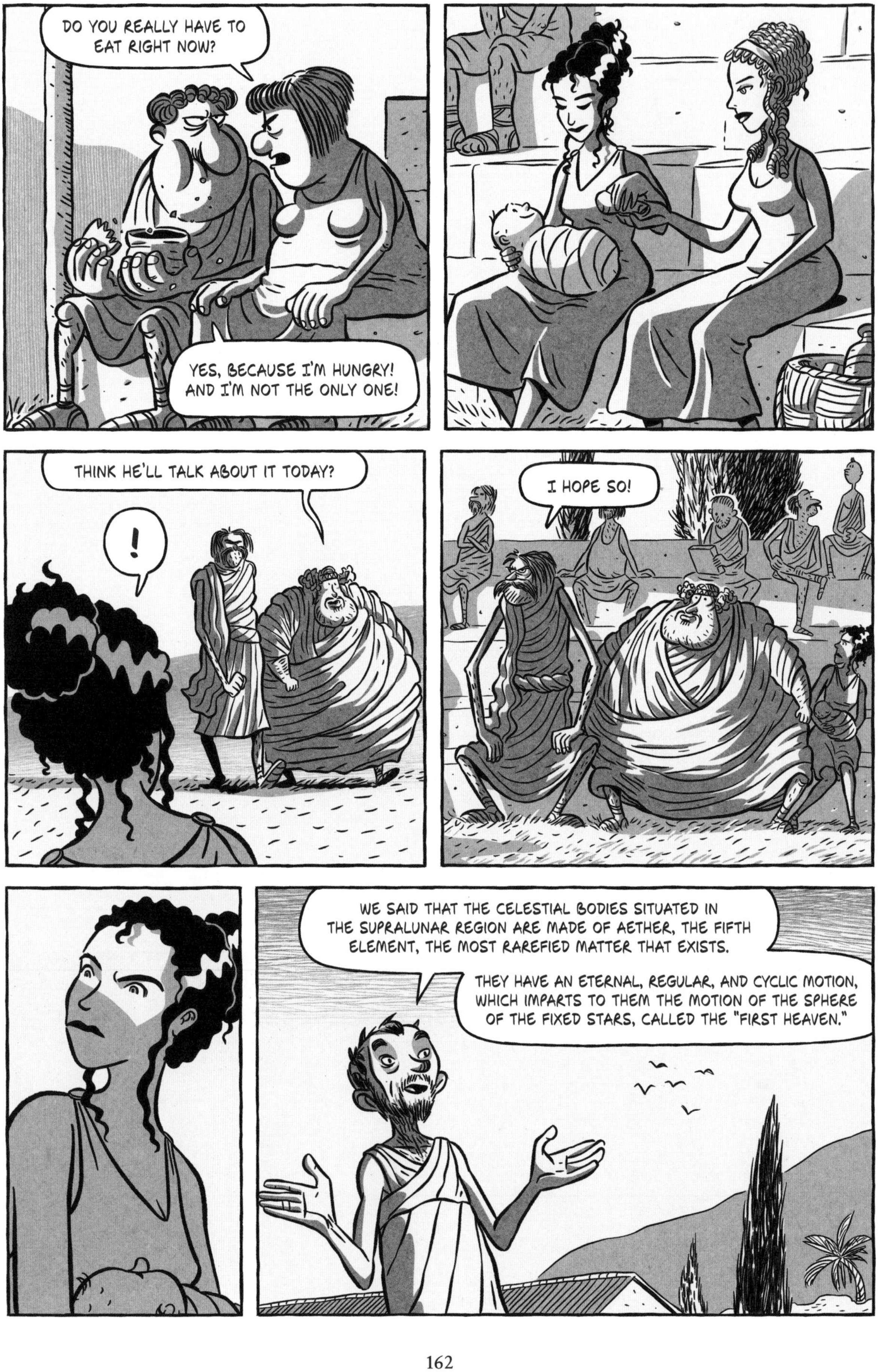
DO YOU REALLY HAVE TO EAT RIGHT NOW?
YES, BECAUSE I'M HUNGRY! AND I'M NOT THE ONLY ONE!
THINK HE'LL TALK ABOUT IT TODAY?
!
I HOPE SO!
WE SAID THAT THE CELESTIAL BODIES SITUATED IN THE SUPRALUNAR REGION ARE MADE OF AETHER, THE FIFTH ELEMENT, THE MOST RAREFIED MATTER THAT EXISTS.
THEY HAVE AN ETERNAL, REGULAR, AND CYCLIC MOTION, WHICH IMPARTS TO THEM THE MOTION OF THE SPHERE OF THE FIXED STARS, CALLED THE "FIRST HEAVEN."

WHAT SETS THE FIRST HEAVEN INTO MOTION?

HERE WE GO!

IT MUST BE "SOMETHING" THAT IS NOT LOCATED WITHIN THE SUPRALUNAR REGIONS BECAUSE, IF IT WERE, IT WOULD HAVE MATTER AND MOTION JUST LIKE THE OTHER CELESTIAL BODIES.

IT WOULD NOT BE ABLE TO SET INTO MOTION THE FIRST HEAVEN. THUS, THIS "SOMETHING" HAS TO BE EXTERNAL TO THIS REGION, AND IMMATERIAL.

SINCE IT ENGENDERS AN ETERNAL MOTION, IT HAS TO BE PERPETUAL AND UNMOVING!

'CAUSE IF IT MOVED, GO FIGURE WHO MOVED IT!

AND SINCE IT'S IMMATERIAL, IT WILL ONLY BE FORM. IT WILL THUS BE INTELLIGIBLE. PURE THOUGHT!

THIS "SOMETHING," I CALL IT THE "UNMOVING PRIME MOVER."

UNMOVING PRIME MOVER!

NICE NAME! WHAT DO YOU THINK?

TODAY WE WILL SEE HOW IT IMPARTS MOTION TO THE FIRST HEAVEN AND, WITH IT, TO THE ENTIRE UNIVERSE!

IT'S COMING!

I'LL START WITH TWO EXAMPLES. WHAT IS IT THAT DRIVES SOMEONE TO GO TO THE BAKER TO BUY SOME CRISPY, DELICIOUS BISCUITS?

THE DESIRE TO EAT THEM!

EXACTLY! DESIRE. NOW, LET'S TAKE A MAN WHO'S IN LOVE WITH A YOUNG LADY. EVERY EVENING HE GOES TO HER NEIGHBORHOOD IN THE HOPE OF RUNNING INTO HER!

WHO TOLD YOU?

SIT DOWN! EVERYONE'S LOOKING AT US!

WHAT GUIDES HIS STEPS?

LOVE!

YOU'LL PAY FOR THIS!

THAT'S IT EXACTLY! SO YOU CAN SEE THAT DESIRE, THAT LOVE, ENGENDERS MOTION.

THE UNMOVING PRIME MOVER, BECAUSE IT IS PERFECT, IS ADMIRABLE. IT THEREFORE REPRESENTS, FOR THE FIRST HEAVEN, AN OBJECT OF LOVE AND DESIRE! THAT IS THE REASON FOR ITS MOTION!

YOU HAVE CERTAINLY GRASPED THAT THE UNMOVING PRIME MOVER TOUCHES THE FIRST HEAVEN, WHICH DOES NOT IN TURN ALTER THE PRIME MOVER.

THAT'S LIKE SAYING: "HER BEAUTY TOUCHED ME, BUT I DIDN'T TOUCH HER!"

WE'RE GOING!

HOW RIGHT YOU ARE!

AREN'T YOU ASHAMED, A WISE MAN LIKE YOU, SAYING THAT THIS PHILANDERER IS RIGHT?

LET'S GO! YOU'VE GOT SOME EXPLAINING TO DO!

EXCUSE ME...

BUT IF THE FIRST HEAVEN DESIRES SOMETHING, THAT WOULD IMPLY THAT THE CELESTIAL BODIES ARE CAPABLE OF DEVELOPING EMOTIONS.

AND ARE THUS BEINGS.

THEY ARE ANI—

?

!! ! !
!! !!
!!!

PYTHIAS!

MAN! HE WAS GOING TO SAY IT!

NO LUCK!

PYTHIAS, WHAT'S WRONG?

NOTHING'S WRONG! I JUST WANTED TO KEEP YOU FROM FINISHING YOUR SENTENCE! I HAD SUSPICIONS ABOUT THOSE TWO RIGHT AWAY AND YOU WERE ABOUT TO SAY THAT CELESTIAL BODIES ARE ANIMATE BEINGS!

BUT THEY ARE. IF NOT, THE UNMOVING PRIME MOVER WOULDN'T BE ABLE TO INSTIGATE THEIR MOTION, NOR WOULD IT BE RESPONSIBLE FOR ALL THE CHANGES THAT ARISE IN THE UNIVERSE.

FOR THE UNMOVING PRIME MOVER IS THE SUPREME OBJECT OF DESIRE AND ADORATION FOR ANIMATE BEINGS. YES...

IT'S GOD! THE PERFECT AND ETERNAL BEING.

AND SINCE ITS ACTIVITY IS THOUGHT, IT CAN ONLY THINK PERFECTION.

IT CAN ONLY THINK ITSELF, GOD! IT IS THE THOUGHT OF THOUGHT!

OH MY...! IT'S A GOOD THING WE'RE AT HOME!

ALL THE SAME, REASONING THAT IS JUST MUST BE EXPRESSED!

BUT NOT RIGHT NOW. NOT ABOUT SUCH MATTERS! IF ARISTOTLE HAD FINISHED HIS SENTENCE...

HE'D HAVE BEEN ACCUSED OF INTRODUCING NEW GODS! AND THEN... HAVE YOU FORGOTTEN WHAT HAPPENED TO SOCRATES?

PERHAPS PYTHIAS IS RIGHT!

FOR THE GOD OF PHILOSOPHY DOESN'T CREATE, NOR DESTROY, NOR JUDGE, NOR PUNISH. IT'S NOT INTERESTED IN HUMAN AFFAIRS.

MEN THEREFORE DO NOT KNOW IT AND ORDINARY PEOPLE WILL NEVER UNDERSTAND IT!

IT WILL STAY THE GOD ONLY OF PHILOSOPHERS!

- ALL THE SAME, ARISTOTLE RESPECTS THE GODS OF THE CITY AND FULFILLS ALL THE RITES.

- BUT HE HAS NO RESPECT FOR THE GODS OF MYTH, THOSE WHO ARE JEALOUS, WHO HATE, WHO FALL IN LOVE WITH EACH OTHER OR BECOME INFATUATED WITH MORTALS!

- LIKE ALL RELIGIONS, FAITH IN THE TWELVE OLYMPIAN GODS RESTS UPON CONCEPTIONS THAT HAVE NOT BEEN PROVEN.

- WHEREAS PHILOSOPHY, ON THE OTHER HAND, HESITATES, DOUBTS, SEEKS, AND PROVES WITH REASONING.

- RELIGION AND PHILOSOPHY ARE TWO DISTINCT WORLDS!

A year later...

- CALLISTHENES SENT A LETTER.

- WHAT DOES HE SAY?

- THEY CROSSED THE HELLESPONT ON A BRIDGE MADE OF BOATS. WHEN HE GOT TO TROY, ALEXANDER WENT TO PRAY AT THE TOMB OF ACHILLES, AND HEPHAESTION AT PATROCLUS'S!

- DON'T LOOK AT ME LIKE THAT! CONTINUE!

- THEY CONQUERED CITY AFTER CITY. THEY ABOLISHED ALL OF THE MONARCHIES AND ESTABLISHED DEMOCRACIES.

- BRAVO! WISE MOVE!

- FIRST VICTORY ON THE GRANICUS RIVER. CLEITUS SAVED ALEXANDER'S LIFE.

- CLEITUS HAS ALWAYS BEEN BRAVE!

- THEY CROSSED THE TAURUS RANGE. ALEXANDER CUT THE GORDIAN KNOT WITH HIS SWORD!

- THE LEGEND TELLS THAT HE WHO "UNTIES" THE GORDIAN KNOT WILL RULE OVER ASIA. IT SAYS NOTHING ABOUT "CUTTING" IT! HA HA HA!

- BESIEGED AND TOOK TARSUS. BATTLE OF ISSUS. KING DARIUS HIMSELF FLED ALONGSIDE THE PERSIAN ARMY, WHILE HIS MOTHER, WIFE, AND TWO DAUGHTERS WERE TAKEN PRISONER. ONE HUNDRED THOUSAND DEAD. MUCH LOOT!

- AN ENORMOUS VICTORY... AND A VERY LONG LETTER!

At that time, Aristotle had everything he needed to be happy. In addition to Pythias, he had his daughter by his side, and he adored her. At the Lyceum, everything was running wonderfully in the three areas that were dearest to him: teaching, research, and writing. He had become a serene scholar and was more understanding toward others. He of course taught, but he also wrote an enormous amount! He revisited his old theories in order to improve them, and he followed the research and work of his associates closely.

It was during this period that he was the first to ask, "What is art?" in order to define it, and more importantly, he was the first to describe "what art does." He separated beings into two new categories: those that are the products of nature, such as trees and rocks, and those that are made by man. He in turn divided this second category into two: that which is made by man to complement nature, such as tools and furniture—he called these creations "necessary arts"; and that which is made to imitate nature and to render it more beautiful, such as statues and paintings—he called these creations "fine art."

FINE ART DOES NOT ONLY BRING PLEASURE TO MAN. IT CONTRIBUTES TO THE RELAXING OF THE MIND AND TO THE DEVELOPMENT OF CHARACTER.

BUT THE FINE ARTS MUST NOT BE A PROFESSION FOR CITIZENS. OTHERWISE, THEY'LL BECOME IDENTICAL TO ACTIVITIES THAT ARE NECESSARY.

FINE ARTS ARE TO BE RESERVED FOR THE VERY WEALTHY, TO AMUSE THEIR FRIENDS GRATUITOUSLY, OR FOR SLAVES!

!

DADDY!

The word "poetry" comes from the verb "poieo" (ποιέω), meaning to make, create, shape.

When Aristotle talks about poetry, he means tragedy, comedy, epic, or lyric poetry.

I THINK THAT POETRY, ESPECIALLY TRAGEDY, IS CLOSER TO PHILOSOPHY THAN, FOR EXAMPLE, HISTORY.

YES, OF COURSE, BECAUSE HISTORY PRESENTS EVENTS AS THEY ACTUALLY TOOK PLACE...

...WHEREAS POETRY PRESENTS WHAT COULD HAVE HAPPENED, BEYOND THE LIMITS OF TIME AND SPACE.

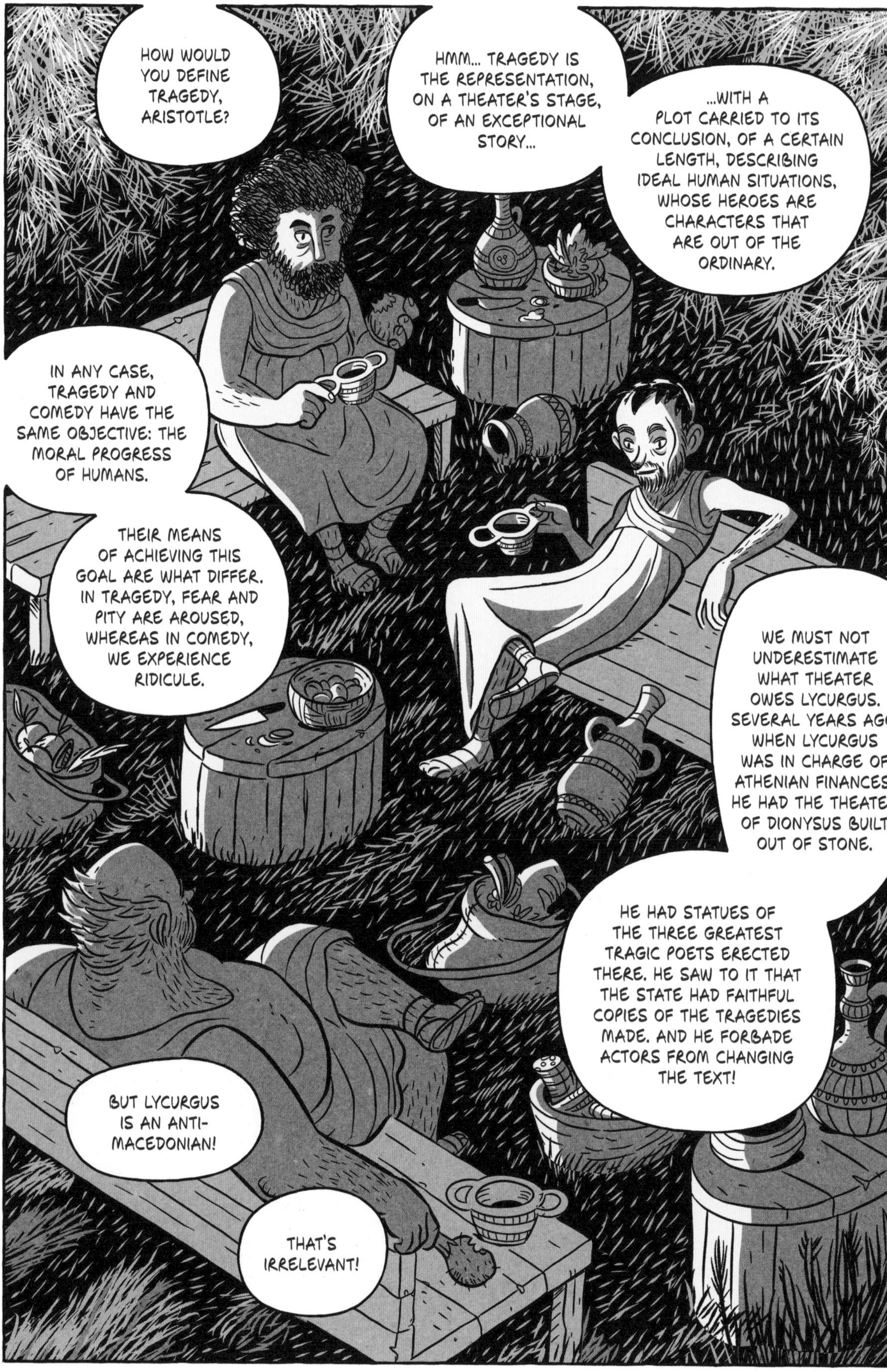

HOW WOULD YOU DEFINE TRAGEDY, ARISTOTLE?
HMM... TRAGEDY IS THE REPRESENTATION, ON A THEATER'S STAGE, OF AN EXCEPTIONAL STORY...
...WITH A PLOT CARRIED TO ITS CONCLUSION, OF A CERTAIN LENGTH, DESCRIBING IDEAL HUMAN SITUATIONS, WHOSE HEROES ARE CHARACTERS THAT ARE OUT OF THE ORDINARY.
IN ANY CASE, TRAGEDY AND COMEDY HAVE THE SAME OBJECTIVE: THE MORAL PROGRESS OF HUMANS.
THEIR MEANS OF ACHIEVING THIS GOAL ARE WHAT DIFFER. IN TRAGEDY, FEAR AND PITY ARE AROUSED, WHEREAS IN COMEDY, WE EXPERIENCE RIDICULE.
WE MUST NOT UNDERESTIMATE WHAT THEATER OWES LYCURGUS. SEVERAL YEARS AGO, WHEN LYCURGUS WAS IN CHARGE OF ATHENIAN FINANCES, HE HAD THE THEATER OF DIONYSUS BUILT OUT OF STONE.
HE HAD STATUES OF THE THREE GREATEST TRAGIC POETS ERECTED THERE. HE SAW TO IT THAT THE STATE HAD FAITHFUL COPIES OF THE TRAGEDIES MADE. AND HE FORBADE ACTORS FROM CHANGING THE TEXT!
BUT LYCURGUS IS AN ANTI-MACEDONIAN!
THAT'S IRRELEVANT!

The words and deeds in tragedy arouse feelings of terror and pity in the spectator: pity for the hero who suffers, terror because he imagines what he would go through if he were in the hero's place. Thus, with the plot's denouement, the spectator is liberated from the suffering provoked throughout the play. This liberation comes at the end if justice has been rendered to the hero or if the moral order has been re-established. Liberation and moral progress are the author's goals, and the audience members should be better beings when they leave the show.

Tragedy presents men as being nobler than they are in real life. As for comedy, it shows them to be baser. In fact, comedy stages a representation of the most common situations and individuals, provoking laughter through the excesses of language and mimicry. The audience is amused by mistakes, blunders, and ridiculous situations, which are also shown as things to be avoided, thus leading the audience to moral progress.

- WHEN I SAY SUMMARIZE, I MEAN SUMMARIZE!
- I'M SUMMARIZING! RIGHT... HE RAZED TYRE. SHOULDER SERIOUSLY WOUNDED IN GAZA. SURVIVED. PERSIAN FLEET SURRENDERED. IN EGYPT, WAS RECEIVED AS A LIBERATOR. THEY CALL HIM PHARAOH!
- YIKES! I DON'T LIKE THAT!

- HE FOUNDED A CITY THAT HE CALLED ALEXANDRIA. AT THE OASIS OF SIWA, THE PRIESTS OF ZEUS AMMON NAMED HIM "SON OF ZEUS" AND "GOD ON EARTH"!
- I DON'T LIKE THAT, EITHER! NOT GOOD!
- HE TOOK SUSA, BABYLON, PASARGADAE, PERSEPOLIS.
- SEIZED ROYAL TREASURES OF A VALUE OF TEN THOUSAND TALENTS!
- NOW I'M REALLY STARTING TO GET WORRIED!

- BATTLE OF GAUGAMELA. DARIUS, BEATEN, FLED. CONQUEST OF THE PERSIAN EMPIRE IS COMPLETE.
- THE GOAL OF THE CAMPAIGN HAS BEEN ACHIEVED. IT'S TIME TO COME HOME.
- THE SATRAP BESSUS KILLED DARIUS. ALEXANDER KILLED BESSUS. HE HAD DARIUS'S BODY TAKEN TO PERSEPOLIS SO HE COULD BE BURIED WITH ROYAL HONORS.
- A GREAT LEADER!
- PHILOTAS, ACCUSED OF CONSPIRACY, WAS PUT TO DEATH, AS WAS HIS FATHER, PARMENION.
- **PARMENION?**
- IN ADDITION TO THE CAMPAIGN JOURNAL CALLED THE "ROYAL JOURNAL," CALLISTHENES IS WRITING A WORK TITLED "THE GREAT DEEDS OF ALEXANDER," WHERE HE SINGS HIS PRAISES AND ALSO CALLS HIM "SON OF ZEUS"!
- I DON'T LIKE ANY OF THAT!
- HE FOUNDED OTHER CITIES, WHICH HE NAMED AFTER HIMSELF!

172

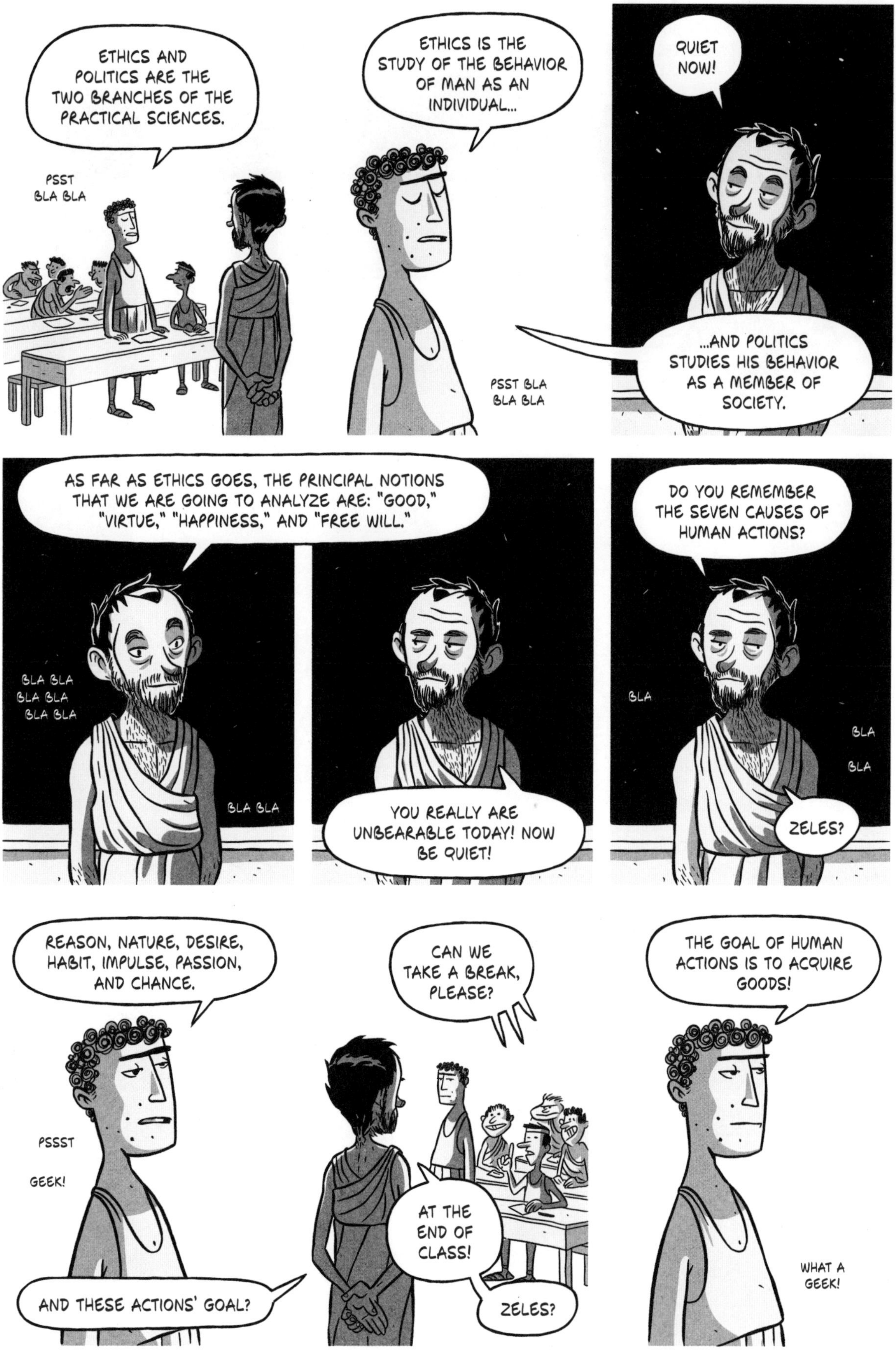
ETHICS AND POLITICS ARE THE TWO BRANCHES OF THE PRACTICAL SCIENCES.
PSST BLA BLA
ETHICS IS THE STUDY OF THE BEHAVIOR OF MAN AS AN INDIVIDUAL...
PSST BLA BLA BLA
QUIET NOW!
...AND POLITICS STUDIES HIS BEHAVIOR AS A MEMBER OF SOCIETY.
AS FAR AS ETHICS GOES, THE PRINCIPAL NOTIONS THAT WE ARE GOING TO ANALYZE ARE: "GOOD," "VIRTUE," "HAPPINESS," AND "FREE WILL."
BLA BLA BLA BLA BLA BLA
BLA BLA
YOU REALLY ARE UNBEARABLE TODAY! NOW BE QUIET!
DO YOU REMEMBER THE SEVEN CAUSES OF HUMAN ACTIONS?
BLA
BLA
BLA
ZELES?
REASON, NATURE, DESIRE, HABIT, IMPULSE, PASSION, AND CHANCE.
PSSST
GEEK!
AND THESE ACTIONS' GOAL?
CAN WE TAKE A BREAK, PLEASE?
AT THE END OF CLASS!
ZELES?
THE GOAL OF HUMAN ACTIONS IS TO ACQUIRE GOODS!
WHAT A GEEK!

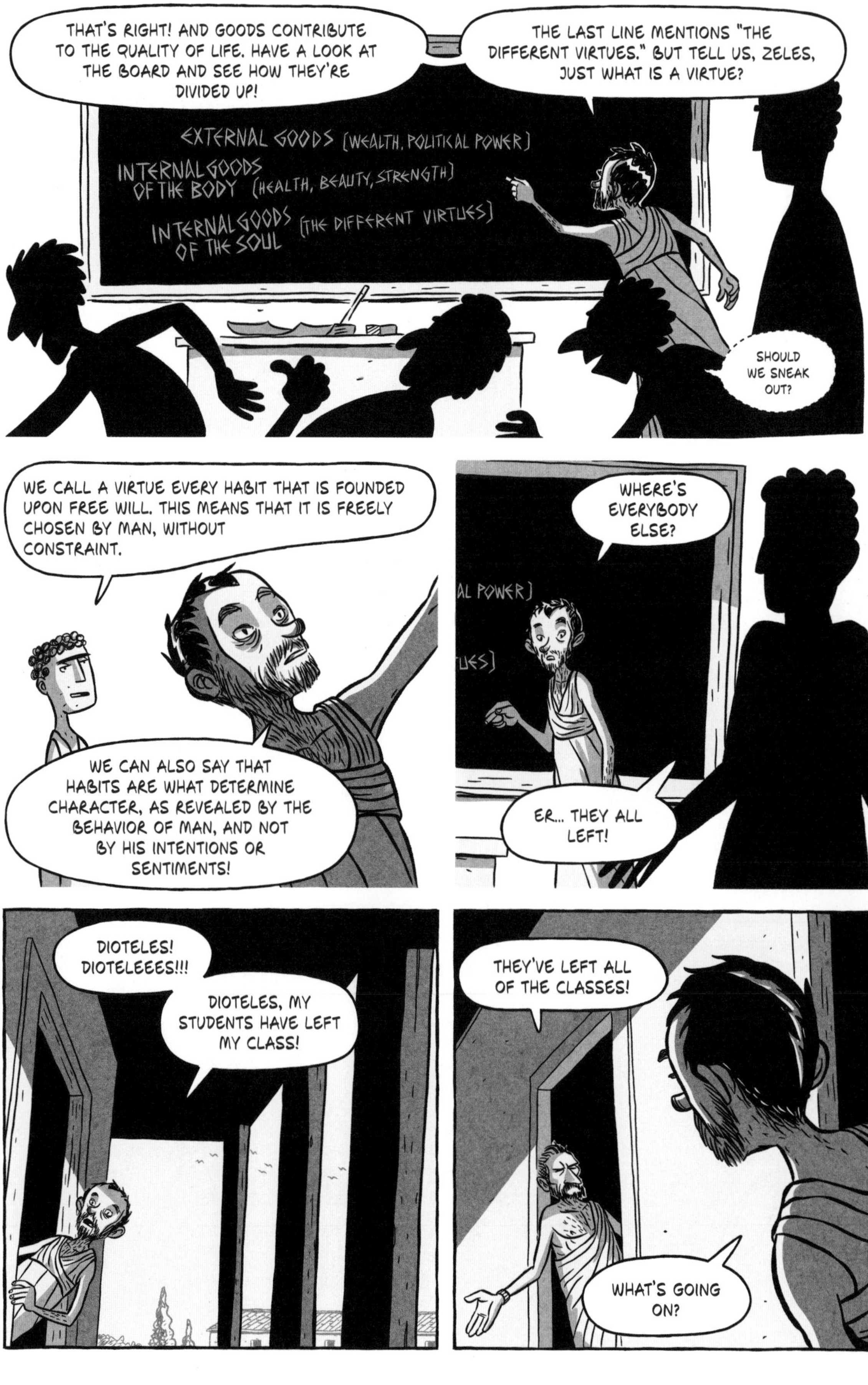

THAT'S RIGHT! AND GOODS CONTRIBUTE TO THE QUALITY OF LIFE. HAVE A LOOK AT THE BOARD AND SEE HOW THEY'RE DIVIDED UP!
THE LAST LINE MENTIONS "THE DIFFERENT VIRTUES." BUT TELL US, ZELES, JUST WHAT IS A VIRTUE?
EXTERNAL GOODS (WEALTH, POLITICAL POWER)
INTERNAL GOODS OF THE BODY (HEALTH, BEAUTY, STRENGTH)
INTERNAL GOODS OF THE SOUL (THE DIFFERENT VIRTUES)
SHOULD WE SNEAK OUT?
WE CALL A VIRTUE EVERY HABIT THAT IS FOUNDED UPON FREE WILL. THIS MEANS THAT IT IS FREELY CHOSEN BY MAN, WITHOUT CONSTRAINT.
WE CAN ALSO SAY THAT HABITS ARE WHAT DETERMINE CHARACTER, AS REVEALED BY THE BEHAVIOR OF MAN, AND NOT BY HIS INTENTIONS OR SENTIMENTS!
WHERE'S EVERYBODY ELSE?
ER... THEY ALL LEFT!
DIOTELES! DIOTELEEES!!!
DIOTELES, MY STUDENTS HAVE LEFT MY CLASS!
THEY'VE LEFT ALL OF THE CLASSES!
WHAT'S GOING ON?

UP THE HILL, AT THE SOURCE OF THE ERIDANUS, APPARENTLY TWO NYMPHS APPEARED. SO THEY WENT TO SEE THEM.

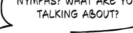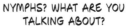

NYMPHS? WHAT ARE YOU TALKING ABOUT?

SEND THE TEACHERS TO GO GET THEM!

THEY ALSO WENT UP THERE!

OH!

THEY'RE SO PRETTY!

OOH!

OOH!

!

OH! OH!

OOOOH!

LOOK AT HOW THEIR WET TUNICS SHOW OFF THE SHAPE OF THEIR BODIES!

WOW!

OH YEAH! OH YEAH!

WELL, DIOTELES?

I WENT TO GET THEM.

AND HOW WERE THE NYMPHS?

UH, WELL... THEY WEREN'T ACTUALLY NYMPHS, JUST A FEW SLAVES WHO WERE WASHING RUGS IN THE RIVER!

GOOD HABITS ARE CALLED "VIRTUES," BUT THERE ARE ALSO BAD HABITS, WHICH WE CALL "VICES," SUCH AS INJUSTICE OR GREED... AMONG OTHERS!

BUT I CONSIDER IT ALSO A VICE NOT TO RESPECT ONE'S PARENTS, THE DEAD, ONE'S COUNTRY, OR...

...ONE'S TEACHERS!

WE ACQUIRE A GOOD IN ORDER TO USE IT TO ACQUIRE ANOTHER, AND THEN STILL ANOTHER, AND SO ON.

AN INDIVIDUAL, FOR EXAMPLE, WORKS...

...IN ORDER TO EARN MONEY...

...IN ORDER TO BUY MATERIALS...

...IN ORDER TO BUILD A HOUSE.

WE THEREFORE HAVE A SUCCESSION OF MEANS AND ENDS, WHICH EVENTUALLY COMES TO COMPLETION.

IT COMES TO COMPLETION WHEN THE SUPREME GOAL OF HUMAN ACTIONS IS ACHIEVED, NAMELY THE ULTIMATE GOOD OF A LIFE.

HAPPINESS, THEREFORE, IS A GOOD THAT WE SEEK FOR ITS OWN SAKE, NOT AS A MEANS TO OBTAIN ANOTHER GOOD!

ACHIEVING HAPPINESS REQUIRES CONSTANT EFFORT! DO NOT BELIEVE THAT IT IS ONLY OBTAINED ONCE WE'RE VERY OLD!

QUITE THE OPPOSITE. IT IS EARNED EVERY DAY, AT EVERY INSTANT, THROUGH VIRTUOUS BEHAVIOR.

WHAT'S WRONG?

IT'S NOTHING! JUST DIZZY!

CLINIAS?!

- CLINIAS, I'M SO HAPPY TO SEE YOU!
- ARISTOTLE!
  MEET ARISTOTLE, MY SON!

- WOW, WE'VE GOT THE SAME NAME! YOU
  LOOK A LOT LIKE YOUR FATHER!
- AND MY UNCLE!
- HA HA HA!

- SPEAKING OF WHICH, HOW IS PHILOLAUS?
  ARE YOU TWO STILL INSEPARABLE?
- WE SURE ARE! WE'VE OPENED A SCHOOL
  ON SAMOS. YOU KNOW, RHETORIC,
  PHILOSOPHY. BUT I'D LIKE MY SON TO
  COME STUDY WITH YOU. THAT'S WHY
  WE'RE HERE.

- HOW OLD ARE YOU?
- FIFTEEN.

- FIFTEEN! THAT'S A LITTLE YOUNG!
- STILL, HE'S READ EVERYTHING YOU'VE
  WRITTEN. WE EVEN ATTENDED YOUR
  CONFERENCE TODAY.

CAN I ASK YOU
A QUESTION?

OF COURSE!

- THERE ARE NUMEROUS
  VIRTUES, JUST AS THERE ARE
  NUMEROUS HUMAN ACTIONS,
  AND THEY ARE THE MEANS
  TO ACHIEVING HAPPINESS,
  RIGHT?

- THAT'S RIGHT!

- WELL, THEN, SHOULDN'T
  VIRTUES BE CONNECTED
  TO THE FUNCTIONS OF
  THE SOUL?

- BUT THEY ARE! YOU SEE, THERE ARE TWO CATEGORIES OF VIRTUES: "MORAL VIRTUES" AND "INTELLECTUAL VIRTUES." MORAL VIRTUES, SUCH AS COURAGE AND KINDNESS, ARE CONNECTED TO THE NON-RATIONAL PART OF THE SOUL AND CONCERN OUR DESIRES, OUR EMOTIONS, AND OUR ACTIONS.

- WHICH MEANS THEY DETERMINE HUMAN ETHICS AND ENSURE "HUMAN HAPPINESS," WHEREAS INTELLECTUAL VIRTUES, SUCH AS WISDOM, PRUDENCE, AND COMMON SENSE, ARE TIED INTO THE INTELLECTUAL FUNCTION OF THE SOUL.

- THAT'S RIGHT! AND OF COURSE, THESE INTELLECTUAL VIRTUES, ACQUIRED THROUGH RIGOROUS EDUCATION, ALSO HAVE A DIVINE ASPECT, WHICH ENSURES "DIVINE HAPPINESS."

ALLOW ME TO INTRODUCE YOU TO PYTHIAS, MY WIFE, AND PYTHIAS TWO, OUR DAUGHTER.

I'M CLINIAS, A COLLEAGUE OF ARISTOTLE'S FROM THE ACADEMY. AND MY SON, ARISTOTLE TWO.

GLAD YOU'RE HERE!

WHAT DO YOU SAY? CAN HE ENROLL AT THE LYCEUM?

PERHAPS YOU NOTICED, HE'S ENROLLED ON HIS OWN!

MORAL VIRTUES LEAD US TO HUMAN HAPPINESS, INTELLECTUAL VIRTUES LEAD US TO DIVINE HAPPINESS.

???

KID THINKS HE'S CLEVER!

Intellectual virtues reflect the excellence with which man exercises his intellectual abilities. Aristotle placed them above moral virtues because those indicate the middle ground between excess and lack, just as courage is between cowardice and recklessness.

It's what we call the "golden mean."

Intellectual virtues, on the other hand, can be indefinitely cultivated. They don't have to be contained within certain limits.

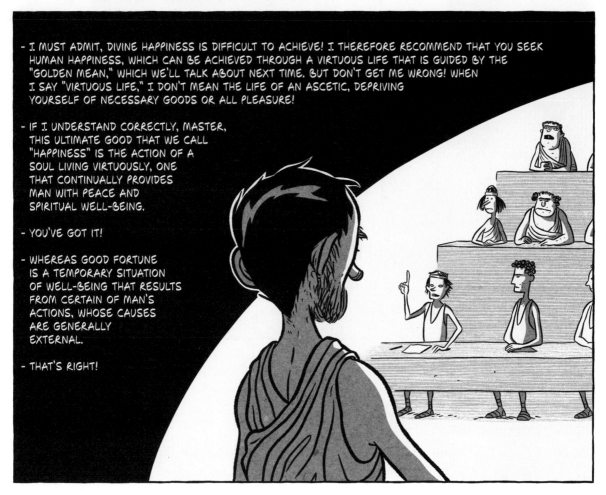

- I MUST ADMIT, DIVINE HAPPINESS IS DIFFICULT TO ACHIEVE! I THEREFORE RECOMMEND THAT YOU SEEK HUMAN HAPPINESS, WHICH CAN BE ACHIEVED THROUGH A VIRTUOUS LIFE THAT IS GUIDED BY THE "GOLDEN MEAN," WHICH WE'LL TALK ABOUT NEXT TIME. BUT DON'T GET ME WRONG! WHEN I SAY "VIRTUOUS LIFE," I DON'T MEAN THE LIFE OF AN ASCETIC, DEPRIVING YOURSELF OF NECESSARY GOODS OR ALL PLEASURE!

- IF I UNDERSTAND CORRECTLY, MASTER, THIS ULTIMATE GOOD THAT WE CALL "HAPPINESS" IS THE ACTION OF A SOUL LIVING VIRTUOUSLY, ONE THAT CONTINUALLY PROVIDES MAN WITH PEACE AND SPIRITUAL WELL-BEING.

- YOU'VE GOT IT!

- WHEREAS GOOD FORTUNE IS A TEMPORARY SITUATION OF WELL-BEING THAT RESULTS FROM CERTAIN OF MAN'S ACTIONS, WHOSE CAUSES ARE GENERALLY EXTERNAL.

- THAT'S RIGHT!

- I SAY WE CALL HIM "LITTLE MISTER RIGHT"!
- OH, YEAH! THAT'S FUNNY! HA HA HA!
- ADMIT IT, ZELES! THE KID'S A GENIUS AND YOU'RE JUST JEALOUS!

I SAW AND HEARD ALL OF THAT!

THE FIRST RULE IS THAT STUDENTS ARE ALL FRIENDS.

EACH PERSON MUST RECOGNIZE ANOTHER'S VALUE, NOT CRITICIZE HIS WEAKNESSES, AND EXCUSE HIS MISTAKES.

FRIENDSHIP MEANS MUTUAL AFFECTION THAT UNITES TWO INDIVIDUALS. IT GROWS AS THEY SPEND TIME TOGETHER.

A TRUE FRIEND IS ONE WHO SHARES BOTH OUR JOY AND OUR SADNESS.

IT WAS ARISTOTLE WHO ASKED HIM TO SAY THAT TO US!

- IN ATHENS, THERE ARE THREE GYMNASIA: THIS ONE, "LYCIAN APOLLO'S," THE ACADEMY'S, AND THE ONE OVER AT THE "CYNOSARGES."

GYMNASIA ARE PLACES DEDICATED TO THE PHYSICAL AND SPIRITUAL EDUCATION OF THE YOUNG.

THEY ARE PLACES FOR SOCIALIZING. AT THEM, YOUNG PEOPLE MEET PHILOSOPHERS, ARTISTS, AND POLITICIANS, AS WELL AS ORDINARY CITIZENS. AND THEY EXCHANGE THEIR POINTS OF VIEW!

WE ARE JUDGED BY WHAT WE CREATE. THIS IS WHAT KEEPS US SHARP. FOR ITS SAKE, WE DO NOT HOLD BACK ON OUR EFFORTS NOR ON THE TIME WE DEVOTE TO IT!

WORD IS THAT ALEXANDER KILLED CLEITUS AND HAD CALLISTHENES ARRESTED FOR CONSPIRACY.

WHAT?

CLEITUS SAVED HIS LIFE AND CALLISTHENES SINGS HIS PRAISES IN HIS WRITING! DON'T BELIEVE RUMORS! GENERALLY SPEAKING, THEY'RE NOT TRUE!

KNOCK KNOCK

But alas, those were true!

Alexander had changed a lot. Conquest, wealth, and glory had turned him into a despot and he was dressing like a Persian king.

He married Roxana, daughter of the satrap of Bactriana. He made everyone bow down before him, even the childhood friends who were his generals!

During a hunt, one of them—Hermolaus—killed a wild boar Alexander was targeting. This angered the king. He whipped and humiliated him in front of the officers' eyes.

Hermolaus, deeply outraged, decided to kill Alexander and instigated a plot, which was found out.

When he was brought before the assembled army for judgment, he knew what awaited him and he let it all out: the unjust execution of Philotas and Parmenion, Cleitus killed by a completely drunk Alexander, the obligation to bow down before him, the way Alexander commanded, and his taste for clothing, wine, and pleasure!

Hermolaus was sentenced to stoning. As he had a penchant for philosophy and Callisthenes was his friend, he, too, was arrested as an instigator and sentenced to death.

?

CALLISTHENES, SENTENCED TO DEATH?! OH, NO!

THE MAN'S ACCOUNT IS RELIABLE. HE'S ONE OF THE FIRST VETERANS THAT ALEXANDER ALLOWED TO RETURN HOME.

CALLISTHENES!

ANOTHER RUMOR SAYS THAT YOU HAD REGULAR CORRESPONDENCE WITH CALLISTHENES, THAT YOU WERE AWARE OF HIS PLOT WITH HERMOLAUS, AND THAT YOU SUPPORTED AND ENCOURAGED THEM!

BE CAREFUL!

UNBELIEVABLE! THEY SHOULD BE ASHAMED FOR EVEN THINKING THAT!

The death of Callisthenes, the rumors about his own supposed involvement in the plot, plus his responsibilities at the Lyceum were wearing Aristotle down. He taught less and wrote more.

At the time, he was working on the practical sciences. He considered ethics to be complemented by politics, especially in its social dimension. He thought that it was only possible for a man to become moral in the city, the "polis."

He deduced that ethical virtue was also political virtue, so ethics was a part of politics. Aristotle divided the citizens according to two criteria: first, their profession, and then their economic situation—"rich," "poor," and "belonging to the intermediary class."

THE RELATIONS THAT ARE FORMED BETWEEN DIFFERENT SOCIAL CLASSES DETERMINE THE FORM OF GOVERNMENT.

WHEN WE SAY "FORM OF GOVERNMENT," WE MEAN THE ORGANIZATION OF THE CITY, WHICH DETERMINES POWERS AND RESPONSIBILITIES, AS WELL AS THE RHYTHM OF THE RESIDENTS' LIVES.

IN THE END, THE RIGHT FORM OF GOVERNMENT IS THE ONE THAT ENSURES FOR SOCIETY DOMESTIC ORDER AND PROTECTION AGAINST ENEMIES, AND GIVES EACH CITIZEN THE POSSIBILITY OF ACHIEVING HAPPINESS.

TIRED?

NO! I FEEL DIZZY AGAIN!

MOM AND I ARE AT THE PART WHERE ODYSSEUS SEES HIS DAD, LAERTES.

THAT'S A VERY MOVING SCENE!

To protect itself against a Macedonian attack, the Athenians had decided to repair the city's walls.

Demosthenes wanted to show off his patriotism and donated three talents.

So then, as proposed by Ctesiphon, the Assembly decided to honor Demosthenes with a golden crown during a great ceremony at the theater of Dionysus.

Aeschines, his constant political opponent, condemned the decision as highly irregular, claiming that Demosthenes didn't deserve the honor because his anti-Macedonian position had harmed Athens.

ARISTOTLE, AESCHINES IS HERE.

AESCHINES? BUT HE'S IN EXILE!

HE CAME IN SECRET IN ORDER TO SEE YOU!

HE'S WAITING IN "PAN'S GROTTO."

I'VE GOT CLASS!

FINE, I'M GOING!

HAVE EUDEMUS TAKE THE STUDENTS TO THE ACROPOLIS.

FROM UP THERE, WE CAN SEE: THE WALLS GOING ALL THE WAY TO PHALERUM AND PIRAEUS; THE SIX HILLS OF ATHENS, THE HIGHEST BEING LYCABETTUS; THE THREE RIVERS; THE PNYX; THE AGORA; AND VARIOUS NEIGHBORHOODS.

- ARISTOTLE, THERE WAS A TRIAL!

- I KNOW. YOU GAVE YOUR SPEECH, "AGAINST CTESIPHON," TO DEFEND YOUR POSITION... AND DEMOSTHENES GAVE HIS, "ON THE CROWN," TO DEFEND HIS.

- HE CLAIMED THAT MY PRO-MACEDONIAN POLITICS WERE TREASONOUS! I WAS SENTENCED TO A FINE OF A THOUSAND DRACHMAS AND STRIPPED OF MY CIVIL RIGHTS FOR THREE YEARS.

THE CITY IS A MATERIAL CONSTRUCTION, BUT ALSO A NATURAL ONE. WHICH MEANS THAT IT'S WITHIN MAN'S NATURE TO BUILD CITIES WITH A GOVERNMENT AND INSTITUTIONS, IN ORDER TO LIVE IN THEM.

I WENT INTO EXILE BECAUSE I COULDN'T AFFORD TO PAY, WHICH BRINGS AUTOMATIC IMPRISONMENT. MOST OF ALL, THOUGH, I DIDN'T WANT TO SEE DEMOSTHENES CROWNED.

THAT IS WHY ARISTOTLE DEFINES MAN AS BEING A "POLITICAL ANIMAL," THAT IS TO SAY, A "LIVING POLITICAL ORGANISM."

I WAS INVITED TO RHODES TO FOUND A SCHOOL OF RHETORIC AND TO HELP THE CITIZENS IMPROVE THEIR GOVERNMENT. AND SO I'VE COME TO YOU TO ASK FOR ADVICE!

WITH NO SOCIETY AROUND HIM, MAN CANNOT FULFILL HIMSELF. HE WHO CHOOSES TO LIVE ALONE, OUTSIDE THE CITY, IS EITHER A GOD OR A SAVAGE BEAST.

THOSE WHO WISH TO HOLD HIGH PUBLIC OFFICES MUST BE ABLE TO GOVERN. THEY MUST HAVE INTEGRITY AND POSSESS VIRTUES SUCH AS CAUTION AND JUSTICE. THEIR PRINCIPAL CONCERN MUST BE THE CITIZEN.

THE CITIZEN WHO KNOWS HOW TO LEAD, AND ALSO BE LED, IS NOT INDIFFERENT! HE TAKES PART IN THE CITY'S DECISIONS, AND HE'S ALWAYS READY TO SERVE BOTH POLITICAL AND JUDICIAL FUNCTIONS.

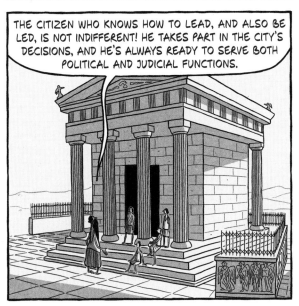

I WOULD PROPOSE A FORM OF DEMOCRACY THAT I'LL CALL AN "INTERMEDIARY REGIME," IN WHICH ALL CITIZENS WOULD BE EQUAL BEFORE THE LAW. MEMBERS OF THE INTERMEDIARY CLASS...

...FULFILL THEIR DUTIES WITH CAUTION. THAT IS HOW THEY ARE USEFUL TO THE CITY AND EARN THE RESPECT AND RECOGNITION OF THEIR FELLOW CITIZENS.

THEY ALSO ENSURE BALANCE BETWEEN THE POOR AND THE RICH. IN SO DOING, THEY PREVENT SOCIAL ANIMOSITY, WHICH CAN LEAD TO REVOLT.

YES, BUT IN A DEMOCRACY, THE GOVERNMENT IS IN THE HANDS OF THE MAJORITY, WHOSE ABILITIES AND KNOWLEDGE ARE ARGUABLE, BECAUSE THOSE ARE RESERVED FOR A VERY FEW—THE BEST!

YES, BUT THE MAJORITY'S OPINION IS MORE CORRECT THAN THE OPINION OF THE MINORITY! THE IDEAL WOULD BE FOR THE BEST TO GOVERN, BUT FOR THESE SAME BEST TO STILL BE ELECTED BY THE PEOPLE.

I HOPE THAT YOU ALL SINCERELY WANT TO BE USEFUL CITIZENS. SO DON'T EVER FORGET THAT THE GOOD OF ALL MUST ALWAYS BE PLACED ABOVE THE PARTICULAR GOOD OF EACH INDIVIDUAL CITIZEN!

BUT MOST OF ALL, IT IS THE LAWS THAT MUST GOVERN, NOT PEOPLE.

YOUR ADVICE IS PRECIOUS!

BUT MOST OF ALL, CITY AND CITIZENS MUST PURSUE THE SAME GOAL: HAPPINESS!

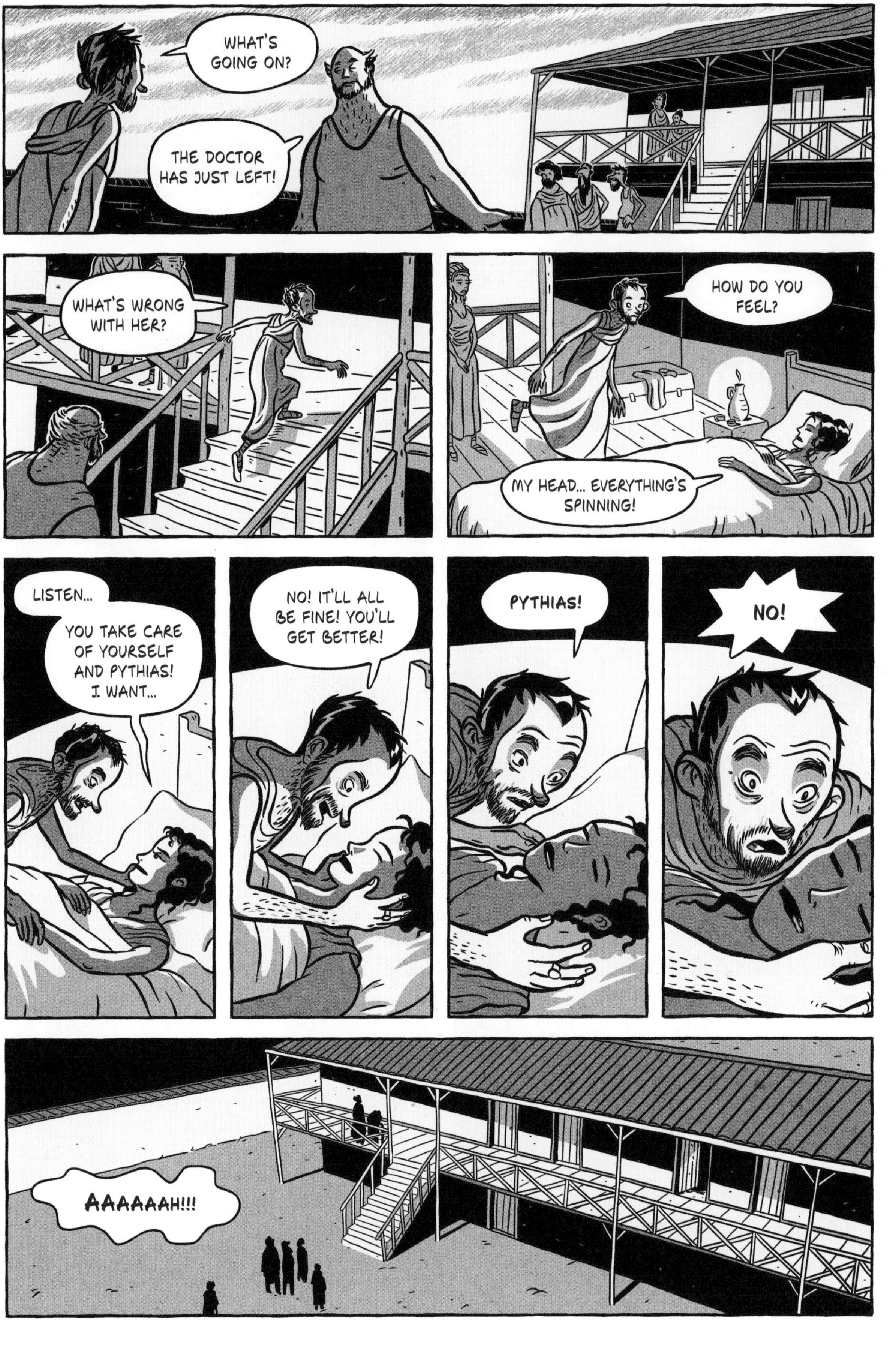
WHAT'S GOING ON?
THE DOCTOR HAS JUST LEFT!
WHAT'S WRONG WITH HER?
HOW DO YOU FEEL?
MY HEAD... EVERYTHING'S SPINNING!
LISTEN...
YOU TAKE CARE OF YOURSELF AND PYTHIAS! I WANT...
NO! IT'LL ALL BE FINE! YOU'LL GET BETTER!
PYTHIAS!
NO!
AAAAAAH!!!

THIS HAS GONE ON FOR A MONTH! HE ONLY GOES OUT IN THE EVENING, TO THE WOODS.

HE SPEAKS TO NO ONE!

TOMORROW, DURING EVENING WALK, I'LL SPEAK.

And so...

THE MEANING OF "VALUES" IS RELATIVE. IT IS DETERMINED BY ECONOMIC AND POLITICAL CONDITIONS.

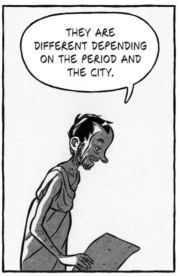

THEY ARE DIFFERENT DEPENDING ON THE PERIOD AND THE CITY.

IN A DEMOCRA...

IN A DEM...

IN A DEMOCRACY, FREEDOM IS CONSIDERED TO BE A "VALUE," WHEREAS IN AN OLIGARCHIC REGIME, WEALTH IS, AND IN AN ARISTOCRACY, VIRTUE IS.

ARISTOTLE, WHAT IS THE PREREQUISITE CONDITION FOR THE EXISTENCE AND PROSPERITY OF A CITY?

THAT WOULD BE AUTONOMY! THE FACT THAT IT DOESN'T NEED ANY EXTERNAL AID TO MEET THE NEEDS OF ITS INHABITANTS.

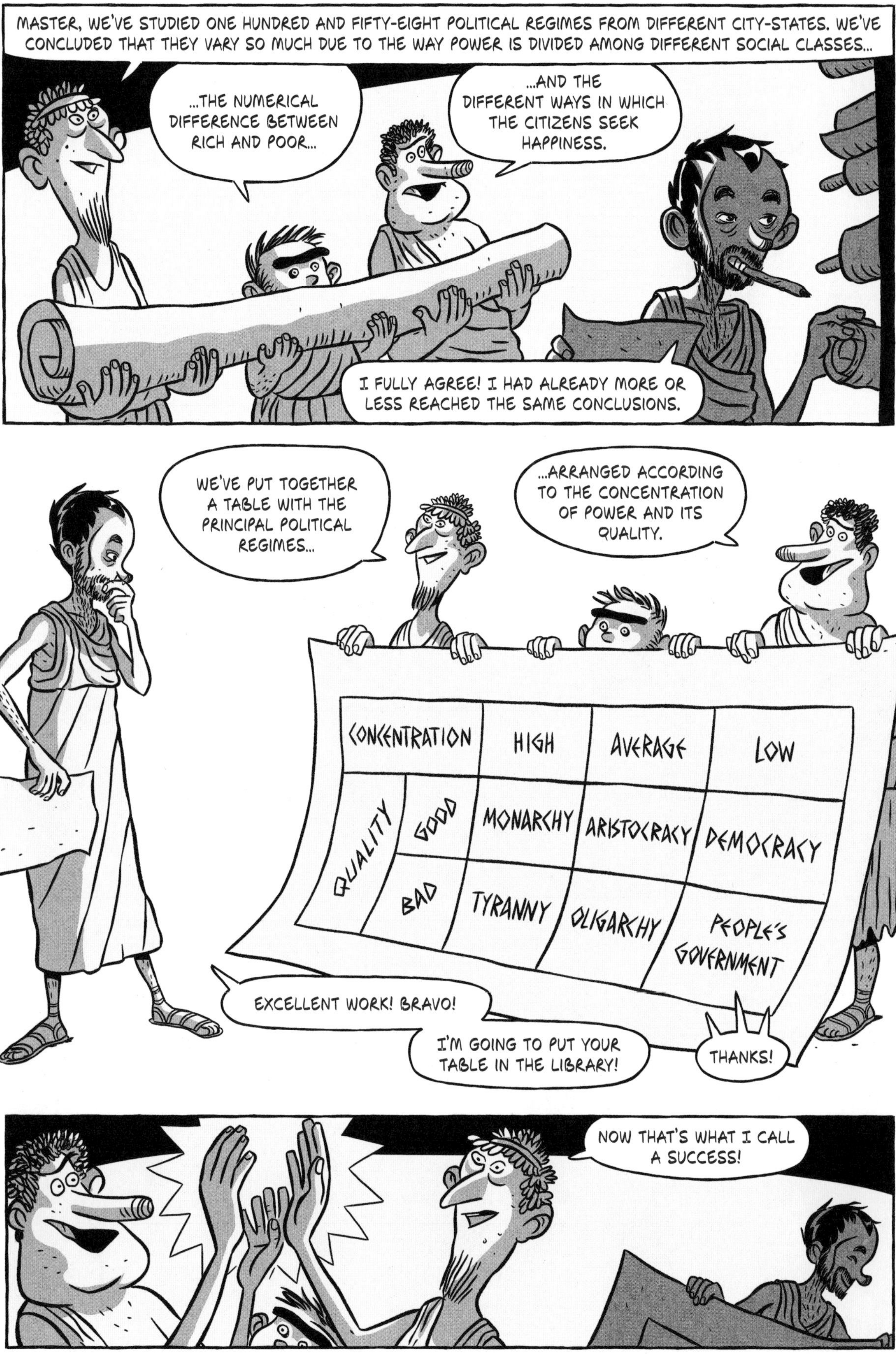

MASTER, WE'VE STUDIED ONE HUNDRED AND FIFTY-EIGHT POLITICAL REGIMES FROM DIFFERENT CITY-STATES. WE'VE CONCLUDED THAT THEY VARY SO MUCH DUE TO THE WAY POWER IS DIVIDED AMONG DIFFERENT SOCIAL CLASSES...
...THE NUMERICAL DIFFERENCE BETWEEN RICH AND POOR...
...AND THE DIFFERENT WAYS IN WHICH THE CITIZENS SEEK HAPPINESS.
I FULLY AGREE! I HAD ALREADY MORE OR LESS REACHED THE SAME CONCLUSIONS.
WE'VE PUT TOGETHER A TABLE WITH THE PRINCIPAL POLITICAL REGIMES...
...ARRANGED ACCORDING TO THE CONCENTRATION OF POWER AND ITS QUALITY.
CONCENTRATION
HIGH
AVERAGE
LOW
QUALITY
GOOD
MONARCHY
ARISTOCRACY
DEMOCRACY
BAD
TYRANNY
OLIGARCHY
PEOPLE'S GOVERNMENT
EXCELLENT WORK! BRAVO!
I'M GOING TO PUT YOUR TABLE IN THE LIBRARY!
THANKS!
NOW THAT'S WHAT I CALL A SUCCESS!

HERPYLLIS, YOU'LL MAKE A COPY OF IT FOR ME TO PUT IN THE LIBRARY, THEN WE'VE GOT TO BEGIN WRITING!

I'LL THEN DICTATE IT.

BUT... I DON'T KNOW HOW...

PLEASE, FORGIVE ME! I HADN'T REALIZED.

PLEASE, DON'T YOU CRY!

IT'S NOT YOUR FAULT!

Several months later...

HAVE YOU SEEN ARISTOTLE?

HE WENT ON A WALK ALONG THE RIVER WITH HIS DAUGHTER AND HERPYLLIS.

THAT WOMAN HAS LITERALLY SAVED HIM!

IT'S TRUE. SHE'S SUPPORTED HIM THROUGH DIFFICULT TIMES!

AND IT'S ALSO TRUE THAT SHE'S BEEN LIKE A MOTHER TO LITTLE PYTHIAS!

I HEAR LAUGHTER: HERE THEY COME!

HA HA HA

SHE'LL GIVE BIRTH ANY DAY NOW!

YES, BUT NO TALK OF MARRIAGE! HE'LL BE HAPPY JUST LIVING WITH HER!

HA HA HA!

Harpalus, if you'll remember, was one of Alexander's friends in Mieza. He had a lame leg and couldn't go into battle. Alexander trusted him completely and assigned him to manage the Persian Empire's treasure, some seven hundred thousand talents.

Harpalus, however, proved to be unworthy of the king's trust. He began living a life of debauchery and pilfering money. He eventually embezzled five thousand talents, recruited an army of six thousand mercenaries, outfitted thirty triremes, and sought asylum in Athens, in exchange for the mercenaries, the fleet, and part of the stolen money.

The Athenians decided to imprison him in the Acropolis for embezzlement, while waiting for Alexander to make a ruling on his fate. They assigned a commission to count the money Harpalus had on him. The first day, they counted seven hundred talents; the second, three hundred fifty; and on the third, Harpalus had gone missing. Members of the commission were suspected of corruption, Demosthenes in particular, and he was sentenced to exile.

IN ANY CASE, JUSTICE PROVED ITSELF UP TO THE TASK!

PERFECTLY! SO LET'S NOT BE ALL DRAMATIC!

ARISTOTLE...

AN OFFICER FROM THE MACEDONIAN GUARD IS HERE.

PLEASE, CONTINUE! I'LL BE RIGHT BACK!

HAS SOMETHING HAPPENED?

HEPHAESTION SUDDENLY FELL ILL IN ECBATANA AND HAS DIED!

HE'S DEAD?

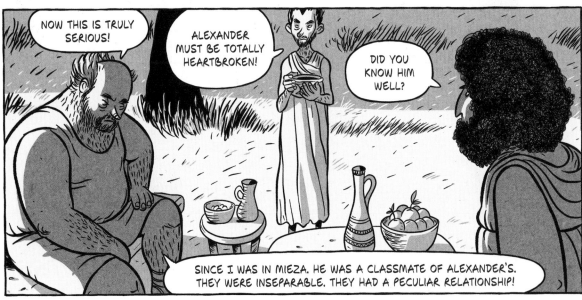

NOW THIS IS TRULY SERIOUS!

ALEXANDER MUST BE TOTALLY HEARTBROKEN!

DID YOU KNOW HIM WELL?

SINCE I WAS IN MIEZA. HE WAS A CLASSMATE OF ALEXANDER'S. THEY WERE INSEPARABLE. THEY HAD A PECULIAR RELATIONSHIP!

THE "GOLDEN MEAN" IS THE MIDDLE GROUND BETWEEN TWO EVILS: LACK AND EXCESS. WE CAN DETERMINE THE MIDDLE GROUND THROUGH REPETITIVE VALIANT ACTIONS.

THEOPHRASTUS IS LEADING THE EVENING WALK. LET'S GO LISTEN TO HIM!

THIS EXPLAINS HOW VIRTUE IS ACQUIRED OUT OF HABIT, FROM MAKING A CONSTANT EFFORT.

THAT'S EXACTLY WHAT I'M GOING TO SAY...

...IN A COUPLE OF DAYS, TO MY STUDENTS ON THE MORNING WALK.

I WOULD SIMPLY ADD THAT OFTEN, THE MIDDLE GROUND THAT LEADS MAN TOWARD EXCELLENCE IS NOT MEDIOCRE, TEPID BEHAVIOR, BUT IT IS RATHER A SUMMIT.

THINK ABOUT THAT!! GOODBYE!

Indeed, several days later...

LIFE IS NEVER A PERFECTLY STRAIGHT ROAD!

WE OFTEN FIND OURSELVES AT A CROSSROADS.

AND AT THOSE MOMENTS WE MUST CHOOSE WHICH DIRECTION WE'LL GO, GUIDED ONLY BY A "MUST" OR A "MUST NOT"!

In Chalcis...

THE WAY YOU LOOK AT THE WATER, YOU MUST BE A FOREIGNER.

YES. A FOREIGNER.

THE WATER GOES THIS WAY, THEN IT GOES THAT WAY. IT CHANGES DIRECTION FOUR TIMES A DAY AND NO ONE KNOWS WHY!

ON TOP OF THAT, EVERY MONTH, FOR SIX OR SEVEN DAYS, IT CHANGES DIRECTION AT LEAST FOURTEEN TIMES A DAY. WE CALL THAT THE "CRAZY WATERS" AND THAT'S WHEN YOU CATCH A LOT OF FISH!

LOOK! I OPENED THE SNAIL TO SEE WHAT IT'S LIKE INSIDE!

WHAT'S WRONG?

I'VE GOT A BELLYACHE! I'M GOING TO FINISH THIS LETTER TO ANTIPATER.

YOU KNOW, I CAN TAKE ANY DICTATION YOU WANT NOW!

BUT... UH... HOW IS THAT...?

I LEARNED TO READ AND WRITE IN ATHENS. IN SECRET. I WANTED TO SURPRISE YOU!

MY DARLING!

In Pella...

ANTIPATER, WHEN YOU'VE FINISHED READING ARISTOTLE'S LETTER, I'LL GIVE YOU THE LATEST NEWS FROM ATHENS. THEY'VE CALLED DEMOSTHENES OUT OF EXILE!

SMELLS LIKE REVOLT! STAY ON ALERT!

"THREE MONTHS HAVE PASSED AND I FEEL VERY ALONE! I'M TALKING TO MYSELF."

"I TALK TO MYSELF AND I ALONE HEAR WHAT I SAY!"

At Zeus's temple in Chalcis...

THE MORE I'M ALONE, THE MORE I FEEL THE NEED TO TALK TO SOMEONE.

HELLO! WHAT'S YOUR NAME?

DADDY, DADDY, GUESS WHO'S HERE!

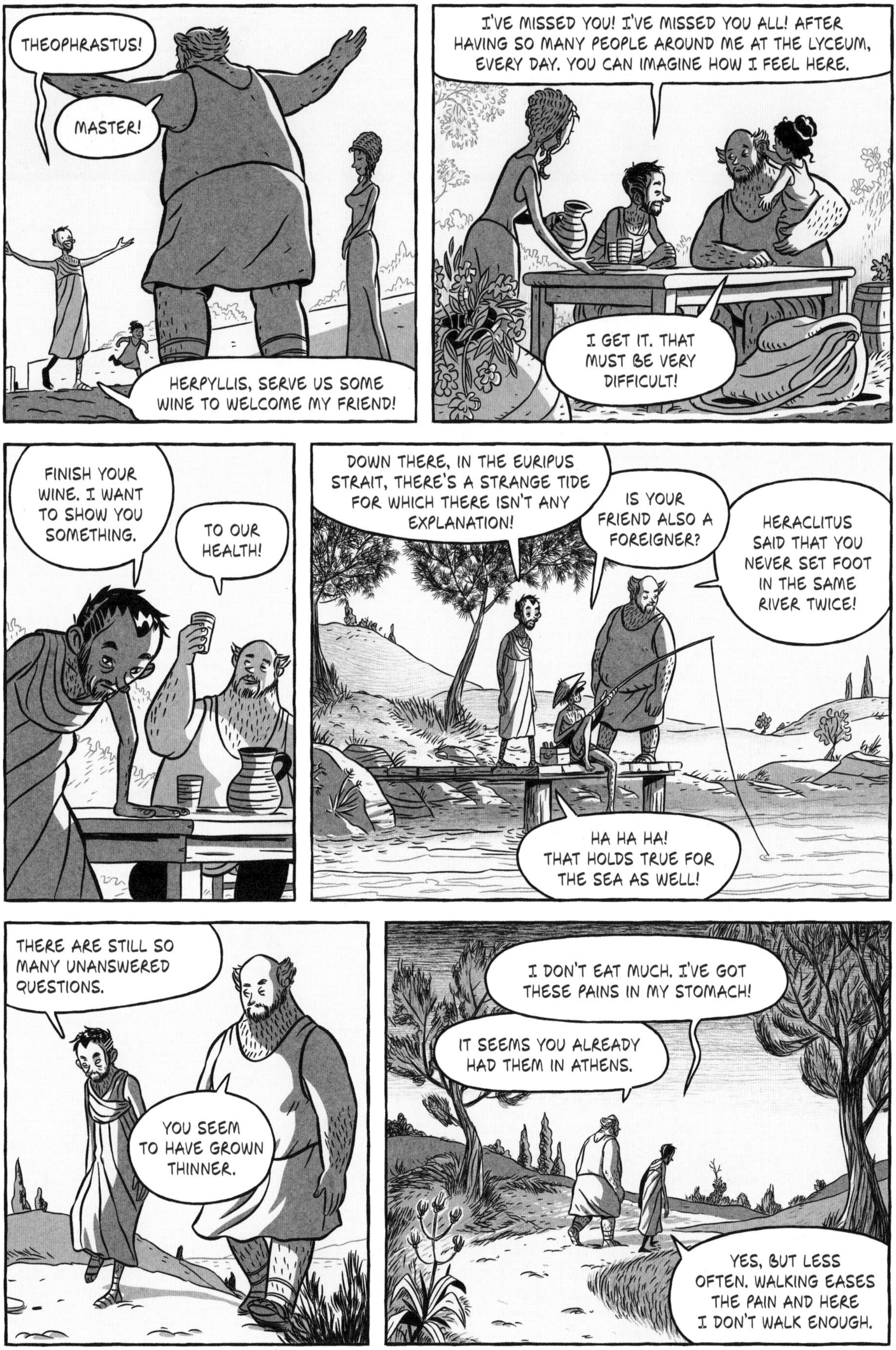
THEOPHRASTUS!
MASTER!
HERPYLLIS, SERVE US SOME WINE TO WELCOME MY FRIEND!
I'VE MISSED YOU! I'VE MISSED YOU ALL! AFTER HAVING SO MANY PEOPLE AROUND ME AT THE LYCEUM, EVERY DAY. YOU CAN IMAGINE HOW I FEEL HERE.
I GET IT. THAT MUST BE VERY DIFFICULT!
FINISH YOUR WINE. I WANT TO SHOW YOU SOMETHING.
TO OUR HEALTH!
DOWN THERE, IN THE EURIPUS STRAIT, THERE'S A STRANGE TIDE FOR WHICH THERE ISN'T ANY EXPLANATION!
IS YOUR FRIEND ALSO A FOREIGNER?
HERACLITUS SAID THAT YOU NEVER SET FOOT IN THE SAME RIVER TWICE!
HA HA HA! THAT HOLDS TRUE FOR THE SEA AS WELL!
THERE ARE STILL SO MANY UNANSWERED QUESTIONS.
YOU SEEM TO HAVE GROWN THINNER.
I DON'T EAT MUCH. I'VE GOT THESE PAINS IN MY STOMACH!
IT SEEMS YOU ALREADY HAD THEM IN ATHENS.
YES, BUT LESS OFTEN. WALKING EASES THE PAIN AND HERE I DON'T WALK ENOUGH.

IT'S ALSO ONE OF THE REASONS WHY I HAD US WALK DURING SOME OF OUR CLASSES!

IF I HAD ONLY KNOWN! HA HA HA!

I ALSO COME BEARING BAD NEWS!

OUT WITH IT.

IN DELPHI, THEY'VE RESCINDED YOUR HONORARY TITLE AND THEY THREW THE VOTIVE COLUMN INTO A WELL!

The next morning...

I'D LIKE IT IF YOU CAME MORE OFTEN, BUT I THINK THEY NEED YOU MORE AT THE LYCEUM.

I'LL RETURN SOON!

NEXT TIME, BRING EUDEMUS WITH YOU!

I'LL BRING HIM.

OH! WHAT YOU SAID YESTERDAY ABOUT DELPHI... IT BOTHERS ME, YET AT THE SAME TIME, IT DOESN'T BOTHER ME!

MY GREAT ACHIEVEMENT IN PHILOSOPHY IS TO HAVE CREATED WHAT I CREATED—NAMELY, A LARGE BODY OF WORK. AND I DID IT BECAUSE I WANTED TO, NOT OUT OF OBEDIENCE OR FEAR OF THE LAW.

NO ONE ELSE COULD HAVE PRODUCED SUCH AN IMPORTANT BODY OF WORK!

PHILOSOPHY'S BEAUTY LIES IN THE FACT NOT THAT IT IS TAUGHT, BUT THAT IT IS LIVED. WITH IT, WE GO ON THIS AMAZING JOURNEY, HIGHLIGHTED BY ENDLESS NEW DISCOVERIES.

THOSE WHO THINK THEY POSSESS ENOUGH VIRTUES DO NOT FIND HAPPINESS IN MATERIAL GOODS, FOR NO MATTER HOW MUCH THEY MAY ACQUIRE...

...THEY'LL NEVER HAVE ENOUGH!

LOOK! PYTHIAS IS READING HOMER TO NICOMACHUS!

I KNOW. SHE DOES IT EVERY DAY! LET'S CONTINUE!

OFTEN, CARRIED AWAY BY OUR DESIRES, WE COMMIT ACTIONS THAT WE KNOW FULL WELL TO BE WRONG!

OTHER TIMES, IT REQUIRES A GREAT DEAL OF STRENGTH TO RESIST TEMPTATION.

NEITHER OF THESE TWO SITUATIONS IS PLEASING. THE IDEAL WOULD BE FOR US NEVER TO SUCCUMB TO TEMPTATION OR FOR US TO FIND IT EASY TO RESIST.

IT SEEMS AS IF YOU'RE GIVING ADVICE TO SOMEONE.

TO OUR SON!

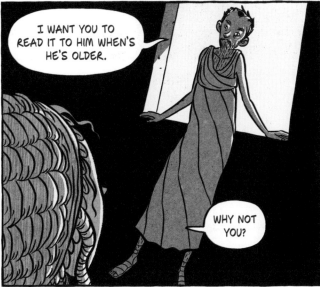

I WANT YOU TO READ IT TO HIM WHEN'S HE'S OLDER.

WHY NOT YOU?

WE ACT WELL WHEN EACH OF OUR ACTIONS IS DONE AT THE RIGHT MOMENT, FOR THE RIGHT REASON, IN THE RIGHT WAY, FOR THE RIGHT PEOPLE.

SO TRUE! WHEN THE MOON IS FULL, YOU DON'T GO FISHING BECAUSE THERE AREN'T ANY FISH.

THE MAN WHO ACQUIRES KNOWLEDGE HAS A MORE PLEASANT LIFE THAN HE WHO STILL SEEKS IT.

KNOWLEDGE IS KNOWING TO GO FISHING WHEN IT'S A QUARTER MOON. IT'S AT THAT TIME THAT THERE'S THE CRAZY WATERS AND A LOT OF FISH.

Six months later...

CONSTRAINED BY CIRCUMSTANCES OR PURSUED BY MEN, I HAVE WANDERED FOR MANY A LONG YEAR! ALWAYS A METIC!

IN ATHENS, ASSOS, LESBOS, PELLA, MIEZA, STAGIRA, DELPHI, ATHENS AGAIN, AND NOW IN CHALCIS!

I'VE SEEN SO MANY DEAR TO ME DIE! MY PARENTS, PLATO, PROXENUS, HERMIAS, CALLISTHENES, PYTHIAS, ALEXANDER...

HE'S BEEN THROUGH SO MANY ORDEALS. A NORMAL MAN WOULD HAVE BEEN DESTROYED OR SUNK INTO MISERY.

BUT HE'S NOT MISERABLE!

THE CONQUEST OF INTELLECTUAL VIRTUES HAS BROUGHT HIM DIVINE HAPPINESS!

THERE HE IS!

MASTER!

WELCOME, WELCOME!

TODAY, I TELL YOU, TODAY I'M DOUBLY HAPPY!

WAIT UNTIL YOU SEE WHAT WE BROUGHT YOU!

WINE FROM OUR RESPECTIVE LANDS!

I HAD YOU COME IN ORDER TO TELL YOU WHO I'VE CHOSEN AS MY SUCCESSOR AT THE LYCEUM.

BUT THINGS ARE STARTING TO CALM DOWN AND—

YOU TWO ARE MY ASSOCIATES AND MY DEAREST FRIENDS.

That was his way of telling us which one of us he'd chosen.

He gave me all his writings that he'd left at the Lyceum: six hundred cylinders containing a hundred seventy works, more than four hundred forty thousand lines altogether.

    The works of Aristotle can be divided into two groups.

His "esoteric" or "acroamatic" writings were intended for students at the Lyceum. They were mostly made up of notes and comments on advanced subjects of physics, metaphysics, ethics, and politics. At first he used them for his classes, but he later corrected and added to them.

    His "exoteric" writings were intended for a larger audience and addressed simpler subjects in ethics, rhetoric, and art.

    With the exception of his scientific writings, a good number of his works don't offer any new knowledge, but they do guide human intelligence toward a better way of thinking.

Two months later...

ARE YOU MAKING COPIES?

NO, I'M WRITING. AND IT HAS TO BE IN MY OWN HAND.

ARE YOU TAKING A TRIP?

I ALREADY TOLD YOU: I'M LEAVING WITH THE KIDS FOR TWO OR THREE DAYS. I HAVE TO MAKE AN OFFERING.

IN AULIS, TO THE TEMPLE OF ARTEMIS!

THAT'S WHERE IPHIGENIA WAS A PRIESTESS, AFTER ESCAPING FROM THE SACRIFICE AND BEFORE GOING TO TAURIS.

YES, RIGHT. SAFE TRAVELS!

BYE-BYE, DAD!

GOODBYE!

YOU TAKE CARE NOW!

I KNOW SO MANY THINGS. AND I'VE ATTEMPTED TO PROVIDE ANSWERS TO EVERY QUESTION.

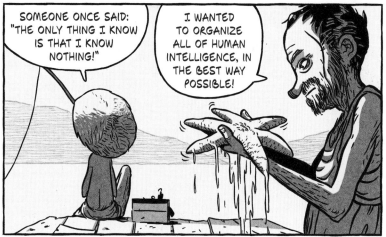

SOMEONE ONCE SAID: "THE ONLY THING I KNOW IS THAT I KNOW NOTHING!"

I WANTED TO ORGANIZE ALL OF HUMAN INTELLIGENCE, IN THE BEST WAY POSSIBLE!

THAT'S LIKE ME WITH MY LITTLE TACKLE BOX. EVERYTHING IS ARRANGED PROPERLY SO I CAN EASILY FIND WHATEVER I NEED!

I WAS THINKING, YOU MAYBE COULD COME HERE TOO WITH A FISHING ROD AND A NEAT LITTLE TACKLE BOX, AND WE COULD DO SOME FISHING TOGETHER...

...AND ALSO TALK!

The next day...

?

YOU FISH, MASTER?

EVERY TIME YOU VISIT IT'S A PLEASURE!

I CAN'T SIT STILL. I NEED TO GO SOMEWHERE, I NEED TO DO SOMETHING!

WELL, EVERYTHING'S FINE AT THE LYCEUM, SO DON'T WORRY ABOUT THAT! I'M HERE ABOUT DEMOSTHENES.

THE ATHENIANS RECALLED HIM FROM EXILE. HARPALUS, THE THEFT—ALL FORGOTTEN.

BUT DEMOSTHENES DID LEAD A CAMPAIGN AGAINST THE MACEDONIANS.

FAILURE!

CONDEMNED TO DEATH BY ANTIPATER, HE ESCAPED AND TOOK REFUGE ON THE ISLAND OF CALAURIA, IN POSEIDON'S TEMPLE.

BUT THEY FOUND HIM, A MONTH AGO.

TO AVOID ARREST, HE CHOSE INSTEAD TO DIE BY DRINKING HEMLOCK.

DEMOSTHENES DRANK HEMLOCK? HOW IRONIC!

WHAT ARE YOU LOOKING AT?

UH... NOTHING! YOU COMING OVER?

I GOT A RIDE WITH A FRIEND WHO'S DELIVERING SOME JARS OF OIL. WE HAVE TO LEAVE AS SOON AS HE'S DONE UNLOADING.

THERE HE IS NOW!

COME BACK SOON!

AH, YOU'RE HOME! WE'VE JUST NOW ARRIVED!

YES, I SAW THE WAGON OUT FRONT.

DAD, IT WAS REALLY, REALLY GREAT. YOU HAVE TO COME WITH US NEXT TIME!

I CAUGHT SNAILS, AND FLIES, AND BUTTERFLIES!

DON'T YOU FEEL WELL?

IT'S MY STOMACH STILL. I'M GOING FOR A LITTLE WALK.

WHILE YOU DO THAT, I'LL MAKE US SOMETHING TO EAT.

WE BROUGHT BACK SOME CHEESE AND SOME FIGS. THE FIGS RIPEN IN THE FALL IN AULIS.

DON'T BE TOO LONG! IT'S GOING TO RAIN SOON.

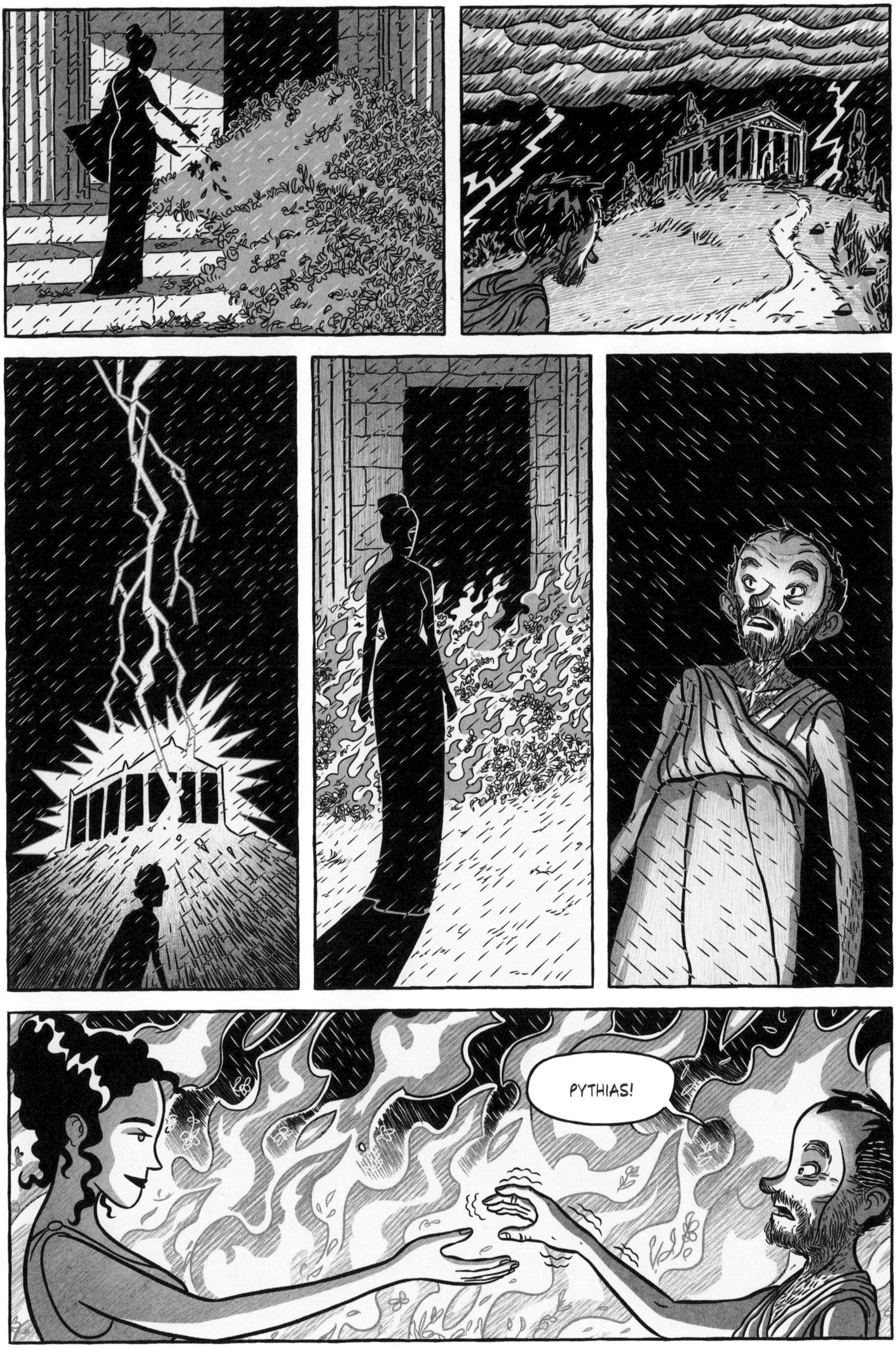
PYTHIAS!

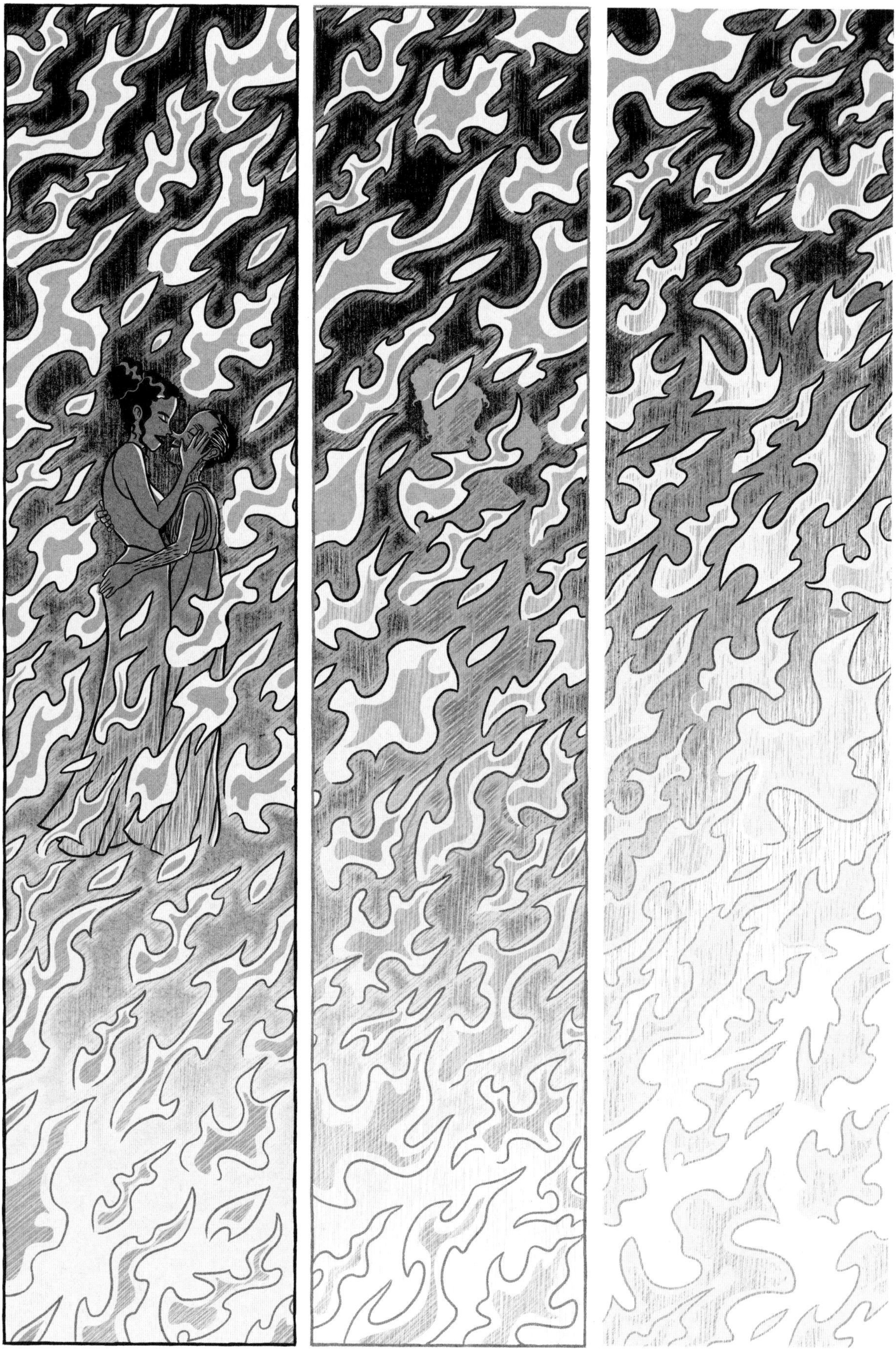

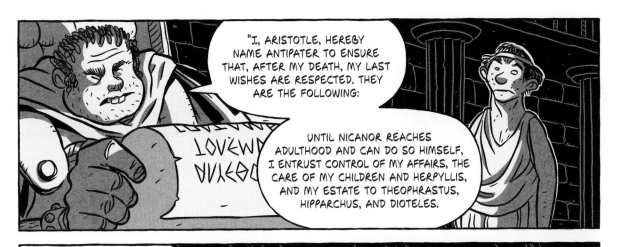

"I, ARISTOTLE, HEREBY NAME ANTIPATER TO ENSURE THAT, AFTER MY DEATH, MY LAST WISHES ARE RESPECTED. THEY ARE THE FOLLOWING:

UNTIL NICANOR REACHES ADULTHOOD AND CAN DO SO HIMSELF, I ENTRUST CONTROL OF MY AFFAIRS, THE CARE OF MY CHILDREN AND HERPYLLIS, AND MY ESTATE TO THEOPHRASTUS, HIPPARCHUS, AND DIOTELES.

WHEN PYTHIAS IS OF MARRYING AGE, I WOULD LIKE HER TO MARRY NICANOR. I ALSO WANT THE NEEDS OF HERPYLLIS, WHO MEANT SO VERY MUCH TO ME, TO BE PROVIDED FOR. IF SHE WISHES TO MARRY, MAY SHE TAKE A SPOUSE WORTHY OF OUR FAMILY AND MAY SHE BE GIVEN ONE TALENT OF SILVER.

IF SHE WISHES TO REMAIN IN CHALCIS, SHE MAY KEEP THE HOUSE AND GARDEN. IF SHE PREFERS STAGIRA, SHE MAY LIVE THERE IN THE FAMILY HOUSE AND HAVE IT FURNISHED ON SITE.

I DO NOT WANT THE SLAVES OF THE HOUSEHOLD TO BE SOLD, BUT RATHER COMPENSATED AND FREED ONCE THEY REACH ADULTHOOD!

AND, ACCORDING TO HER LAST WISHES, MAY THE ASHES OF PYTHIAS BE PLACED NEXT TO MINE, WHEREVER MY FINAL RESTING PLACE MAY BE."

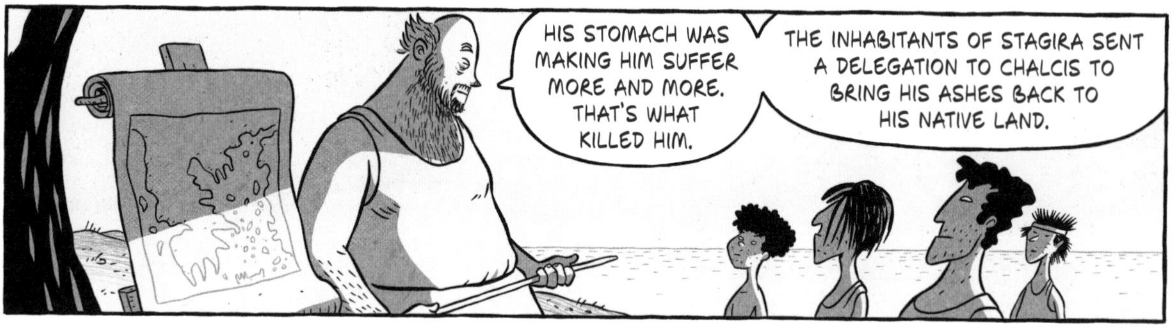
HIS STOMACH WAS MAKING HIM SUFFER MORE AND MORE. THAT'S WHAT KILLED HIM.
THE INHABITANTS OF STAGIRA SENT A DELEGATION TO CHALCIS TO BRING HIS ASHES BACK TO HIS NATIVE LAND.

He was buried with the highest honors.
His fellow citizens officially declared him the "founder" of the city for, as you remember, he was the one who urged Philip to rebuild it. The bronze urn with his ashes was placed in a very lovely grave, upon which an altar was erected. The place was named "Aristotelion," and when the Stagirites have difficult decisions to make or problems to resolve, it is there that the assembly of citizens gathers.

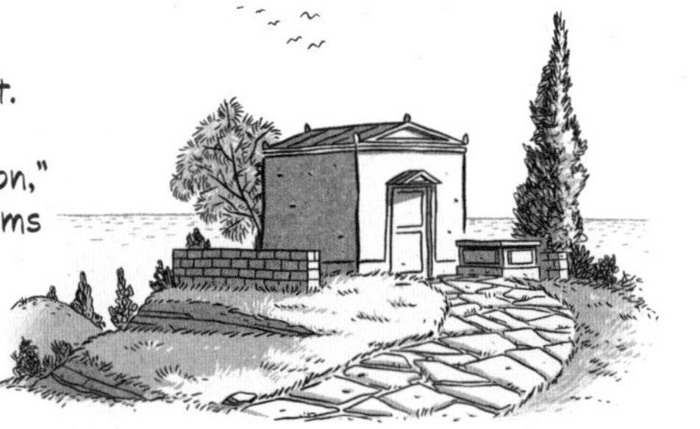

They've instituted a festival—the "Aristoteleia"—in his honor, and they've given his name to a month of the year.

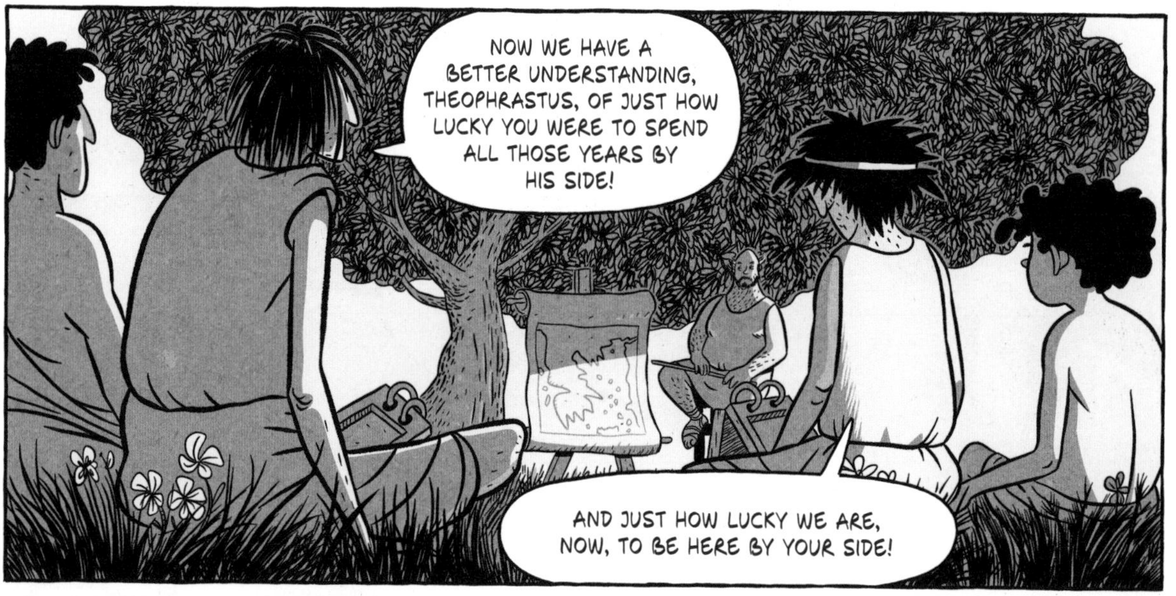
NOW WE HAVE A BETTER UNDERSTANDING, THEOPHRASTUS, OF JUST HOW LUCKY YOU WERE TO SPEND ALL THOSE YEARS BY HIS SIDE!
AND JUST HOW LUCKY WE ARE, NOW, TO BE HERE BY YOUR SIDE!

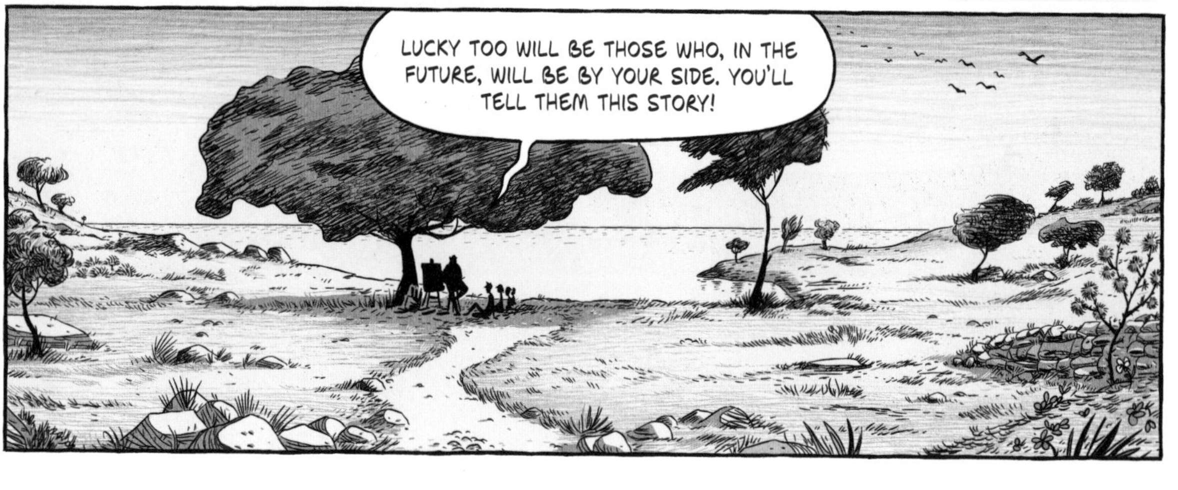
LUCKY TOO WILL BE THOSE WHO, IN THE FUTURE, WILL BE BY YOUR SIDE. YOU'LL TELL THEM THIS STORY!

Everything is endlessly
changing and transforming,
Bringing us
Now joy, now sorrow...

PINDAR

PRINCIPAL WORKS OF ARISTOTLE

ORGANON
  Categories
  On Interpretation
  Topics
  On Sophistical Refutations
  Prior Analytics
  Posterior Analytics

PHYSICS AND BIOLOGY
  Physics
  On the Heavens
  On Generation and Corruption
  Meteorology
  History of Animals
  Parts of Animals
  Generation of Animals
  Movement of Animals
  On the Soul

METAPHYSICS
  Metaphysics

ETHICS
  Eudemian Ethics
  Nicomachean Ethics
  Great Ethics

POLITICS
  Politics
  Constitution of the Athenians

RHETORIC AND POETICS
  Rhetoric
  Poetics

COMPLETE WORKS

Loeb Classical Library, Harvard University Press, Heinemann (bilingual editions).
Aristotle, *The Complete Works of Aristotle*, Princeton University Press.

BIBLIOGRAPHY

BONAN, RONALD
Apprendre à philosopher avec Aristote, Ellipses, 2018.

COULOUBARITSIS, LAMBROS
La Physique d'Aristote, Ousia, 1997.

CRUBELLIER, MICHEL & PIERRE PELLEGRIN
Aristote. Le philosophe et les savoirs, Seuil, 2002.

DIOGENES LAERTIUS
Lives of Eminent Philosophers (numerous editions available).

PELLEGRIN, PIERRE
Le vocabulaire d'Aristote, Éclipses, 2009.

ANTHOLOGY
Les Lettres grecques. Anthologie de la littérature grecque d'Homère à Justinien,
Les Belles Lettres, 2020.

ADLER, MORTIMER JEROME
Aristotle for Everybody, Macmillan, UK, 1978.

BARNES, JONATHAN
Aristotle: A Very Short Introduction, Oxford University Press, UK, 1982.

HALL, EDITH
Aristotle's Way: How Ancient Wisdom Can Change Your Life,
Rogers, Coleridge and White Ltd., 2018.

HUGHES, GERARD
Routledge Philosophy Guidebook to Aristotle on Ethics, Routledge, 2001.

MCLEISH, KENNETH
Aristotle's Poetics, Routledge, 1995.

LEROI, ARMAND MARIE
The Lagoon: How Aristotle Invented Science, Bloomsbury, 2009.

O'ROURKE, FRAN
Aristotelian Interpretations, Irish Academic Press, 2016.

ROSS, DAVID
Aristotle, Methuen & Co Ltd, 1977.

VLASTOS, GREGORY
Studies in Greek Philosophy, Princeton University Press, 1995.

HEIDEGGER, MARTIN
Phainomenologische Interpretationen zu Aristoteles, 1922 Freiburg classes.

HEIDEGGER, MARTIN
Vom Wesen und Begriff der Physis, in *Wegmarken*, 1939.

PACHYMERES, GEORGIOS
Scholien und Glosen zu De partibus animalium des Aristoteles (Cod. Vaticanus Gr. 261).

Our very warmest thanks go to Ms. Sfendoni-Mentzou, Professor Emeritus of the Philosophy of Science and President of the Interdisciplinary Center for Aristotelian Studies at the Aristotle University of Thessaloniki (Greece), for her judicious suggestions and remarks.
—**Tassos Apostolidis** and **Alecos Papadatos**

Editor: Rodolphe Lachat
Designer: Josh Johnson
Art Director: Shawn Dahl
Managing Editor: Logan Hill
Production Manager: Anet Sirna-Bruder
Translation: Tom Imber
Scholarly review (French): Alice Gaumer
Scholarly review (English): Katerina Ierodiakonou, University of Athens / Geneva
Handwritten lettering: Alecos Papadatos
Inking: Annie Di Donna
Digital lettering: Cromatik, Ltd.

Library of Congress Control Number: 2024936636

ISBN: 978-1-4197-7701-1
eISBN: 979-8-88707-415-3

ABRAMS The Art of Books
195 Broadway, New York, NY 10007
abramsbooks.com

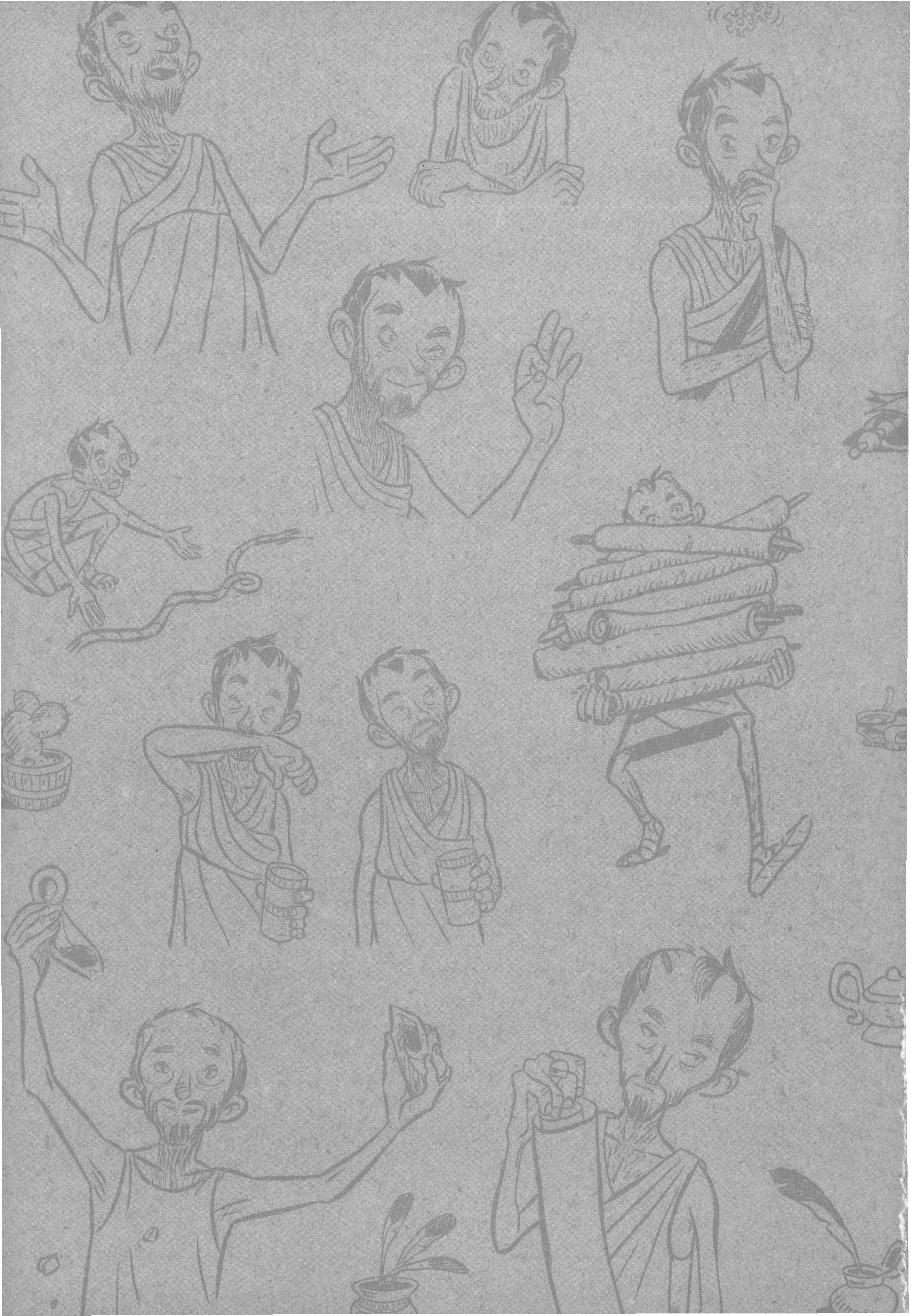